The Journey of G. Mastorna

The Journey of G. Mastorna

THE FILM FELLINI DIDN'T MAKE

FEDERICO FELLINI

with the collaboration of **Dino Buzzati, Brunello Rondi** and **Bernardino Zapponi**

Translated and with a commentary by **Marcus Perryman**

berghahn
NEW YORK • OXFORD
www.berghahnbooks.com

First English edition published in 2013 by
Berghahn Books
www.berghahnbooks.com

Originally published as *Il viaggio di G. Mastorna*
© Federico Fellini, Dino Buzzati,
Brunello Rondi and Bernardino Zapponi

© of the English-language edition Berghahn Books, New York/Oxford

© of the Introduction and essay 'Imagining *Mastorna*' Marcus Perryman
© of the Preface Peter Bondanella

All rights reserved. Except for the quotation of short passages
for the purposes of criticism and review, no part of this book
may be reproduced in any form or by any means, electronic or
mechanical, including photocopying, recording, or any information
storage and retrieval system now known or to be invented,
without written permission of the publisher.

Library of Congress Cataloging-in-Publication Data

Fellini, Federico.
 [Viaggio di G. Mastorna. English]
 The journey of G. Mastorna : the film Fellini didn't make / Federico Fellini ; with the collaboration of Dino Buzzati, Brunello Rondi and Bernardino Zapponi ; translated and with a commentary by Marcus Perryman. -- First English edition.
   pages cm
 Screenplay and commentary on an unproduced motion picture.
 Includes bibliographical references and index.
 ISBN 978-0-85745-970-1 (hardback : alk. paper) -- ISBN 978-0-85745-971-8 institutional ebook)
 1. Fellini, Federico--Criticism and interpretation. I. Buzzati, Dino, 1906-1972. II. Rondi, Brunello. III. Zapponi, Bernardino. IV. Perryman, Marcus, translator, writer of added commentary. V. Title.
 PN1997.3.F44313 2013
 791.43'72--dc23
                                                                    2013006043

British Library Cataloguing in Publication Data

A catalogue record for this book is available from the British Library

Printed in the United States on acid-free paper

ISBN 978-0-85745-970-1 (hardback)
ISBN 978-1-78238-230-0 (paperback)
ISBN 978-0-85745-971-8 (institutional eisbn)
ISBN 978-1-78238-231-7 (retail eisbn)

Contents

Foreword	vii
Preface by Peter Bondanella	ix
Acknowledgements	xiii
Introduction	1
The Journey of G. Mastorna by Federico Fellini, with the collaboration of Dino Buzzati, Brunello Rondi and Bernardino Zapponi	15
Imagining *Mastorna*	137
Selected Bibliography	203
Index	209

Foreword

The following pages present an important film script written by Federico Fellini in 1965/6 in collaboration with Brunello Rondi, Dino Buzzati and Bernardino Zapponi, translated for the first time into English. The script has been available in Italian since 1995.

The introduction includes an excerpt from a letter by Fellini to his producer Dino De Laurentiis, explaining his intentions for the film. It discusses the roles of the co-scriptwriters and the difficulties Fellini encountered with Buzzati, in particular. I also briefly discuss how the unmade film might have completed a trilogy of films with *La dolce vita* and *8½*. Without over-anticipating details of the script, Fellini's habit of plundering *Mastorna* for ideas and scenes for the rest of his films is illustrated.

After the script, 'Imagining *Mastorna*' discusses how Fellini intended to make the film, with what crew and cast, its pace and some possible techniques, based on his films of the same period. Also discussed are the events from 1965 to 1967 that led to Fellini abandoning the project. I briefly summarize and contextualize the three other scripts written by Fellini not turned into film at the time of *Mastorna* (or, in fact, subsequently). The final sections are dedicated to a famous film and a not-so-famous novel that influenced the script and may have significantly shaped the ending.

Throughout, I have tried to provide background information of use to specialists and non-specialists, and to stimulate curiosity leading, hopefully, to further study. Only once have I given in to the temptation to 'direct' a scene. I hope readers will similarly be drawn into imagining how Fellini might have shot the film. My thoughts have been influenced at times by a film made a few years before Fellini set to work on *Mastorna*: Orson Welles's *The Trial*. Also tempting is to ponder how a director – Martin Scorsese, Terry Gilliam or a film-maker not so evidently influenced by Fellini, such as Marc Forster or Lars von Trier – might set about making *Mastorna* today.

Preface

Peter Bondanella

Like the monstrous whale in Melville's *Moby Dick* that haunted Captain Ahab and nearly caused the death of the novel's narrator, Fellini's unrealized film, *The Journey of G. Mastorna*, became his white whale after the smashing popular and commercial successes of *La dolce vita* and *8½* and the relative failure of *Juliet of the Spirits*. The initial stages of this project's birth involved not only dramatic personal changes in Fellini's usual collaborators on and off the set, but they also raised legal problems and may well have contributed to a near-fatal illness that almost ended the director's life. All of the fascinating details surrounding the creation and ultimately the abandonment of Fellini's project are minutely and dramatically described by Marcus Perryman in his excellent critical essay, 'Imagining *Mastorna*' and the introduction to his new English translation of the Italian script. For the rest of his life, Fellini would have the production of this film in the back of his mind, and although he never succeeded in making it, almost everything he did during the last three decades of his long and eventful career shows some sign that this unrealized film had left a mark on those that followed. The Mastorna project became, in Fellini's own description, a kind of storehouse of themes and images that were sometimes brushed off and employed in a very different context from *Fellini Satyricon* through *Toby Dammit*, *Roma*, *Amarcord*, *The City of Women*, *Ginger and Fred*, *Interview* and *The Voice of the Moon*.

Because Fellini continuously considered turning his script into a film but never succeeded in doing so, a number of myths about the role this failure played in the director's life grew up. In particular, there was speculation that Fellini's superstitious nature prevented him from making a film about death because he thought that it might lead to his own demise in the process! Such a superficial estimation of Fellini's emotional, spiritual, and artistic capacities must rule out any such explanation for the Maestro's ultimate failure to complete his film. His continuous concern with this project during a period of over three decades would argue against such a simplistic theory. Moreover, even a cursory examination of Fellini's recently published *Book of Dreams* reveals how *Mastorna* played a major role in the director's dreamlife, frequently illustrated by the marvellous kinds of magic-marker coloured drawings typical of Fellini's style as a cartoonist. In fact, Fellini always visualized his dreams in cartoons and caricatures, not as realistic and polished sketches, and those visions from his subconscious immortalized in his dream notebooks that concern Mastorna are first and foremost cartoons before they are serious and disturbing ruminations on the meaning of death and what awaits us beyond death.

The Journey of G. Mastorna is an oneiric narrative about a musician who finds himself in an ultra-earthly dimension after an airplane crash and who begins, despite himself, a journey of life and death in which the line between this world and the next is so faint and thin that he does not initially realize he is in the Afterworld. In the long tradition of Virgil's *Aeneid* and Dante's *Divine Comedy*, Fellini's film would thus have been an original treatment of the theme of the katabasis, a journey to the Afterlife, and as was the case in the classical antecedents to Mastorna, such a journey would have necessarily been concerned with a growth of understanding during the course of the journey. This subject was one of continuous fascination to the director; another unrealized script that he toyed with making during the last years of his life was, not surprisingly, based upon Dante's *Inferno*. Making a film about the ultimate meaning of life after death would be a daunting task for a theologian, not to mention a film director.

Marcus Perryman not only furnishes the reader without access to the Italian script a fine translation of the original but also offers an infinite amount of information about almost everything surrounding the place of Mastorna in Fellini's life. He provides an invaluable contribution to the critical literature on Fellini – a mass of reviews, essays, books and editions that continues to grow and grow year after year. Adding something really substantial, original and useful to this mountain of material is truly an accomplishment. Even without the completed film, the reader fascinated with Fellini's universe will find this unrealized script quite an adventure and a delight.

The Journey of G. Mastorna was the Maestro's final and perhaps greatest dream. There are currently plans to make a feature-length motion picture loosely based on Fellini's treatment for *The Journey of G. Mastorna*. Ermanno Cavazzoni – author of the screenplay for Fellini's last film, *The Voice of the Moon* (1990) – is understood to be working on the script. Damian Pettigrew, director of the highly praised documentary film, *Fellini: I'm a Born Liar* (2002), will concurrently prepare another documentary on both Fellini's attempts to make *The Journey of Mastorna* and the creation of this new production of Fellini's unrealized project. Marcus Perryman's new edition and translation is therefore not only an intrinsically interesting work of impeccable Fellini scholarship and a good read, but it is also timely as well. It should prepare the lover of Fellini's cinema for two cinematic treats, both indebted to the last and most enigmatic creation of Fellini's fantasy.

Peter Bondanella is Distinguished Professor Emeritus of Comparative Literature, Film Studies and Italian; a member of the European Academy of Sciences and the Arts; and past President of the American Association for Italian Studies. The author of numerous publications on Fellini and Italian cinema, he is best known in this regard as the author of *The Cinema of Federico Fellini* (1992; preface by Federico Fellini). He is currently working on a collection of essays for the British Film Institute, *The Italian Film Book*.

Acknowledgements

The cover photograph and all other photographs in the book were taken by Tazio Secchiaroli during the screen test of Marcello Mastroianni for *Mastorna*, which was re-enacted for the 1969 NBC documentary *A Director's Notebook*. These and other photographs regarding *Mastorna* by Tazio Secchiaroli can be found in *G. Mastorna opera incompiuta* (Palermo: Sellerio editore, 2000). Many thanks to David Secchiaroli and the Photomovie website for permission to use the photos.

I am grateful to Peter Bondanella, expert on all things Fellini, for his Preface, to Umberto Rondi for his unwavering support and to Carlo Patrizi for obtaining permission to publish this translation from Fellini's heirs and rights-holders.

Special thanks to Mark Stanton of Berghahn Books for his patience and understanding.

"Mastorna goes over to it, opens the case very carefully, lovingly takes out the cello, as if it were a living being."

Introduction

In 1965 Federico Fellini signed a contract with the producer Dino De Laurentiis to make a science fiction film based on Fredric Brown's *What Mad Universe*.[1] The cover of the 1949 edition of the novel shows a very Fellini-like lady – Betty Page face and Anita Ekberg body – in the foreground, as if she has just stepped out of a shower and is going to dry her hair. In the background a dwarfed, wide-eyed extraterrestrial is waving, next to a rather inadequate-looking phallic rocket. For all that this might have interested Fellini after his pretend spaceship and red-herring escape scenario in *8½*, he quickly changed his mind; instead of *What Mad Universe* he began writing an original script of his own, *Il viaggio di G. Mastorna*, based on an idea by Dino Buzzati, whose collaboration he sought and secured.

He sent De Laurentiis a long letter which amounted to a first draft of the script. The letter began:

Dear Dino,

I don't think this draft is the most useful thing for you to assess either the cost of the film or what kind of film it is; as you'll realize, it is a story that can't be summarized in episodes because there are no episodes, and it is my intention to tell the story of the film lucidly but at an ever faster pace, without a moment's respite, right to the end, which cannot be the end of the story, although it is the end of the film. I mean the film really has no end.

I also imagine (but I'm not sure) that the film should be told in the first person by the main character, who is thinking out loud, commenting on what is happening, talking to himself, in an effort to clarify things, to understand and find something to latch onto during his journey, in the absurd labyrinth he is caught up in.

On the basis of this little talk, it won't even be easy for you to work out which scenes will require a stage set and which will need to be shot on location.

My idea is that the film should be very realistic and avoid stage sets as much as possible.

Mostly the film takes place in airports, railway stations, the Underground, sea ports, modern and ancient city streets, swamps, the sea and certain districts of Rome, New York, Amsterdam, Berlin, the Vatican, some towns in Lazio and Venice.

Don't be alarmed by this list which could actually be longer; I've got an idea of how to use the scenery to avoid location costs and trips abroad. But I'll tell you more about this later, when we're closer to the shooting.

I expect this introductory preamble has already put you off and you'd like to know something about the story. As I said I would have preferred to send you the final script because it's the kind of story that needs details.

But I'll try to give you an idea of what I'm thinking of doing and what seems to me something close to the film we want to make.

A few words about the main character and then the story proper. I haven't yet decided his profession but he will be called, at least in this story, 'M'.

Initially I thought he should be a musician, someone in an orchestra, someone who wanted to be a composer when he was young and had even composed some symphonies, but then, quite early on, had given up his artistic dreams, and now just plays the cello in an orchestra.

Why a musician?

I can't explain it exactly (and I might still change my mind), but I think the world of music, the atmosphere of an orchestra, the rehearsals, the cherished instrument closed in a case that has the shape of a woman's hips, the humility of a job which consists in joining in at the right moment, not a second earlier or later, and joining a collective effort, perhaps playing just two notes, no more, and then waiting in silence, immobile until the next moment for another two notes, your eyes glued on the slightest movement of the conductor's baton, this, as I was saying, strikes me as a condition which might symbolically represent a highly religious attitude to life.

Introduction

> I'll try to explain this better. A musician goes about his business with humility and modesty, without trying to understand the overall sense of things, confident that the conductor who is leading him knows more than he does.
>
> But I've also been dabbling with other ideas, a painter or even a businessman like yourself, Dino. I mean someone used to living his life in a very concrete way, filled with enthusiasm, with no melancholy metaphysical thoughts.
>
> Whichever he may be, musician, painter or industrialist, the story of the film is the same.
>
> We can decide which at a later date, when I have a better idea of what I want.
>
> You'll object: 'Just what is it that you want?' Let me try to explain, with the apparently arbitrary rhythm of a long dream, what happens to M. ...

There followed over seven thousand words in which Fellini narrates the action of the film, describes its main characters and indicates its mood and spirit, collecting some of the episodes under headings. For example under THE LANDSCAPE OF FEELINGS, SENSATION AND THOUGHT he writes: 'The Region of thought with its cultural leaders; the fantastic Classical world of secondary school, the pagan world, Greek gods, Homer's heroes. His guide in this world is his old schoolmaster, a materialist, follower of Carducci, atheist.'[2] So, here, in a couple of sentences we have Homer, Dante and a nineteenth-century poet of anti-clerical revolutionary zeal, a quick swing through the history and culture of Europe. This part of the letter to De Laurentiis shows Fellini thinking aloud, putting down his thoughts in large blocks. It is a sort of hypertext, or key to vertical and horizontal intertextuality (according to whether we see the script as a text or a film).

Fellini signs off repeating his perplexity about the ending. It's not hard to guess what De Laurentiis made of this uncertainty. Fifteen years earlier, he had sent back a script on Ulysses to Orson Welles, because it lacked commercial appeal. But De Laurentiis had backed out of *8½*, yielding to Angelo Rizzoli one of Fellini's greatest successes, and the mistake still smarted. Despite the hiccup of *Giulietta degli spiriti*, Fellini was still a film-maker De Laurentiis could bet, if not bank, on.

Several months later, with help from Brunello Rondi and the contribution of Dino Buzzati, the script had grown to over thirty-three thousand words. A few scenes had been dropped, many added, and the ending had been put in place, introduced by one of the few cinematic instructions in the script, a voice-over. Much has been made of Fellini's scripts, or lack of them. His co-scriptwriter and lifelong friend Tullio Pinelli has said that, contrary to popular belief, Fellini stuck closely to them. And this from a man who created the Steiner character in *La dolce vita* to commemorate his friend Cesare Pavese, only to see Fellini radically alter the sense of his suicide, on the set. Pinelli's remark indicates that this kind of rethinking of an entire character must have been an exception rather than the rule. Why is it then that many actors have declared that Fellini worked virtually without a script? The thirty-three thousand words of *Mastorna* stand in open contradiction to this claim.

Perhaps the truth of the matter can be seen in the difficulties Fellini and Buzzati encountered in collaborating on *Mastorna*. The novelist sought to pin down the film-maker's drifting narrative and atmospherics, which Fellini wanted to leave loosely unstructured. Buzzati found the dialogue vacuous; Fellini shrugged. The writer scratched his head over a significant name for the protagonist, the director picked the name out of the Milan phone book.[3]

Buzzati's idea of a script was not Fellini's. A novelist works with words; they're all he has. Not so a film-maker. Fellini was well known for improvising on the set, writing dialogue on a napkin the evening before shooting, overdubbing lines to fit the expressions of the actors, and generally paying little regard to the printed page. He had learnt to improvise from neorealism, and specifically from Rossellini, and the overdubbing was inherited from even before that, the Fascist period. Stories abound in this connection: actors (not only the English speakers) saying or mouthing 'one, two, three' for dialogue to be added later. When Mastroianni asked to see the script of *La dolce vita* he was presented with a somewhat lewd sketch of a male bather and sirens; and Claudia Cardinale, who had no more idea of her role in *8½* than her namesake in Guido's non-existent film, was asked to improvise the dialogue in the car with Mastroianni. While making *E la nave va*, Fellini confiscated any copies of the script he found on the set and declared his open admiration for the English cast, which didn't bother him with pointless questions about roles and dialogues. Later, he was appalled to discover the actors just hid their copies whenever he came by.

Evidently, Fellini didn't think scripts were for actors. For him they were accurate descriptions of the scenes that would be shot, verbal storyboards, giving the rhythm and architecture of a film; they didn't need to indicate anything about the mechanics of shooting (camera movement, lighting, depth, and so on) or give the actors their lines. This is reflected in the *Mastorna* script, which only indicates 'Exterior' or 'Interior', and a generic location, without further shooting guidelines. The dialogues are sometimes perfunctory, at other times utterly critical. However, they often have the feel of interleafed monologues, two people talking at cross purposes, part, of course, of the nightmare world being portrayed. Buzzati wanted the dialogue to fizzle; instead it simmers.

If Fellini had made the film in or around 1966, as he originally intended, apart from some inevitable serendipity on the set, it would have substantially followed the script in this book, if not always the dialogue.

* * *

Mastorna was meant as a sequel to *8½*. Some critics go further, believing it would have completed a trilogy begun with *La dolce vita*: all in black and white, starring Marcello Mastroianni, and Dantescan in tone and content.

The film would have presented a man more isolated and in a deeper and more intractable personal crisis than either Marcello or Guido. It would have made seamless transitions from dream to reality to memory to vision, without the sepia coloration used in *8½* to alert the film-goer to the changes. The women in the film would have been variants and multiples of the water-gatherer Claudia, mocking and enticing Beatrices, invitations to a vitality that is denied them, spectral, illusory (not exactly visions), throw-backs to Gelsomina and Cabiria, with the shapes of Anita (from another script, written in 1956/7, *Viaggio con Anita*) and Sylvia, sensual but unsexed. In support of the trilogy theory, *Mastorna* would have repeated and magnified Emma questioning Marcello about his love for her; exemplified Steiner's remark that we don't know how to listen; asked on a grander scale who manipulates who, as in the phoney miracle sequence of *La dolce vita*. Most tellingly, it would have built on the image of the fish washed up on the shore. In that penultimate scene, the monster fish's eye is fixed open, its mouth gaping cannibalistically with other fish. Marcello seems afraid of the eye, as if somehow he feels its scrutiny. In 1966 Fellini told Dario Zanelli he wanted Mastorna to look at the world like a fish looks at human beings, utterly estranged.

Mastorna would have used a technique from *Le tentazioni del dottor Antonio* (The Temptations of Doctor Anthony, 1962), where the effect of the wind and the rain on the giant poster of Anita Ekberg convinces Mazzuolo that the picture is real and Anita is beckoning him. In *Mastorna* a baby on a poster was to be enlivened in the same way, but with a series of different expressions, almost like a cartoon book, where the pages are flicked over quickly to produce the illusion of movement. In *Lo sceicco bianco* (The White Sheikh), Fellini had produced the effect of a photo-book through his editing; now the technique was to be, as it were, incorporated into the visual world through the subtle changes in advertising hoardings. In *Mastorna* messages of this kind would have been inscrutable, detached from the adjacent scenes, sudden enigmas, patches of light and dark in Mastorna's mind, of uncertain provenance.

The expressionless crowds in the traffic jam opening *8½* would, in *Mastorna*, have become almost faceless, featureless, indistinguishable, as semi-jokingly suggested by the producer, Pace, in *8½* when he describes the apocalyptic film Guido is supposed to be making: 'What remains of humanity looks for a safe haven on another planet. More than 10,000 extras ... maybe 15,000. ... You understand, a tragic crowd that abandons forever ...'

The meeting in the sanatorium with Mezzabotta would have involved a still more shocking recognition; the male/female cabaret singer would have become Mastorna's first accuser; the loudspeaker announcement 'Attention please, attention please, His Excellency is expecting you' would have become: 'Attention please, due to technical difficulties, we have been forced to make an emergency landing' (as shot for the NBC documentary, *A Director's Notebook*, in 1968). Guido and Mastorna's wives would have had the same name. Mastorna would have been charged with what Guido attempted to do: 'bury everything that's dead in us'. An alternative final scene to *8½* would have been important too. Originally the carousel scene was shot as a trailer; Fellini wanted to end the film quite differently in the restaurant car of a train: Guido looks up and sees all the characters encountered in the film looking at him in a spectral light, ambiguously smiling, with uncanny expressions, a kind of limbo, between life and death,[4] the precise feel created in the script of *Mastorna*.

If *La dolce vita* was Hell and *8½* Purgatory, *Mastorna* should have been Paradise. Progressing through the script, readers may wonder what sort of Paradise, however: the world of *Mastorna* often recalls the petty expediency and estrangement of Kafka's *Amerika*; sometimes it plunges into Nazi regimentation and a total disregard for individuality, humanity seen as species, bureaucratically reduced to an amorphous mass. This is often how Fellini portrayed Fascism, with the faces of the officers and petty officials frozen into death-masks. The satire reserved for Mussolini's face in *Amarcord* associated his regime with the kind of myth-making operating in Hollywood. Mastorna anticipates this insight with a scene in which the protagonist is made up to look like anyone (his features are rearranged cartoon-style to produce this or that effect under the spotlights) and then sent on stage to receive an award as the screen projects the photograph of someone else and the citation bears no relation to his life. In the corresponding scene in *Toby Dammit* (from *Spirits of the Dead*), the first of the many half-films and films Fellini made instead of *Mastorna* and Fellini's first collaboration with Bernardino Zapponi,[5] Dammit launches drunkenly into Macbeth's speech: 'Life's but a walking shadow, a poor player that struts and frets his hour upon the stage and then is heard no more. It is a tale told by an idiot, full of sound and fury …' and his voice trails away. The viewer finds himself inevitably completing the quotation, amplifying the (non-)signification by silence, filling in the gaps, as in *8½* confronted by Guido's blank expression, his substantial absence. Here, Dammit mutters, 'It isn't true', as if to contradict Macbeth or to deny his own prowess as an actor: the words tumble out of him and he then resumes his self-fixation, his demolition of the image foisted upon him.

Everyone Mastorna meets appears to be reflecting back a sense of guilt and shame. How this could be Paradise is one of the puzzles of the script. Its very last, essentially cinematic, image is one plucked from Fellini's recollections of his psychoanalyst Ernst Bernhard's studio in Rome: 'I went to see him most willingly of all at sunset when the sun illuminated the small dust particles in the air and gave them a gold colour.'[6] These particles – dust that could be gold dust – are the last things we see in Mastorna's world, a mixture of the sacred and profane, muck and brass, richness and plenitude that may – or may not – be found in the humblest and lowliest things of life.

Bernhard was the Jungian psychoanalyst who encouraged Fellini to believe that dreams are as much part of existence as waking life. In the four years Fellini was in analysis with him, the two men became close friends; Fellini said of Bernhard that he always gave him 'a great sense of peace'. His death in the summer of 1965 certainly lies close below the surface of Fellini's *Mastorna* script.

Bernhard was an esoteric student of the soul, consulting the oracular Chinese text, the *I Ching* (preface by Jung), and practising palmistry and astrology, predilections that cost him a visa to enter Britain in 1936. Unwisely he moved to Rome and was interned in a concentration camp in Calabria in 1938 when Italy copied Germany, promulgating its own Race Laws. After meeting Bernhard, Fellini became an adept of the *I Ching* and began to record his dreams in what he called his Dream Book. His interest in the esoteric was shared by Buzzati, another reason perhaps he was invited to work on the script. When they met to discuss *Mastorna*, Buzzati had just returned from Mumbai where he had been interviewing magicians and shamans, in whom Fellini had always taken a close, Wellesian interest.

Bernhard declared himself an exponent of the psychology of the individuation process, a theory which posits gender-opposite soul images (i.e. the female anima for a man and the male animus for a woman).[7] His only book was a collection of conference addresses, recorded conversations and diaries dealing with therapy and self-narration, with a title that might have been suitable for Fellini's entire oeuvre: *Mitobiografia*. It investigates entelechy, 'life with a design' as the author called it, a concept that led him to recommend that people suffer their deaths in full consciousness. In the English-speaking world the concept was espoused by the American philosopher Kenneth Burke, who Fellini probably hadn't read but whose works, nonetheless, have affinities with his art. In *Language as Symbolic Action* (1966), Burke wrote that reality has been 'built up for us by nothing but our symbol system'. *Mastorna* can be read, in part, as an investigation of Bernhard's ideas, as well as a form of mourning his death.

* * *

Vincenzo Mollica calls *Mastorna* the most famous unmade film in Italian cinema. Such were the accidents and deaths associated with it that he came to think of it as jinxed: food poisoning after he had met Buzzati, the death of Bernhard and then of the cinematographer Gianni Di Venanzo, almost Fellini himself in April 1967, when he was misdiagnosed and became sick enough to prompt a telegram from, of all people, the Pope. He shrouded the film in mystery partly to keep open the option of making it. Every new project he worked on after his *Satyricon* had first to get past the recurring thought, illusion or delusion of *Mastorna*. After the initial failure, Fellini tinkered with the script for the next ten years. He showed it to new co-writers Bernardino Zapponi and Tonino Guerra. He came close to returning to it after *Il Casanova*, which his analyst considered to be an important step in his self-therapy and one that *Mastorna* would have extended further. By his own admission, he repeatedly plundered the script for his new films: for the airport scene and award ceremony in *Toby Dammit*, for the pope's regalia in *Fellini Roma*, for verbatim inclusions and characters in *Amarcord*.[8] *Prova d'orchestra* investigates the world of orchestral music, to which *Mastorna* belongs, albeit focusing more on the conductor as dictator than the musician as acolyte; *La città delle donne* has numerous affinities with the unmade film. The bus and motel in *Mastorna* are very much like Ginger's bus and motel and *Mastorna* includes one of Fred's dance routines. Some said *E la nave va* was *Mastorna* in disguise. Perhaps, he actually did make the film, only hid scenes from it in his other work, unravelling from it what Dorothée Bonnigal calls the 'distortions that a mystified vision imposes on reality',[9] which Fellini explored throughout his career. Fabrizio Borin calls Mastorna the character Fellini 'thought about, continually returned to, abandoned, repudiated, sought out, feared, hated and never created – but Fellini's *entire* cinema can be thought of as *the oneiric journey* of Mastorna-Fellini'.[10]

He read the fabulous tale that inspired his script – Buzzati's story for children, *Lo strano viaggio di Domenico Molo*, serialized in the magazine *Omnibus* – when he was eighteen. At school he precociously challenged Dante's vision of the Inferno: too neat and tidy. Landing in a blizzard in New York in 1964, he was gripped by sudden panic, and this became the opening scene of *Mastorna*. Mastroianni screen-tested for the film, paid a large penalty to release himself from theatre commitments in order to make it, re-enacted the screen test for an NBC documentary and then found himself without a film. He joked that they would make *Mastorna* in the afterlife. Bernardino Zapponi made his contribution to the script after the attempt to make the film had been abandoned. Mike Nichols offered a large sum for the script, which Fellini turned down.[11] In the early 1990s Giorgio Strehler proposed making his directorial debut in film with Fellini's script,[12] and in 1993, the year of his death, Fellini encouraged Milo Manara to turn the idea into a comic strip, only once again to give up on the project after the first episode. By some mistake the first book finished not with 'to be continued' but with 'the end', which Fellini, once again, took as a bad omen, the last.

In 1980 he published *Fare un Film*, part autobiography, part assembly of interviews, in which he tells a dream about *Mastorna* that reads like a parable from Fellini's beloved Kafka:[13]

> There's a film, I mean the idea, the feeling, the suspicion of a film I have been carrying in my mind for fifteen years and has still not allowed me to get close enough to, trusted me enough, for me to understand what it wants. At the end of every film I make, there it is again, apparently claiming that now it's his turn; it stays with me for some time, studies me a little, and then disappears. I'm relieved every time it goes away: it's too serious, committed, uncompromising, not like me at all, who knows which of us would be willing to change. Now that I think about it I've never done so much as a sketch for this film, a scrawl; clearly when he makes up his mind he'll tell me in a different way.
>
> Sometimes I even get the idea that it isn't a film at all, but something else which I'm not yet able to understand, and then it frightens me a little, but I'm immediately comforted by the idea that probably, for me, the film is a pilot, in the sense that it is some sort of bizarre spiritual guide, ushering in other stories, other imaginings; and, in point of fact, when it goes away, unfailingly it leaves me with the film I'm going to make next.
>
> I had a dream a long time ago, perhaps about this chimera of a film, or rather my attitude towards it, a mixture of fascination and scepticism, which gives me energy and diffidence and has always attracted and repelled me: the very feelings I had in the dream. It was about a mysterious man from China, who arrived in the dead of night in a huge aeroplane, full of passengers. I was the Airport Director. I was sitting behind my desk in a gigantic, empty office, and, through the windows, could see the runway lights, the starry sky and the massive outline of the plane that had just landed. As Airport Director I was also in charge of the Immigration Department and had to decide who got visas, who was to be allowed in. I'm going about this business when I notice one of the passengers and I'm unable to attend to anyone else. He's alone, some way away from the others, dressed in a shabby but ostentatious kimono that gives him

a priestly, vagabond air. He has no luggage. Quietly, with solemnity, he approaches my table and now is standing in front of me, his hands hidden in his ample sleeves, eyes closed. I look at his face: the face of an Oriental aristocrat fallen on bad times, his hair greasy and dirty, foul-smelling, clothes soaked, like wet leaves and rubbish, but the nobility he exudes fascinates and dismays me. He could be a king, a saint, or a gypsy, a tramp, who has become indifferent to the disdain of others through lengthy mortification and poverty. An indefinable feeling of anxiety and unease takes me by the throat, makes me speechless, and my heart beats faster. I know the foreigner is waiting for my decision but he asks nothing, makes no demands, says not a word. I am increasingly uncomfortable and at a loss, but he counters this with the undeniable, silent, fact of his arrival, his physical presence. What is happening concerns me, not him; all he had to do was arrive and now he is here. I have to decide whether to let him in or not, whether to grant or deny him a visa. This feeling that it is me, not him, who is being tested, increases my anxiety and unease. I find myself mumbling some hypocritical excuse, childish lies; I say I am not the real head of the airport, the decision isn't mine to take, I take my orders from others, superiors, experts, who know what to do in such circumstances, I am just a clerk. A sense of shame and self-pity forces me to lower my head, I don't know what else to say, I look at the plaque on my desk which says 'Director General'. Everyone falls silent. The passengers at the other end of the room are an indistinct, silent mass. I don't have the courage to raise my head. It feels like a long time has passed, too long; a lifetime. Painstakingly slowly in the dream I formulate this thought: what will I fear most when I raise my eyes? The fact that he is still there, covered in dust yet shining, close yet unreachable, the fact that the mysterious Oriental is still there, waiting, or that he has gone?[14]

Notes

1. De Laurentiis produced *Il disco volante* (The Flying Saucer) in 1964, *Barbarella* in 1968 and *Flash Gordon* in 1970. In *8½* Guido is apparently trying to make a sci-fi film about a space colony that escapes the earth's destruction.
2. Further lengthy excerpts from the letter are given in the notes after the script.
3. So Fellini said. Some believed the word to be a collapsed version of 'Mastroianni ritorna'. According to the poet Andrea Zanzotto, who worked on the script of *Il Casanova*, it was Spanish ... 'che màs torna'.

Introduction

4. This scene is described and briefly discussed by Alessandro Casanova in *Scritti e immaginati – I film mai realizzati di Federico Fellini* (Rimini: Guaraldi Universitaria, 2005), 68–69.
5. Zapponi (1927–2000) went on to work with Fellini on *A Director's Notebook*, *Satyricon*, *I Clowns*, *Roma*, *Il Casanova di Federico Fellini* and *La città delle donne*. He was a novelist and prolific screenwriter, with credits for films by Risi, Monicelli, Argento, Bolognini and many others. In 1999, he wrote a theatre adaption of *La strada* with Tullio Pinelli.
6. Fellini's description continues: 'The large windows offered an endless view of Rome. The church bells rang out. It was like being in a big balloon, suspended in mid-air.' The similarity with the opening scene of *8½* is evident.
7. In *Federico Fellini, Essays in Criticism*, edited by Peter Bondanella (New York: Oxford University Press, 1978), Carolyn Geduld analyses *8½* and *Giulietta degli spiriti* in terms of Guido's anima and Giulietta's animus. Writing at about the time of *Il Casanova* she concludes: 'Fellini has not made another film about his anima. The clearest indication of his rejection of Jung occurs in *Roma*, in which the ancient frescoes discovered in the evacuation are destroyed as soon as they are exposed. Evidently, for Fellini, the past can no longer be called upon to heal the present in quite the same way as it could in *8½* and *Giulietta degli spiriti*.' The same scene is recalled by David Grossman in *Writing in the Dark* (London: Bloomsbury, 2008) in the essay 'Books That Have Read Me', where, however, it appears to indicate how the past may sputter into life only to be snuffed out. Intriguingly *Roma* was the first time that Fellini portrayed 'himself' as a young man in the correct historical era: *I vitelloni* is set in the 1950s although the memories are of the pre-war period and in *La dolce vita* Marcello is much younger than Fellini at the time. Fellini's first entry in his dream book states that at forty he sees himself as a man of twenty.
8. *Amarcord* is probably the film that borrows most heavily from *Mastorna*, reproducing Fellini/Mastorna's memories of his old school, the Fulgor cinema, the teacher of religious education, the philosophy teacher (De Cercis), a childhood flame (Margherita/Bianchina), his father's house and the order of provisions 'Brunello Casati Brunello Casati, Cesena, 400 kilos of coffee, 10 sacks of Japanese rice, 200 kilos of jam …'
9. In her contribution to *Federico Fellini: Contemporary Perspectives*, edited by Frank Burke and Marguerite R. Waller (Toronto: University of Toronto Press, 2002), 147.
10. In *Visionaria, il cinema fantastico tra ricordi sogni e allucinazioni*, edited by Dario Marzola (Alessandria: Edizioni Falsopiano, 2008), 134. The chapter is dedicated to Tarkovsky and Fellini.
11. According to Giuseppe Rotunno, between $500,000 and $1,000,000. Rotunno says he was working on a Nichols film at the time the offer was made. Alas, that only marginally helps to understand the entity of the offer and Fellini's resistance to selling the script because Nichols and Rotunno made two films together, *Carnal Knowledge* in 1971 and *Regarding Henry* in 1991, worlds apart.

12. On 29 June 1996, *Il Corriere della Sera* reported that after a failed attempt to make the film by Terence Stamp and American backers, Strehler had not given up on the project and was negotiating with Fellini's heirs to finally turn *Mastorna* into reality.
13. In April 1993, Fellini told Goffredo Fofi and Gianni Volpi that before Kafka 'we may have felt threatened, had a confused feeling, an uneasy, convoluted sensation but we didn't think such moments were part of our existence, or pertained to our effort to live life in full consciousness and to interpret it; we believed they were fleeting moments associated with an ill-disposition, a disturbance of the psyche, unbearable feelings. These sensations, these contradictory feelings, fears and hopes, the cruelty of them, are what Kafka gave a sense and meaning to; above all, he showed us the way to find that sense in our everyday lives.' Federico Fellini, *L'arte della visione* (Turin: Donzelli Editore, 2009), 5. This tribute to Kafka appears to coincide strongly with Fellini's intentions in *Mastorna*.
14. Federico Fellini, *Fare un film* (Turin: Einaudi, 1980), 67–68.

The Journey of G. Mastorna

FEDERICO FELLINI, with the collaboration of
Dino Buzzati, Brunello Rondi and **Bernardino Zapponi**

"Not good to use music to betray. He and esposa big admiration for your... for your frin frin...You everything bad..."

Interior. Aeroplane.

A large commercial passenger plane, high over an unending sea of clouds.

Here and there, the rays of the setting sun dazzle the windows of the huge passenger compartment.

On board the packed plane, they're showing a film: Laurel and Hardy trying to climb the steep sides of a giant bathtub.

Some passengers are asleep, their eyes masked. Others are having dinner, others still reading intently.

Mastorna, a man of about forty-five, takes off the headphones he is using to follow the film and continues to watch the silent images on the small screen, absent-mindedly, bored.

Suddenly, everything goes dark: the plane has entered a large black cloud; it vibrates and shakes violently.

The seat-belt light comes on. A steward makes an announcement in several languages:

– *Please return to your seats and fasten your seat belts.*

Lazily, Mastorna fumbles about and retrieves the buckle from somewhere deep down. He fastens his seat belt.

Outside it's almost dark. Through the oval window Mastorna looks at the huge outline of the wing, at first grazing over, then cutting through, enormous puffs of cloud and murky vapour. Blinding lightning flashes followed by deafening claps of thunder rapidly create a feeling of anxiety and dread.

The film has been switched off, the small screen rolled up.

Air hostesses are attempting to remove trays and the leftovers of dinner. There is a sudden jolt: glasses and tableware fall to the ground.

A steward turns the loud-speaker system on and a merry, ridiculous, piece of music can be heard off and on as the hail beats down on the fuselage and thunder claps roll in the immense skies.

The lights suddenly fail.

On the other side of the windows, beaten by rain and slush, the fog and vapour lift, leaving the view of a huge chasm. Instantaneously, a flash of lightning conjures from the darkness the terrifying image of mountains, apparently only feet away.

As if dizzy and out of control, slowly but surely, the wing begins to drop.

Vibrations, creaking, the droning guttural voice over the loudspeakers that comes and goes, not a word intelligible, heighten the sense of an imminent, dreadful catastrophe.

His face covered in sweat, Mastorna surveys his fellow passengers: like him, they are strapped into their seats, eyes bulging, mouths drawn.

Then, as if by magic, everything is still; no thunder shakes the heavens, no flashes of lightning cut across the air; a profound silence falls over the enormous sightless aeroplane, which now moves on effortlessly, accompanied only by an eerie whirring sound, as if the engines had been cut. The plane continues to plummet, enveloped in ever darker vapours.

The characteristic metallic sound before a passenger announcement comes from the pilots' cabin, and a few moments later, the voice of an air hostess, slow and clear, delivers these words:

> – *The Captain would like to inform all passengers that, for technical reasons, in a few moments we will be landing at an airfield for this 'eventuality'. Please keep your seat belts fastened and refrain from smoking. Thank you.*

In the thick twilight that has invaded the passenger cabin, only partially lit by a whitish shimmer filtering through the oval windows, the voice of a passenger can be heard, saying in anguished dismay:

For this eventuality? Did she say for this 'eventuality'?

No-one answers. Only the slow whirr of the plane can be heard as it continues its descent.

The passengers are huddled around the windows, looking out.

As if backlit, slipping rapidly past, shrouded by the remaining vapours, with the plane apparently flying no more than seventy feet above the ground, the outlines of skyscrapers, towers, domes and bell-towers can be made out.

The dark buildings flash past more slowly, without the slightest ruffling of the plane.

Then, suddenly, the crash to ground, passengers, hand luggage and overcoats thrown everywhere, pandemonium.

Jolting, shuddering and skidding in all directions, the plane ploughs on, the brakes screeching in a high-pitched whistle, as it desperately tries to come to a standstill.

Another terrifying jolt and the plane, as if snagged by its own power, begins to turn crazily on itself. On the other side of the windows, buildings, skyscrapers, roads opening out, rotate and merge into one another.

In their seats, the passengers are petrified, eyes closed, hands like claws sunk into the armrests.

The frenzied roller-coaster ride slows. The engines fall silent, only the whirr of the plane is audible, as it turns continuously on its axis.

One last lurch, like a shock wave, and the plane comes to a halt.

In the unnatural silence, Mastorna opens his eyes: the plane is motionless. The passengers, their faces still terrified, can hardly believe a catastrophe has been averted. It's a miracle.

On the other side of the windows, the frontages of houses become visible, their windows closed, then pavements, the outlines of streets, and beneath, the paving stones of the huge square where the plane has landed, undamaged.

It's a large square which the darkness of night renders indistinct, no more than an outline. There's no lighting. Gusts of rain and sleet give the paving a metallic dazzle. Above, way up high, in one of the buildings, windows start to open noisily, violently. Voices in an unknown language can be heard, surprised, in wonder. Far away, a siren can be heard approaching quickly. At the end of the main road, two headlights blaze across the darkness.

The ambulance skids into the square as the siren stops. Men in white overalls get out.

Another siren wails close by, cutting the night air like a knife. A fireman's truck arrives, lighting up the slippery paving and throwing huge beams against the facades of the buildings where groups of people are now standing at the windows, shouting in stupefaction and fear, pointing at the gigantic plane below, its wings stretching across the square from side to side, almost as far as the surrounding buildings.

Another two ambulances, small as kiddies' toys, have reached the crash scene and have pulled up under the fuselage.

Above, one of the plane's hatches begins to open. From somewhere in the city a church bell sounds, pealing faster and faster, either in warning or rejoicing, announcing festivities.

Against the outline of the hatch – now clear – the shapes of people can be made out. Words go back and forth between the ambulance men and the plane crew. They appear to be speaking a language similar to German.

– *Anyone injured?*

– *A few. Nothing serious.*

The fireman's truck is hoisting a ladder towards the hatch to get the passengers off the plane, whilst the long plastic emergency chutes are unfurled. A few passengers have already plunged to the ground. Below, the ambulance men are helping the first passengers from the chutes.

Meanwhile, Mastorna is disembarking via the fireman's ladder.

In the hatchway the captain, a handsome man of about fifty, stands waving both hands at the crowd below, reassuringly. Brave, strong, he beams at the crowd.

Below, the grateful crowd bursts into spontaneous applause; soon the entire square is swarming with people. Out of admiration and gratitude, people at the windows of the surrounding houses also clap their hands.

Motionless on the fireman's ladder, swaying in the gusts of frozen wind, Mastorna, too, looks up towards the captain, who has now disappeared inside the plane after one final wave. In the distance, the outline of a huge Gothic church can be made out and behind it, glass skyscrapers and tall chimney stacks.

Some wounded passengers are put into the ambulance, others onto waiting coaches with engines ticking over, headlights off.

Mastorna holds his hat to his head to fight off the wind and, buttoning up his overcoat, heads towards one of the coaches which is feebly lit inside.

From the huge belly of the plane they're unloading suitcases, trunks, bags. Torch lights play up and down the undercarriage, the siren of a departing ambulance starts up, there are voices, announcements over a loudspeaker, in various languages:

> – *Passengers will be taken to a motel where they will spend the night before resuming the flight first thing tomorrow morning. Suitcases and bags …*

The sliding doors of the coach, inside which Mastorna has taken his place, close and the large vehicle moves off silently.

Already far away, under the dark outline of the plane, the crowd and crew wave before being swallowed up by the night.

Interior. Coach. Night.
A gloomy carriage, illuminated dimly by a roof light, without seats, towed by a truck. The passengers are standing, squeezed together. The windows are covered with smoke and streaked with rain. Through them, Mastorna sees the fronts of houses and entrances of streets pass by, cloaked by the night. The architecture looks like a northern city. The truck's headlights light up closed doorways, lowered shutters, shop signs that are switched off, a rain-drenched advertising hoarding with a chubby baby's zany laugh. It is visible only for a split second but Mastorna notices that photo. Someone behind asks:

— *Where on earth are we? Germany?*

— *Must be Switzerland, we were over the Alps.*

— *That big church at the end of the square is Cologne Cathedral.*

— *We've been going backwards?*

Hands are trying to clean the misty windows. But it's too dark outside to read the street names or shop signs. The headlights once more hit the advertising hoarding with the baby, now with a different, yet still clownish, expression: he's winking cunningly, tiny finger raised.

A voice quietly says:

— *My wife told me not to go, not to take the plane. … She'd had a dream …*

Mastorna turns round, trying to catch the eye of the person speaking. His companions don't move. They're a blur of shapes. All you can hear is a squeaking noise from the windscreen wipers, back and forth, back and forth. Another photo of the baby boy, bundle of joy, arms open. The rain beating on the paper makes it look like he is pulsating, alive: he laughs and cries, pulls a face, breaks out into a smile.

The houses peter out. Now, they're in open country, flat, a waste land, where suddenly a cube-shaped building appears, hyper-modern, impersonal: the motel.

Motel. Night. Interior and exterior.
The two coaches have stopped in front of the motel's large cantilever roof. The passengers get off the coaches in a ramshackle manner, torch lights dancing over them. Porters and other members of the hotel staff bustle about, welcoming the unexpected arrivals.

Through the large motel windows we can see the lobby and its long divans, upon which numerous passengers have settled for the night. There are candles here and there, everywhere.

Mastorna is given a lit candle and an apology in a language he doesn't understand.

He follows other passengers through to the entrance and heads towards the porters desk.

Porter:

— *Spanish? Deutsch?*

The man flashes a dazzling set of gold teeth.

Mastorna nods with an inappropriate air:

— *Italian. I absolutely must resume my journey. At once. Is there any other transport?*
— *No sir, not at this time of night. Tomorrow morning.*

Mastorna appears vexed, impatient.

— *Call this number in Rome, 572 …*
— *I'm sorry. The phones are out of order … It is not possible to call Italy. The bad weather …* (indicating the candle Mastorna is holding) *… we also have a power cut …*
— *A telegram. Give me a form.*

With one hand the porter gives him a room key and with the other points towards a long line of people in the corner of the lobby, standing in front of desks with glass fronts.

Accompanied by the motel staff, some passengers are heading for the lifts, others for the bar.

Others still are sleeping in armchairs dotted around the lobby.

In the background members of the hotel staff are pushing trolleys toppling over with piles of baggage.

Mastorna raises himself onto tiptoe and, over the queue of waiting people, sees that there is nobody behind the glass on the other side of the desk. Someone in front of him protests:

— *We have got to send a telegram!*

On the other side of the desk, emerging from behind a partition, a young man appears, wearing a black apron, a napkin tucked into his collar. In French he says:

– We're having dinner. A little patience.

And he disappears.

There is loud applause from somewhere in the lobby and Mastorna, curious, still holding his candle, goes down two steps into a crowded night-club, wrapped in a dense penumbra. At the centre of the stage two actors, a man and a woman, are going through what must be a comedy routine, judging by the laughter and applause of the spectators. What the comedians are doing and saying is utterly incomprehensible to Mastorna, who is standing near a thick curtain, looking round: the tables are all occupied by elegant ladies and gentlemen in smoking jackets and coat tails.

At an oval table, larger than the others, there appears to be some kind of birthday party; a man is standing and is about to propose a toast; quietly, in order not to disturb the show, he is giving a speech of thanks, that, it would appear, he is addressing to Mastorna. The man has a long, pink face, and moves with delicacy.

Someone suddenly blows out Mastorna's candle. Sitting next to the wall, behind the curtain, is a young woman with an air hostess's cap. Mastorna looks at her and smiles witlessly as if to apologise for disturbing her with the candle, but the woman shifts over on her seat, inviting him to sit next to her. She laughs until she cries at one of the comedians' jokes, then looks at Mastorna, who looks back, as if to indulge her. She tries to speak, translating her words into a language which is a mixture of French, Spanish, English and a smattering of Italian:

– Oh, lui très funny. Funnyissimo. You don't understand? Pas compriso? Io ti esplico a ti.

The young woman with the intelligent face is very expressive: alternately serious, ironic, motherly, provocative. She laughs again at another joke, childishly, merrily, and continues to translate into her bizarre language. Mastorna smiles with enjoyment and attempts to help.

— Oh, lui mucio stupido! Como tu dir dans ton langage: 'To leave?' 'Livare?' 'Livire?' Uno momento; partire. Lui partito but nada arriveto, arrived?

— Arrived.

— Nada arrived porchè ... maitresse de lui ... Dimanche ... domeniga? Como grante fiesta ...

Laughing once more she points to the actress on stage who is miming something funny. Then, all of a sudden, the actress looks at Mastorna, stops moving, stares at him, appears to have an increasingly aggressive, violent, expression. She motions sharply to her partner not to move and then strides over to where Mastorna is sitting. Everything is a hush. The actress, who, under the heavy make-up, is now recognizably a man, is panting hard. With a ferocious look, he hisses a sentence that strikes Mastorna like the lash of a whip.

— Abe nisch maine mutter interzeen. Baus?

Mastorna chuckles amused and makes as if to clap his hands but the hostess has gone pale and lowered her eyes. Out of the side of her mouth she drops a short phrase to the transvestite as if to calm him as he bears down on Mastorna threateningly; he answers abruptly with the same violence as before, making it clear there is going to be no peaceful solution to this altercation. So the hostess, still embarrassed, decides to translate what the transvestite had said to Mastorna:

— He ask where is his esposa.

Mastorna is still smiling broadly, but the smile turns to ice as he notices that, all around, the audience is behaving strangely: some look on with half-smiles, others have turned away as if out of embarrassment, shame, or discretion. The hostess says with a serious tone of warning:

— He still muy in love with his esposa.

Mastorna is dumbfounded and half smiling says:

— *So where is his 'esposa'?*

The hostess raises her eyes and looks at Mastorna with unfeigned reproach. As if the transvestite had understood Mastorna's question, with a violent movement, he removes his wig and sits down in front of him, looking at him with a resentment that doesn't soften his aggressive expression. Then he starts talking in his unknown language, panting and spitting out short sentences with ill-disguised anxiety. At the edges of his heavily made-up eyes there is a veil of tears. Embarrassed, the hostess listens, her head bent forward, quietly translating:

— *You musician. He say frin-frin* (she mimes playing the cello). *Not good to use music to betray. He and esposa big admiration for your ... for your frin-frin ... You everything bad: friendship with him, hospitality. Ruined his life ...*

Mastorna is struck by this story and looks closely at the man trying to remember.

Still almost whispering, the hostess says:

— *She called Grete. In Troisdorf. Very long time ago ...*

Mastorna is disconcerted, distressed, as he begins to vaguely remember.

Mastorna (hesitating):

— *True, I've been there.*

Then pointing to the actor:

— *But I have never met this ...*

Perhaps Mastorna was going to say 'clown', but the actor has grabbed his finger and is holding it in an iron grip, spitting out threats and ending in an insult, in Italian:

— *... sporco italiano.*[1]

Mastorna stands up and yanks his finger back, tries to grab the transvestite by the neck, but he jumps to his feet and takes a step back, quick as a flash puts his wig back on, holds his arms up, and waves to the audience, then bows low repeatedly. Applause everywhere, voices calling 'bravo', laughter all around. The transvestite blows kisses of thanks and smiles at Mastorna and invites the audience to show its appreciation.

Still furious, Mastorna looks up; confused, lost, he turns round and marches out.

Interior. Hotel room. Night.
Mastorna goes into his room, in a thick penumbra, only slightly alleviated by a milky light – neon – oozing through a crack in the closed window.

A small TV set stands in the corner of the room.

Mastorna fumbles for the light switch. A bedroom, sober, elegant.

In a corner, the cello case, round sides, propped up, a ghostly presence.

Mastorna goes over to it, opens the case very carefully, lovingly takes out the cello, as if it were a living being. He takes the bow and plays a few notes to make sure the cello has not been damaged, tunes it, polishes its shiny body with his hand.

He catches sight of himself in the large octagonal mirror and, embarrassed, lowers his gaze, thoughtful, genuinely pained. In this room the strings play mutely, as if the sound were somehow rarefied. Mastorna plucks a string with his thumb, the G, and tries to get it to sound right, pure, deep.

The phone rings. Mastorna jumps and goes over to answer it.

A voice he doesn't recognize says with a euphoric, familiar tone:

– *Mastorna? Is that you? Welcome. How long are you staying?*

Mastorna tries to understand who is speaking.

– *Who is this? Who told you I am here? Your name please.*

The voice continues, in amazement:

- *You don't recognize my voice? That's a good one! So? When shall we meet?*

- *Who are you? First, tell me who you are.*

The voice grows irritated:

- *You really don't recognize me? I'm Tubino. I saw your name on the porter's manifest downstairs. So, shall we meet?*

Mastorna tries to concentrate, to remember. But the line goes dead, and the voice of the porter comes on, saying:

- *Porter. How can I help you?*

Mastorna quivers with impatience, protests:

- *I was talking. Why are you butting in? I was talking to a friend, an acquaintance…*

The voice of the porter is icy, impersonal:

- *I beg your pardon. I will call back shortly.*

Annoyed, Mastorna sits down on the bed and reaches forward to switch on the TV. Soundlessly, two faces appear on the screen, staring at him. The reception is bad: horizontal lines appear and the image won't stay still or, if it does, it's off-centre.

Mastorna is lying on the bed, dozing. A long silence. Mastorna is having bad dreams; he is restless, his lips are moving as if he were speaking; he is breathing heavily.

A sharp knock at the door, several knocks; when Mastorna opens his eyes he sees a porter standing in the middle of the room, holding his suitcase and cello.

- *Do you have any other luggage, sir?*

Mastorna sits up bolt upright.

- *What's going on … Are we leaving?*

He is already off the bed, straightening his tie, joyful, excited, muttering:

— ... *the head porter didn't tell me ... or maybe he did ... I must have slept like a baby.*

The porter has gone over to the open window: the first lights of dawn can be seen far off in the darkness. The outlines of trees in an avenue, buildings further away:

— *It'll be a nice day. We can leave through here.*

So saying, the porter climbs through the window and holds out his hand to Mastorna for the suitcase and cello.

Mastorna hands them over and then looks dumbfounded as the porter holds out his hand once more, to help Mastorna through the window. With a look of childish petulance, Mastorna refuses assistance and climbs through the window, stopping for a moment on the sill.

Something has caught his eye. He looks pleasantly surprised.

— *The sea!*

Between two buildings a flat, grey sea can be seen.

He catches up with the porter who has stopped to wait for him in the middle of the deserted road.

— *I'm sorry to have asked you to leave by the window, sir. Who knows what you must have thought. But we're on strike, you see. If they'd seen me, my colleagues, the head porter, the other passengers ...*

The porter is clinging to a wall as if trying not to be noticed.

— *Perhaps you think I am not being very fair with my colleagues ... that I'm a scab ... but I've signed IOUs ...*

Mastorna squints to get a good view of the porter, but he has turned away brusquely and is now striding on ahead towards a minor road flanked by closed shops, the goods displayed in the windows.

Mastorna is following him:

— Are we going on foot? Is it a general strike?

Mastorna quickens his steps to keep up; he is a few yards behind and losing ground.

His attention has been caught by some jewellery sparkling from a shop window. From inside a melody is being played on bells, crystal clear, sombre. Mastorna stops to look at the objects. But immediately he has to tear himself away because the porter hasn't stopped and is walking even faster.

— I wanted to get my wife a present ... I always forget ... Are we really so late?

The porter is now almost running. Mastorna stops for a moment to shout and make him stop. Then he hurries to catch up.

In the silent, deserted streets the two are hurrying along, side by side.

— Stop, stop. I can't run like this!

The porter turns to look at him for a moment and continues running.

Mastorna has the idea that the porter is laughing.

— The luggage! Leave my luggage.

Angrily, out of breath, Mastorna keeps running, closing on the porter who is weighed down by the luggage and tiring. He reaches him, takes him by the shoulder and forces him to stop. Trying to wriggle away, the man lets the baggage go and then falls to the ground. Mastorna jumps on him and the two men fight, rolling about on the pavement. It's an unskilled, untidy struggle between two men who are no longer young and are tired after running.

— What were you up to? Thief!

The porter, with strangled voice:

— We're late. It's no longer leaving ... it's a long way, you know.

— *What's a long way, you rascal?*

Mastorna grabs the porter by the throat and the porter tries to fight him off.

— *That hurts!*

He too takes Mastorna by the throat and manages to throw him down.

— *See what it's like?*

Mastorna is suffocating.

— *Get off me, I'll kill you!*

The porter now shows his face for the first time, as he stops fighting. It's the same man as the evening before in the night-club, the transvestite who had threatened him and babbled about his wife.

— *Yes, me. I have to work as a porter too … two of everything: two jobs, two families …*

He pats at the blood on his cheek. The two men look at each other silently, panting, one beneath the other, still in a jumble from fighting.

The street is deserted. The light is brighter.

The coach arrives.

In the street, at an upstairs window, a rather elderly lady has been talking for some time. She has a tone of reproach, like a farmer's wife. Her words are inaudible but she appears to be upbraiding the two of them, treating them like children.

With some difficulty, Mastorna gets to his feet. The porter is kneeling, stretching an arm out to pick up his beret.

— *She's inviting us in for coffee.*

The porter gets up, picks up the suitcase and, with a studious air, checks it for damage.

The door next to the window clicks open.

Exterior. Street (motel slip road). Day.
It's a first floor window, maybe even a little lower. Looking out from the window, the previous evening's flat wasteland has become a brightly lit up street, with a thronging, oddly assorted, festive, crowd. Streetlamps, lights, garlands, neon signs, spotlights pointed at the facades of buildings, flags, banners, streamers, strange flying deer lit from below. Confused echoing music of some kind, choirs chanting solemnly, organ music, bells ringing, singing from minarets, long trumpet blasts.

Under the cover of the crowd, Mastorna sees the porter slipping away with his suitcase and cello. The porter turns round and beckons to him to come down from the window and look sharp about it.

Exterior. Churches, street. Day.
Mastorna steps through the window into the street.

The kerb is lined solely with churches, enormous, tiny, ancient, modern, Christian, Romanic, Gothic, baroque, Mosques, pagodas, synagogues, Buddhist temples, as well as some giant idols, steaming in the open air, where a swarm of priests are gathered to hold mass.

A restless, yearning multitude is flocking to the spot. Pilgrims arrive on coaches that pull up along the side streets; swiftly, they alight and immediately form processions, carrying sacred images of the weirdest cults.

At the entrance to the various temples, high priests are enticing people in the crowd, shrieking strident appeals so loudly not a word can be made out clearly.

Mastorna makes his way forward along the pavement as people run in all directions. He's lost sight of the porter but occasionally seems to catch a glimpse of the cello case high above the crowd, so he tries to push his way forward, past arms and legs that push back, crash into him, press in from all sides.

In front of a baroque church, like so many in Rome, he thinks he sees his cello case floating atop a crowd entering the church.

But when Mastorna tries to go in, a wall of backs blocks the entrance.

He stands on tiptoe. Over the top of the crowd he faintly sees lights and smoke from the altar, and can hear a Gregorian chant.

Swept along by the throng, he is carried to the front of a primitive temple, some way off the street. The temple is made of huge blocks of stone, one on top of the other, like prehistoric huts in Sardinia.

He wipes some sweat from his brow, then returns to the main street to look about.

He can no longer see the motel, which should be there, at the end of the street.

He approaches a young man in a Norwegian jumper.

— *Excuse me, the airline coach?*

The young man looks at him with a feeble expression.

Mastorna continues:

— *Where does the coach leave from?*

The young man replies in a language Mastorna doesn't understand.

A procession of young, chattering kids swarms around him, holding the lines of fish-shaped, Japanese-style, kites.

The last of them is a long fish, a snake, with a string that seems endless.

Fretful, Mastorna looks for a way through, but a new wave of people arrives, pinning him back against a wall.

It's a procession of nuns, who are almost running and are reciting a prayer that sounds like a tongue-twister, faster and faster, incomprehensible; all that can be made out, here and there, are words of praise.

— *Holiest of women ... dove ... purest ... est ... est ...*

Mastorna catches hold of someone who looks like a traffic warden.

— *How do I get to the airport? Please help me.*

Despite himself, he is close to panicking, barely able to control himself. The traffic warden gives him an encouraging smile. He's a fit-looking young man, part blond, part red-haired, blue eyes, honest looking. He takes Mastorna fiercely by the arm, drags him toward the crowd, strides forward.

> – Is it a public holiday today? What are you celebrating? I really haven't been able to work it out. I would like to stay in this city, and I'll certainly return. I've been promising my wife a trip for many years, but work commitments ... Or maybe it's just that a trip with my wife doesn't seem the perfect holiday. I'm always finding excuses. But this time I want to keep my promise. She has earned it! I haven't been a good husband. Once, I felt remorse, but I don't feel even that any more.

Mastorna has said these things speaking to himself, with empty smiles, stutters, at times down on his knees, as if suddenly tired, and the traffic warden has continued to drag him along, pushing people in the crowd away with his right arm, barking and grunting at them to move.

Exterior. Sentry box/lodge. Day.
In the middle of a crossroads a glass construction, narrow, vertical, a sort of sentry box, houses three or four traffic wardens, squashed together. One of them appears to be in command.

Mastorna and his traffic warden stop in front of the sentry box; the warden knocks on the glass to attract the attention of the Chief, pointing to Mastorna.

> – I must get to the airport. I'm one of the passengers who made an emergency landing here yesterday evening, after the plane developed a fault.

Chief warden:

> – There was no fault on the plane. It was a scheduled landing. What is your name, sir?

— *Mastorna. Giuseppe Mastorna. I am a cellist. I have a concert this evening in Florence. I must get back to Italy before midday. We are rehearsing in the afternoon.*

Saying this, Mastorna hands his passport to the Chief, who doesn't look at it and asks:

— *You have no other papers? This doesn't prove who you are, sir.*

As if anticipating Mastorna's surprised, resentful reaction, he adds:

— *It's just a passport.*

A crowd has gathered around the glass hut and is observing the scene silently. Mastorna looks around and, seeing rows of expressionless faces, he loses control:

— *But this is my passport, it's official: I renewed it two months ago. Look at the stamps. What kind of authority do you represent if you do not consider a passport valid identification? Where on earth am I? A porter who steals my baggage, the telegraph operators at the hotel who refuse to take a telegram because they're eating, the head porter who doesn't wake me in time, although I'd asked him to, and now a representative of the local police, an officer of the law, since that's what you appear to be, who says a passport is not a valid document for the identification of a foreign citizen. Rest assured, I will report all this to my Embassy.*

During this tirade Mastorna noticed the night-club hostess looking into his eyes, making signs as if to placate him, then shaking her head with a look of care and suffering. She just irritates Mastorna all the more and he turns on her violently:

— *What are you doing there? What are you trying to tell me, you insufferable bore?*

The hostess speaks low, shyly, as if she doesn't want the wardens behind the glass to overhear:

> – *Just say you want to leave. That'll be enough for them and they'll be able to help you.*

Suddenly Mastorna's legs feel weak. He has to sit down on the octagonal step at the bottom of the sentry box.

The wardens, still inside the glass construction, seem higher up. They have gone back to their work and are paying no attention to Mastorna.

More and more people have come up. They stand around Mastorna in a circle, silently.

Mastorna (almost to himself):

> – *I've already explained. The airport.*

Then, still quieter, disconsolate, without accusation:

> – *What did you put in my drink last night? What was in that liqueur?*

And he sits there, head bowed, without strength or willpower.

Someone in the crowd has started speaking, at first quite quietly, then louder and louder.

Tiredly looking up, Mastorna sees a bearded man with an authoritarian look about him, addressing the crowd as if he is giving a political speech.

> – *... the airport is under construction, nobody would deny that such a complex project needs lengthy research, a great deal of time, but in all frankness, situations of this sort, which are being brought to our attention right here and now, are extremely embarrassing since they require us to justify to a foreigner the exasperatingly slow progress of the building work at the airport.*

All around, the flowing of the crowd, the arrivals and departures of buses and processions, resume, at a hectic, chaotic rhythm, accompanied by a deafening ringing of bells, liturgical chants, voices all speaking at once, a Babel of languages.

Finally, someone leans down over Mastorna as if taking pity on his bewilderment and with a calm, polite tone, whispers in his ear:

> – *If you like, I can take you to the station. I'm going that way myself.*

The invitation gives Mastorna new strength; he gets up and follows the man, who pushes his way through the crowd.

Exterior. Side street (car). Day.
They walk down a side street which is less well lit and less crowded. The stranger comes to a halt in front of an old banger, a broken-down wreck.

> – *Here's the jalopy. Do get in.*

They get in. The stranger switches on the engine.

> – *You'll be able to take a train from the station. There's an information desk and they will tell you all you need to know.*

Interior. Car.
Now Mastorna looks at the face of his helper as he drives on in silence: an uncomplicated face, with something that is both courteous and strong-minded in the expression. It ought to be the face of an elderly man, were it not for the smooth skin and spirited expression in his eyes. Some wisps of white hair around the temples give him an air of courtesy and dignity.

> – *I have the feeling we've met before.*

A brief pause. The driver smiles slightly as if to say: I don't recall, I dare say.

> – *And this street, I seem to remember it too. Isn't there a school back there, with some steps? And further ahead a cinema, the Fulgor?*[2]

The silent driver turns to look at Mastorna, as if, a split second earlier, he had anticipated this sudden gloominess from his passenger.

Mastorna looks dejected, almost crumpled up on the seat, no longer looking through the windows at the streets and squares.

Slowly the driver begins to speak:

> *– I think I understand your situation and would like to help.*

With sudden self-pity, through the loneliness and sense of abandonment, Mastorna replies, almost to himself:

> *– You are very kind, but at this moment I have the impression that nobody can help* (with a discouraged tone) *… what has happened now?*

On the other side of the glass, in a steady grey light, the streets and squares are going by, the buildings of a city that is both unfamiliar and familiar; some of the architecture is certainly foreign, from another civilization, very different from any that Mastorna has ever seen or come across. Some shop signs are illegible, others console by being recognizable.

For example: some side streets, which might be the oldest part of Rome or Albano Laziale or Venice.

> *– One thing might help you perhaps: try to remember how you got here. I mean, the exact moment you set foot in this city. Try to remember even the tiniest detail, exert yourself a little.*

Mastorna nods obediently, grateful.

> *– It isn't difficult: it all happened just a few hours ago. Yesterday evening. I'm a cellist. Together with the orchestra conducted by Maestro Lucifreddi (you will have heard of him, I presume: he is a famous conductor), we performed a number of concerts in your country. The other day we were in Hamburg. With my colleagues I was supposed to return to Italy by train, to Florence, where we are giving a concert this evening. In Hamburg I met a girl and missed the train. My colleagues left without me. Luckily, yesterday afternoon I was able to book a plane: over the Alps there was a terrible storm. We were all very afraid, it was a frightful moment, and when it was all*

over they told us the plane had developed a fault, I think, and we were forced to make an emergency landing, in an airfield for the 'eventuality', so they said. Strange landing, to be sure. In a city square. But it all happened slowly, smoothly: an excellent pilot I must say. They took us to a motel and this morning, when I was supposed to take the coach, I got lost.

Exterior. Station.
The small car has come to a stop. The driver has got out and is opening the passenger door.

The two men are standing, one in front of the other. The helper is looking into the eyes of Mastorna, a smile hovering about his lips, like someone who is waiting for a sign, an expression, a light to come on in Mastorna's eyes.

But Mastorna has a cold, opaque look and the helper, disappointed, without further ado, takes his leave.

– *This is the station, dear friend. I must hurry. Look for your train.*

And before Mastorna can thank him, the car is far away.

Interior. Station entrance.
Mastorna turns and sees a huge shelter, full of people, and smoke from distant trains, whistling plaintively.

Under the huge smoky vault, trains are incessantly arriving and departing ... on the wide platforms hordes of people board and alight from trains that clatter deafeningly down the tracks as the loudspeakers make uninterrupted, echoing announcements: not a word is understandable.

The posted timetables with destinations and train times are equally incomprehensible.

Everywhere you look, there are advertising hoardings, banners and dummies, huge faces smiling, winking, opening their mouths.

Long queues of passengers stand in front of the ticket counters. It all looks in a state of chaos.

On one wall there is a gigantic map with islands and continents, and moving lights to illustrate routes.

A very beautiful but rather elderly lady, white in the face, her eyes red from crying, is walking in the crowd like a sleep-walker, asking whoever she comes across in a sobbing voice:

- *Anyone arriving from Dijon? I need some urgent information. Are you from Dijon?*

Other passengers shout different questions.

- *Charles de Louvot! Does anyone know, has anyone met, Captain Charles de Louvot?*

An old lady takes Mastorna's arm, follows him almost as if he were dragging her along, and shows him a photo that has gone yellow with age, saying tenderly, almost sobbing:

- *My son ... see, my son. I heard him call out. But I don't see him. ...*

Fending her off, Mastorna tries to carry on in the same direction but a young woman, with a harrowing smile, almost indecent, taps a finger on his chest and says, rather provocatively:

- *Engineer Ribulsi?* (she repeats the question in German).

Mastorna carries on past her, giving a hurried reply:

- *No ... no, pardon me ...*

On the other side of the barriers making long corridors Mastorna can see tables with large, incomprehensible signs, where passengers are being directed. Mastorna makes his way over, surrounded by a crowd of restless, wandering people.

At the tables officials are giving out information rapidly and almost inaudibly, at a feverish pace.

Mastorna turns to a woman who seems to be some kind of hostess, standing by a table. Pointing to the large signs, he asks:

— *What do they say? What is written here? What are they talking about?*

Smiling slightly from the corners of her mouth but looking in another direction, the beautiful hostess replies:

— *If they were about you, you would understand them.* (Then, speaking loudly to the assembled crowd.) *There is no point in taking any baggage. Leave your belongings at the depot.*

The loud-speakers booming underneath the station vault repeat the announcement from time to time.

— *Forbidden to carry any baggage. Leave your luggage at the depot.*

Pushed onward by a wave in the crowd, Mastorna finds himself at a low desk where brutal, stylized orderlies gruffly take the suitcases and bags from the passengers and throw them into a massive pile on a mobile platform. Those who have been deprived of their luggage rebel or complain, protest in bewilderment:

— *Why are you doing this?*
— *Where are you putting them?*
— *We need those bags.*

An elderly man, corpulent, with a white turned-up Stetson hat, desperately tries to get his luggage back, particularly his bag, shouting in a low tenor voice:

— *Not my bag. My papers ... I have all my papers in that bag ... I need them.*

Without reply, one of the orderlies throws his suitcase and bag onto a loading device, like a metal hold which — by remote control — begins to lower into a dark chasm.

Beside himself, the man who is standing right in front of Mastorna runs to the lowering device and waves from underneath it, shouting, begging:

> – One moment. ... No, I beg you, give me back my bag. ... My papers ... I need them. ... If only the photos of my wife, my children!

Finally Mastorna sees a sign that gives him some hope: INFORMATION. With some effort Mastorna manages to push his way through the crowd standing in front of the office but the desk is still a long way off.

Standing on tiptoe, Mastorna sees a female office clerk behind the desk who appears to be signalling to him, then shouting to him, but the noise drowns out her words.

> – ... Mastorna? ... go?

Mastorna gestures in impotence, to show he can't understand, and the other passengers around him react with aggravation; one of them turns to him, his patience tried to the limit.

> – She wants to know where you are going.
> – To Florence. I have to get to Florence.

From a distance the clerk continues to gesticulate and mouth words which he doesn't understand.

> – You don't understand? If you don't say where you're going, there's no point standing in line.

Interior. Station. Papal procession. Day.
Just then, an illustrious arrival: behind Mastorna, heading towards the information desk, comes a procession of ecclesiastical authorities, in full ceremonial dress, hoisting above their heads a luxurious throne, and on the throne, wearing a papal crown and mantle, richly embroidered and studded with gems, a Pope. The smoke of incense from the swaying censers blends with the dark clouds of locomotive steam. A sacred choir of a thousand voices can

be heard, accompanying this extraordinary event. Silk, velvet, huge flabella waving, the whiteness of the robes of altar boys, the black tail-coats of the diplomatic corps, the high combs of the Spanish ladies, the sumptuous make-up of the wives of French and American attachés, and up high, on the chair used to dispense gestures to the crowd, the small white figure of the Pontiff, his face like a wax mask, eyes half-closed, immobile, intent on his own immense pride, like someone who has achieved all he set out to in life.

All around people applaud, kneel.

– *He died a holy man.*

– *He said: 'Leave me in peace. I know very well where I'm going and why.'*

– *He said: 'I am not afraid, I have no doubts, I am well.'*

– *'Everyone has their rightful place. I am going to my place.'*

– *Bless us, bless us.*

A group of altar boys and a large number of priests push through the crowd and reach the Information desk. They shout:

– *He is here. There must be no delay.*

– *He must be the first on the list.*

The kneeling crowd joins in:

– *'Te lucis, ante lucis, ante terminum rerum Creator poscimus.'*[3]

Interior. Station. Day.
Mastorna looks on incredulous.

His attention wanders to a small shadow; from almost out from between his legs a poodle wriggles and slowly trots away, wagging its tail.

Mastorna (with a cry from the heart):

– *Toby! Toby!*

The dog turns his head, wags its tail, then moves away into the distance.

— *Toby!*

Leaving the Information desk Mastorna pushes his way through the crowd and altar boys and follows his dog.

He follows him along a platform, but the dog has disappeared. Mastorna continues to look for him and his eyes fall on …

Interior. Station. A four-decker train. Day.
… the window of a carriage, as high as a building. Behind the glass someone makes a slight movement as if to greet Mastorna but the train is already pulling slowly away; the fifth floor of the carriage is invisible under the smoky roof.

Mastorna looks as if he has turned to stone: he stares at the pale image of the person who greeted him, who now is being taken away by the train.

He's a boy of about fifteen, dressed in school uniform from about forty years ago.

— *My God!*

The boy on the train has lowered the window and is leaning out, he's shouting greetings in the deafening noise, and waving his cap.

— *Mastorna, how come you're here? God be with you … God be with you!*

Interior. Station. Day.
Without saying a word, Mastorna stares at the train disappearing into the distance.

Mastorna (stuttering):

— *Venturini! … But he's dead! … He died forty years ago.*

Shocked by the revelation, Mastorna walks towards the exit like an automaton, as if trying to escape from something terrifying, unacceptable, but which he knows in his heart to be true. The announcements of the loud-speakers, the distant strains of music from the juke-box, the buzzing of the crowds, the voices, become an obsessive chorus. Mastorna walks quicker and quicker, as his anxiety increases.

At each side he sees confused images of the crowd, one person after another.

Mastorna stops, exhausted, in despair. He begins to shout:

> – *No ... it cannot be ... I am not dead! ... I can't be dead! ...* (he touches his face and arms) *... I can feel myself ... touch myself ... I am made of flesh and flood ... my heart is beating ... I can hear ... see ... it can't be true ... can't be true ... take me back! ...*

As soon as he started to yell, a small group of people, ticket collectors, clerks, gathered round him. They look on in silence, expressionless.

Mastorna shouts with increasing vehemence:

> – *I can see ... feel ... I'm thirsty ... hungry ... want to make love. ... If I were dead, would I want to make love? ... Answer me!*

Shouting and tottering on his feet like a drunk, he approaches one of the hostesses, grabs her by the shoulder and embraces her.

> – *Would I want to kiss you, if I were dead? ... would I? ... answer me! ... answer!*

Wildly he throws her head back and presses his lips to hers. The woman acquiesces, moves closer to him.

> – *I can make love to her, right here, in front of everyone, to prove I am alive.*

And greedily he puts his hands into her blonde hair, kisses her, bites her lips.

The woman has long eyelashes that hide the depth of her imperturbable, slightly ironic, eyes and it is in those blue eyes which slowly dilate, until they disappear, that he sees, as if on a screen, a horrifying scene.

Exterior. Mountain range. (Plane wreck).
The peak of a snow-covered mountain. Close-up of crevices in a glacier; between one crevice and another, a peculiar black stain: the wreck of a large aeroplane.

Helicopters hang over the disaster scene, like buzzards in a funereal merry-go-round.

Next to the wreck: torn, charred, twisted bodies.

Now a man lying on his back, head thrown back, his forehead crushed. But the face is intact, the mouth and eyes half-open: it is him, Mastorna. All that remains of his poor body.

The long eyelashes of the hostess lower slightly, the atrocious scene sinks and dissolves into the blue of her eyes.

Interior. Office of the Deputy Station Master.
A pleasant-looking man, with huge nose and tiny gold pince-nez, is taking off his overcoat and hat; he is speaking affably, with amused indulgence, as if he were talking to a child.

Mastorna must have fainted, because he is on a stretcher, surrounded by three or four people. A hostess has rolled up his sleeve and is giving him an injection.

Deputy Station Master:

> — *With a little calm you will understand that our staff merely wishes to be of assistance. The question is far simpler than it might appear. It is we, that is to say, you, who want to make it more complicated than it really is. As you can see, you are inside a station. Here there are trains for every possible destination. But passengers need to have valid documents and must say where they want to go. That is the right and obligation of every passenger.* (In a comic dialect voice.) *My good fellows, if you don't tell us where you want to go, what can we do for you?*

The hostess/nurse has finished the injection and is buttoning up Mastorna's sleeve, smiling at him pleasantly.

– *But the poor man said he wanted to go to Florence.*

The tone is one of slight irony, as if she were making fun of him.

– *Dear fellow, I realize that you may not trust me, or anything that I say, and therefore I have asked these gentlemen to be here. A meeting, a few words between old friends, I imagine that might do you some good. Do you remember your teacher of religious education?*

And saying this, the Deputy Station Master pushes a tall, thin priest towards Mastorna. He has an ascetic air and begins to speak with a lovely bass voice:

– *Come come Mastorna a little courage. A little coherence. What is the matter with you?*

Deputy Station Master (pretending to be scandalized):

– *Imagine, Reverend, have you any idea what this scallywag wanted to do? He wanted to make love to one of our hostesses, here in the station, in front of everyone.* (He bursts out laughing.) *To show that he is alive. What a fellow. What a joker.*

The priest chuckles in genuine amusement.

– *It is excellent evidence. Love is life.*

Seemingly irritated by this idle chitchat, another person steps up impatiently and pushes everyone else away from Mastorna's stretcher-bed. A colonel in Italian Army uniform. He addresses Mastorna unceremoniously:

– *My dear Mastorna I accepted the Deputy Station Masters' invitation very willingly, because I think I know you better than the others, and if I had been allowed to I would have brought here Pelizzi, Rivalta ...*

He says these surnames with an emphatic tone, yet touched, and tries to conceal his feelings, which he considers unmanly.

> – *Longobardi. Tell me, Mastorna, do you remember Longobardi?*

Slowly turning his head to the wall, as if to deny the reality of the people standing by his bed, feebly Mastorna begins to speak:

> – *I don't believe a word any of you are saying. I don't want to recognize any of you. I'm dreaming and I'll wake up any minute. And if I can't wake up yet, I want to change dream. As a child I use to be able to change my dreams as I was dreaming them.*

Maternal, the hostess sweetly and delicately whispers almost into his ear:

> – *What would you like to dream?*

A tapping at the glass windows attracts Mastorna's attention.

On the other side of the glass, behind a backdrop of buildings, the face of a man with curly hair and long black sideburns appears.

Only the head is visible, which from time to time lowers, so only the eyes can be seen. Evidently he is standing on tiptoe to look into the room. The man makes energetic, ironic gestures, which appear to be telling Mastorna to pay no attention to the people around him.

No-one else in the room has noticed him; they carry on talking amongst themselves, sometimes raising their voices.

Deputy Station Master:

> – *... it is advisable to have your situation registered as quickly as possible. Everything depends on this: placement or individualization, as some prefer to call it. Without which continuation ... let us say, of the journey, is impossible.* (Brief pause.) *Oh indeed, my colleagues have told me of some cases in which people have wanted to do as they please, and it appears that they managed to depart all the same, but where did they end their journey?*

Priest (with a conciliatory tone):

> — *Undeniably cases of this sort do exist. There are forms of help even for those who obstinately refuse help. But in your case, Mastorna, I really would advise you …*

But Mastorna is not listening. Now he is sitting up, dedicating his whole attention to the man making faces behind the window, who continues to make fun of what is being said, with grimaces, shakes of the head and shrugs of the shoulders.

Someone who looks like a clerk sitting at a typewriter begins to speak.

> — *It would be sufficient to find a moment, the slightest moment, from your life … listen to me, even an insignificant one … in which you, precisely, were yourself … at least once … just once.*

The face behind the window is sticking out its tongue, like Pulcinella. It blows raspberries, makes obscene gestures, and now invites – orders – Mastorna to come away from there, to follow him, to have nothing to do with these people.

Mastorna stands up, a little unsure on his feet, and goes towards the door. Nobody tries to stop him. Nobody says anything. Mastorna opens the door …

Exterior. Station. (Tree-lined avenue).
… and is back out in the street. Immediately the little man with curly hair, now holding onto the rusticated stone walls of a building, jumps down and comes towards Mastorna, with the air of an old friend.

> — *Ah! Jesus be praised! Finally you understood that all those brainy guys, those half-wits and harlots, with their big words, and wiggling of their asses, just get you more and more mixed up. Heavens above! Have pity on us! Is that any way to treat a man, a man who had a mother! You were good, congratulations. What did you say? I heard you. 'I don't believe*

> *a word any of you are saying. I don't want to recognize any of you.' Hah hah hah!*

And the little man blows a raspberry and makes an obscene gesture with his arm.

> *– I was about to fall for it, too, you bet! (He imitates the voice of the ticket collectors.) Where do you wish to go, who are you, who are you really ... (standing bolt upright). What do you mean who am I? I'm Armandino. Armandino Proboscide. Who else?*

Saying this he shakes Mastorna's hand and, at the same time, waves to two strange individuals, gendarmes or priests, it isn't clear which, on horseback, riding silently, down the tree-lined avenue, rapt in thought. The two horsemen condescendingly return Armandino's greeting and continue unperturbed.

> *– See? Everyone knows me here. Everyone likes me, because they know I'm no fool, and I don't put up with fools and their tricks. They say: 'you are dead!' And so? What of it? Anyway it's not so certain, because I've been here for a long time, dear Sir, I eat, drink, smoke and ...*

With a vulgar wink he makes it clear that he also makes love.

> *– Let's suppose, for the sake of not getting into an argument, that we're dead. Is that any way to ...*

Exterior/interior. Phone box.
Suddenly Armandino trails off and, quick as a cat, pushes Mastorna into a phone box on the pavement.
Armandino (whispering):

> *– Quick. Get in.*

Then, with a booming voice, he speaks to a group of people approaching the phone booth:

> *– I'm terribly sorry, we got here first. Be patient, you will have to wait your turn.*

He winks at Mastorna with a complicit air and laughs, pleased with himself for his quick-wittedness.

– *Did you hear the complicated, convoluted words from those shysters? 'Individualization, identification.' But what I say is, doesn't it enter into your tiny minds that a poor fellow, who hasn't a clue what is happening to him, who is in a country he doesn't know, that speaks a language he doesn't understand, one minute Naples, the next New York, then Bologna, one place then another ... Doesn't it occur to them that a poor wretch might want to phone home? Might want to hear his mother's voice, his wife's, any old harlot's, someone he loves?*

He looks at Mastorna, his eyes filled with tears, like a ham actor, and pinches his cheek with obscene affection.

– *But you were born with a silver spoon. Here is Armandino Proboscide, who is about to connect you to your wife. Here are the coins. See how many?*

So saying, he takes out of his pocket a pile of coins of different shapes and colours.

– *Do you remember your number?*

Mastorna, who has been listening to this lengthy preamble with a feeling of dizziness and sickness, loses control. His nerves get the better of him and he bursts into tears. Armandino, too, is genuinely moved, and whispers, lowering his head:

– *Is that any way to behave dear boy?*

Mastorna continues to sob with his head close to the wall of the telephone booth. Armandino puts the coins into his hand and with a voice choked with emotion says:

– *Call home. I'll be outside.*

And he steps out, closing the glass door behind him.

Interior. Telephone booth.
Alone in the phone booth, Mastorna whispers his home telephone number feverishly, his fingers trembling. Close-up of the telephone. On the dial most of the numbers are missing and the ones that are visible are incomprehensible ideograms. Mastorna feeds in the coins and dials frenetically. At the other end the phone rings repeatedly. Mastorna waits in trepidation. Then there is the metallic sound of the receiver being lifted and a man's voice says clearly:

– *Who is this?*

Mastorna jumps. The voice is exactly like his own, as if someone were imitating him perfectly.

– *The Mastorna residence?*
– *Who is calling?*
– *Answer me, please. Is this the Mastorna home?*

After a little hesitation, the voice says:

– *Yes, who do you want to speak to?*
– *Who are you?*
– *Who are you? You're the person calling.*
– *I'm Mastorna. Giuseppe Mastorna. Who is this?*
– *What an idiotic prank! What do you want?* I am *Mastorna.*
– *I beg you. Listen to me* –

But the line has already gone dead.

Exterior. Telephone booth.
Outside, on the other side of the glass, the faces of unknown people are crowding in; they are waiting to use the phone.

Behind them, Armandino is buying a bag of lupins from an old lady sitting on a small stool. Armandino looks at Mastorna and starts to wink and pull faces of encouragement, as if to say everything is fine.

Interior. Telephone booth.
Mastorna dials the number again but a deafening hiss interrupts him. Then there is a click and a metallic, impersonal, evidently recorded, voice says:

– *The number you have dialled ...*

Then the hiss again, a chiming, a piece of music blasting out, followed, after all this racket, by the metallic voice once more:

– *You are advised not to continue, if first ...*

The hissing becomes high-pitched, drowning out the voice. Mastorna repeatedly bangs on the cradle to free the line and dials again, slowly, biting his lip, his forehead covered in sweat. The phone rings repeatedly and a young woman's refreshing voice comes over the line.

– *Yes, I was going to call you. I'm going out.*

Mastorna tries to keep calm, to give his voice a demure, persuasive tone.

– *I beg your pardon. Is this 572420?*

After a moment, as if puzzled, the voice replies:

– *Yes, of course.*
– *Is Luisa there? Is she resting? I'm afraid I don't recognize your voice young lady. Are you one of my wife's friends? Could you ask her to come to the phone?*
– *You ... are calling the Mastorna household, I imagine? I don't have the new number. They moved. Three months ago. After the accident. We are the new tenants.*

Exterior. Telephone box.
In the meantime, in the square, an ambulance is circling the phone box, closer and closer, its siren howling.

The crowd hurriedly disperses in order not to be run over and forms a large circle around the phone box, watching the ambulance.

The ambulance is now backing towards the phone box, its rear doors open to prevent Mastorna from escaping.

Armandino has managed to squeeze himself between the phone box and the ambulance and signals wildly to Mastorna not to leave the phone box, to wait.

Inside the ambulance a young doctor in white overalls is sitting on a stretcher trolley next to a beautiful nurse, watching Armandino waving his arms and smiling, as Armandino, red in the face, yells:

> – *You should behave like a gentleman. No bullying. You have to tell him the truth. You have to tell him he is free to decide. No no, that is the point …*

He has opened the door to the telephone box and has grabbed Mastorna by the wrist, shielding him with his body.

> – *I've seen them, with my own eyes, taking people away, without a word about the regulations. And the regulations are clear. You don't have to get in. Vaccination is not obligatory.*

Fellini: *"You know sometimes I have had the feeling to have met personally Mastorna. But every time he slips away again."*

The beautiful nurse, who now looks like a mature woman, yet still very pleasing to the eye, a mass of black hair falling loosely over her shoulders, eyes and mouth heavily made-up, gets out of the ambulance and speaks to Armandino with an amused, tolerant tone, like someone used to dealing with this strange, colourful character.

> – *Of course he is free! Nobody has any intention of taking him away against his will.*

Then she speaks directly to Mastorna:

> – *But if you decide to stay in town, postponing your journey, you must be vaccinated. Like everyone. Even you, Armandino.* (Again to Mastorna:) *No hotel would give you asylum, no boarding house. Everybody is given strict instructions not to provide hospitality to foreigners who do not have our certificate.*

> – *He wants to think about it. He doesn't know what he wants to do yet. What do we know? He's just got here. What if he wanted to leave right now? What for? Who says he wants to stay here? What if he doesn't like it here, hates it? What if he's had enough?*

Armandino drags Mastorna along by the wrist and manages to get five or six steps away, through the circle of curious onlookers.

> – *You're so quick to judge, you lot!*

Then staring into Mastorna's eyes he hisses into his face:

> – *Do you trust me? Don't decide anything, not yet. You haven't been able to speak to your wife, right? I'll get you through to her. I know someone who asks no questions. He'll arrange it. Better than on the phone. Because you feel something in your heart. He's a friend of mine. Last year he got me to speak to my brother. What a row we had! I've never got on with my brother. And fifteen years ago, I remember it as clearly as if it was yesterday, I thought about Oreste ... Greta was Dutch,*

she bellowed when she made love. Yes, when she came, she yelled like a tiger. I was in Amsterdam for two months. So, as I was saying, Greta came to mind. What'll she do …? Will she remember me? So I went to him. … You'll see, it's quite extraordinary. He has a machine, an invention of his. You hear them in your heart, the people you're talking to. I swear, that evening, me and Greta we almost made love. Here's our train. Let's get on.

During this long speech, Armandino has been pulling Mastorna along by the hand …

Exterior/interior. Underground steps going down.
… away from the phone box and the ambulance.
They take a dark flight of steps down to below ground.

Interior. Underground passageway.
With rapid movements, as always, Armandino pushes Mastorna onto the Underground train, which immediately starts off again with a deep rumble. The train is packed. But Armandino has managed to grab a seat by first throwing his cap onto it. He pushes Mastorna onto the seat and then, twisting, contorting, dancing and wriggling, with a pyrotechnical series of grimaces and threatening looks, he manages to squeeze into a seat opposite, forcing the others to huddle even closer together.

The train is travelling at high speed. On the other side of the windows neon signs appear and disappear rapidly, underground roads, huge, funereal, deserted car-parks, gigantic junctions criss-crossed with railway lines, and crowds lining the platforms at each station they speed past. The train doesn't stop at any station and continues its clattering headlong journey.

– *What's your wife like? Young? Middle-aged? Do you have children? Do you need them more than your wife? You can tell me.*

Mastorna is angered by his nosiness and over-familiarity and doesn't reply.

– *I don't have a wife, but I have children, how can that be?*

Armandino seems suddenly to have become sad. Leaning forward, elbows on his knees, his head rocking backwards and forwards with the motion of the train, he has lit a cigarette and is smoking in silence.

Now he raises his head and looks at Mastorna and the two look at each other in silence for some time, either far away or very close, brought together by the same mysterious adventure, yet utter strangers with nothing in common.

– *Do you really want to talk to your wife?*

And with a tone of voice which is half discomforted, half tired and sleepless, Armandino adds:

– *Because, if not, we can stay here. Sleep here. It's not so bad here. The train goes round in circles. It might even never stop.*

Suddenly his eyes are veiled with tears. Stretching out a hand he makes an awkward attempt to hug Mastorna's knees.

– *You're good to me. You do me good. You can help me. The others steer clear of me. Don't even talk to me. So Armandino just gets nastier. But you seem to be different. You seem ... if I ran into you there must be a reason for it. Perhaps you can tell me about these journeys everyone is always talking about. ... What do you reckon, is it worth the trouble? Should we go? Sure, here is ok; but I've seen plenty of people like me, some of them my friends, who didn't want to go, they wanted to stay here, they refused to be vaccinated, and I've seen them become ... It's atrocious ...*

Armandino looks terrified, mumbling and curling up like a frightened dog. A voice, with a satisfied tone, says into the silence:

– *Excellent, Armandino.*

It's the ticket collector, a beautiful girl in uniform, a large leather bag over her shoulder.

Armandino pulls himself together.

– Hi, Mariarosa, we don't have tickets, but we're getting off here. We're going to see the Professor, me and this gentleman, a friend of mine. Be kind to us, Mariarosa, slow the train down, we can get off while it's still moving.

Armandino and Mastorna get up and go to the doors. The train slows as it approaches hundreds of neon lights, flickering in the darkness of the tunnel. It looks like Place Pigalle.

Armandino (caught in the wind of the speeding train):

– Come on, let's jump!

And he jumps from the moving train to the ground, followed by Mastorna and ...

Exterior. Street. Night-club.
... together they walk along a street with lamps, lights, neon signs flicking on and off, moving, making patterns, of women, naked, dancing, and the faces of clowns, animals, magicians, devils.

After a few words at the entrance of a tawdry night-club, Armandino goes in, pulling Mastorna behind him.

Interior. Night-club. Night.
Inside there is an unimaginable horde of people, immobile, some standing on chairs, all looking into blazing, focused stage lights, towards the centre of the dance floor of another night-club, not visible from here, but where evidently some kind of primitive, horrendous orgy is taking place, with beastly copulations, judging by the greedy, rapt attention of the onlookers and yelping, barking noises coming from a heaving mass of blonde hair and dogs' tails.

Armandino finds the man they had been so breathlessly looking for, curled up at a dark corner table.

A soft, drooping face, like Oscar Wilde, two swollen lips pasted at the edges into an immobile smile, long greasy hair half way down his neck.

Moving around behind him, Armandino bends down, points to Mastorna and says something passionately into his ear.

The man listens, slowly raising his face from his beer glass, and looks at Mastorna with a diffident, bored air.

Armandino winks at Mastorna and waves his hand with a flurry, commandingly, beckoning Mastorna to approach.

– *I've told him everything already. Luisa is her name, your wife's, right? What a beautiful name. What taste, what distinction!*

Meanwhile the man, from under the table, has taken out a strange-looking machine where all that can be made out is a horizontal cylinder in the middle, covered with signs, and a dial with graduated rods and a tangle of wires, knotted string and a series of metallic receivers opening out like a bunch of tulips.

From that moment on, the man never looks once at Mastorna and speaks whilst continuously fiddling with the machine.

– *Concentrate on a feeling of serenity, uncomplicated, unforced, love, pure and simple.*

On the seat he now occupies, with all his willpower, yet choking with anxiety, Mastorna tries to concentrate. He wrings his forehead with his hands, closes his eyes, holds his breath.

But almost immediately, connecting a plug, the man says:

– *Don't be so shy. I can't hear a thing yet.*

Mastorna screws up his eyeballs and writhes in concentration. Meanwhile the din of the music and the rowdiness of the sad carnival are reaching their climax.

Still fumbling with the receiver, the man says:

– *It's no good. If you don't concentrate, if you don't feel true love. Give me your hands. Call with me: Luisa.*

Trying to concentrate, Mastorna repeats: Luisa!

– *Louder, louder. Luisaaa!*

He addresses Armandino and the others who have gathered round:

– *... Help me, all of you.*

Armandino:

– *Luisaaaa!*

The man:

– *Luisa, I love you!*

Mastorna:

– *Luisa, I love you!*

The man:

– *Louder, everyone together!*

Armandino:

– *Luisa, I love you!*

Now the other customers join in what becomes a jangling, mocking chorus.

– *Luisa, I love you. Oh, how I love you. Ah, I love you so much.*

Everyone else in the night-club has climbed onto the stage, and to the orders of a powerful-looking striptease artist with a mournful face, they are doing a collective striptease. An acrid smell of sweaty, grimy, naked bodies is given off from the infernal exhibition.

Fat, bald men with huge bellies, monkey-like, hirsute women of all ages, some old, with sagging breasts, all wrinkles, take off their clothes in the centre of the stage and, one after another, do a striptease with deliberate, studied motions.

– *Luisa, I love you, I love you ...*

The man holds up his hand to silence everyone and asks Mastorna to put his ear close to one of the trumpet-shaped receivers.

– *Perhaps it's possible. I can hear her coming. Listen closely ... is that the voice of your wife?*

Bending down over the strange contraption, his face covered in icy sweat, Mastorna listens intently, trying to hear a far-away, cherished voice.

But the trumpet-shaped receivers only produce a strained and unrecognizable gurgling that doesn't bear listening to, so much does it sicken and terrify.

The gurgling continues, becoming flaccid sounds, like mud, intolerable to Mastorna's ears and heart. Overcome with nausea, unable to put up with it any longer, he throws up.

A young man, corpulent, powerfully built, bursts into the nightclub. The unbuttoned shirt reveals a large, fleshy, sweaty chest.

His eyes are feverish like someone who has drunk too much and is uncontrollably merry, bawling out in excitement.

– *Fabulous. Hallelujah. I'm dead at last, I've done it! They can't touch us any more, we don't need to be afraid of anything. I no longer have to die! We can't, even if we wanted to! But you lot, what are you doing here? Why aren't you celebrating? Laughing? Shouting? We have nothing to fear now. A whole life with just one thought! A temperature, a slight pain, and that thought came back to ruin any peace of mind.*

He strides over to Mastorna energetically and pokes his finger into his chest.

– *You. What are you making that face for? Why are you sad? What are you afraid of? Aren't you ashamed of yourself? Don't you understand you can't die any more? We were frightened on the train, on the plane, frightened of disease, of cancer, of accidents, we were frightened all night! Fear, a whole lifelong, nothing but fear. But not any more! No moooore! We are no longer condemned. Let's celebrate! Come with me, all of you! Come and play, you too!*

And so saying he opens the wooden shutters of a low, wide window and with a jump he is outside.

Mastorna, as if inebriated himself, infected by the uncontrollable exuberance of the young man, follows him impetuously, going out onto a huge terrace surrounded by rooftops, terraces and chimneys.

Exterior. Night-club and terraces.
The black outlines of houses merge on the horizon in an unending stretch of terraces, each one crowded; even the windows are full of faces and heads.

Laughing madly, the young man throws himself over a balcony and falls head first eight floors to the ground, shouting with joy. He hits the paving with a terrible thud, like a walnut being smashed open.

He has fallen onto the tarmac of the road below. The body is motionless, atrociously twisted out of shape, lying in a pool of blood and spilt brains. He stays like that for a few moments, then jumps up, like the coiling of a spring, alive, young, good-looking, healthier than ever.

– *You too, go on, throw yourself down! You can't die any more!*

A terrible noise begins. The people from the night-club have come out onto the terrace and are now throwing themselves over the balconies in comic poses and – with sinister thuds – are smashing onto the road below. A few seconds later, they get to their feet, unharmed, happy.

Other windows open, there are shouts and greetings, everyone joins in the impossible suicide, a huge pile of human bodies falling downwards, some joyously playing and cavorting, everyone falling to the same spot.

After crashing onto the road, the bodies reform and happily climb back up the ramps to throw themselves over again.

It turns into an endless cycle of people crashing to the ground, climbing back up, throwing themselves down.

Mastorna too is now on the night-club terrace. He leans over to look down and sees people falling everywhere, then picking themselves up.

From the windows people are applauding, laughing, encouraging others. Hands wave, arms reach out, voices shout high-pitched.

– *Down!* ...

– *Down!* ...

– *Everyone down!*

– *What are you waiting for?*

Right in front of Mastorna, a beautiful woman throws herself over head first, flying down, her petticoat acting as a parachute. Laughs come from all the windows, others are clapping as they watch the show.

Another beautiful girl with a determined look about her takes a step forward, looks down and undoes her belt. She ties it around her knees to prevent her skirt billowing as she falls, winks at M. and takes him by the hand.

– *Come on! Together!*

Mastorna hesitates but allows himself to be taken by the hand, then, closing his eyes, he throws himself over the balcony with the girl who, laughing, lets out a shriek and hollers, beating her hand against her mouth, like children imitating red Indians. Mastorna and the girl fly down merrily smashing into the road like two ripe pears. The blood falls in a rather decorative pattern all over the road but, to his surprise, Mastorna is able to stand up again immediately. He feels better than ever, he can hardly wait to climb back up and throw himself over again.

And that is what he does. In his haste and enthusiasm, his heart swelling with wellbeing, he removes his jacket and tie in order to throw himself down more freely.

Street below the night-club.
Now, from the end of the otherwise deserted street, a small, German-style, military band approaches. At that particular place and time the music is exquisite, breathtakingly beautiful. Like all beautiful music it contains and expresses the sufferings of humanity, regret, nostalgia, but it is as if these were overcome by the force of life coming from the trumpet section, with its carefree rhythm, its happy, heroic abandon.

From the rooftops and windows people are throwing themselves into the street, women, old men, children, some fully dressed, others in dressing gowns or pyjamas or completely naked. They smash into the road; blood and intestines spill out onto the tarmac. As they energetically get back onto their feet, the brass band passes, marching in the middle of the road.

And Mastorna? Just look at him. Here he comes again, falling and laughing happily.

Exterior. Window of a large room in Naples.
Three floors down, a handsome woman, fat, sweating, is cooling herself with a frilly fan. Quick as a flash, she reaches out a hand and seizes him by the end of his shirt. Mysteriously, he stops falling. Mastorna is puzzled, upside down, floating in mid-air. With a flabby, lazy voice, affectionately maternal, the fat lady says:

> – *What do you think you're up to? Handsome fellow? You're all sweat. You'll be catching something; come inside, rest a while. Don't listen to all those mush heads.*

Saying this she spits a sweet out onto the pavement.

Mastorna hesitates, holds onto the balcony and rights himself like a jellyfish in the sea.

> – *At your age! Just look at you! What do you think you're doing? Are they paying you for diving over balconies? Get in here!*

The woman moves aside to let him pass. Calm music, guitars and mandolins, the noise of cutlery being washed up, comes from the room, which has a welcoming penumbra.

Floating in the air, Mastorna decides to enter.

Interior. Large room.
It's a huge, all-purpose room: kitchen, living-room, bedroom, bathroom, like some Neapolitan rooms of the petty bourgeoisie: the furniture, wallpaper, light and darkness, create a familiar, tatty, comforting atmosphere. An endlessly long, tattered sofa lines one of the walls, like a station waiting room or, more likely, a brothel.

In point of fact, there is a sort of counter in the corner of the room and behind it, sits a gigantic old lady draped in a cloak, a classic Madam, sleeping and muttering in her sleep.

What else is there? A huge chest of drawers and a high, complicated mirror, decorated with nymphs and sirens; it looks like an altar, with Madonnas and saints, wedding couples, children attending the confirmation service, babies suckling, venerable old men, sailors on deck, cuirassiers, combat soldiers. Around it, to the side and front, lamps have been kindled. They flicker. Olive leaves, garlic, corn on the cob.

A worktable with fabrics and cloth, sewing machines and irons.

On a mannequin an immaculate wedding dress, its train reaching half way across the room.

The fat lady drones on in her complaining voice, wiping some sweat away from her cleavage and combing her hair, which falls to the middle of her back.

> – *Have you seen what you have done to your clothes? Mummy's little boy, poor creature, this cloth is of fine quality!*

She kneels down to wipe something away from Mastorna's trousers with a handkerchief, feels the cloth and then, with a tone that could be of joy or complaint, she almost shrieks:

> *— Fancy that! The very same cloth, the same design as poor Mimì, the day of the outing.*

So saying, she begins to sob. Then she blows her nose and dries her eyes and goes over to a large oven where she is cooking a huge pile of spaghetti. She rinses the pasta and starts to put it into various plates, doling it out with her hands. Then she sprinkles some cheese on top. All the while she has been speaking, complaining, as Neapolitan women do.

> *— We went to the celebration of the Holy Virgin of Health, took an aubergine stew, omelettes and potatoes, and Assunta made some cakes. Do you remember Assuntina?*

Four or five people are sleeping, all jumbled up, in a huge bed. One of them is a sturdy-looking lass, half naked, hair dishevelled, lively mulatto eyes, who suddenly starts to laugh shrilly.

> *— Of course I remember him, Mum.*

She goes back to pushing someone who doesn't seem to want to budge from the bed, continuing to repeat in a childishly sulky voice:

> *— Entertain us. Keep the man who has just arrived amused. Do it for him.*

Meanwhile the fat lady is giving out the plates of pasta to everyone in the house.

> *— It was a spring day. What sunshine, the sea. ... Look here. This is Mimì.*

She has stopped in front of the mirror with the saints and photographs and is showing Mastorna a small photo between two large prints of King Vittorio Emanuele III and Mussolini.

Fat lady (bursting into tears):

> *— Where are you, saintly soul, why don't you come back to us? What do we have to do to find you?*

She continues to sob for a while, shaking her head and its huge mass of hair, then wipes the tears from her eyes and nose with the back of her hand and continues to tell her story in a calmer tone of voice.

> – *The poor dear man, he saved every penny, he'd even given up smoking to be able to buy himself a used 500 on HP. Eight of us could squeeze in. The whole family, everyone. Even granny came with us that day. Granny, do you remember the walks to the Holy Virgin of Health?*

Kicked out of bed by the continuous pushing of Assunta, a poor old man, almost completely naked, his skin yellow and shrivelled, is putting on an MC's coat tails. He swears under his breath about being woken.

He pulls a bowler hat onto his head, takes a walking stick from the wall and, accompanied by the rhythm of a bass drum, leaps about here and there in the room, like a puppet controlled from above, gesturing lewdly.

> – *Ndringhetè ndrà ... ndringhete ndrà ... uè ... uè ... ndringhete ndrà ... uè!*

In the meantime a large number of soldiers, sailors and airmen have entered the room, their legs twisted, bandages poorly wound around their calves, combat troops, some Americans, a few of them black.

They sit on the long divan and smoke, talking quietly and awkwardly amongst themselves.

Fat lady (resuming her story):

> – *God only knows what it was like when we got back. I was sleeping and saw nothing, heard nothing, just a big pain here, you see?* (and she uncovers a huge tit). *I suppose it was better that way, we all died together. I don't know what happened. Maybe Mimì had had a few too many and fell asleep at the wheel. You read about that kind of thing in the papers, don't*

you? Assuntina said she was awake and saw everything, she says we plummeted into the sea at the San Gervasio corner ...

She bursts into tears again.

... Only Mimì isn't with us, only him. (She begins a funeral wail.) *Saintly soul, where are you? Did you stay behind? Have you gone away?*

On a large television set looming at the foot of the bed, Mike Bongiorno[4] can be seen putting on his glasses to read from a folder. He is saying (from the TV):

– *And now for a second song:* Moon and Love in the Night *by Bardazio and Mayer. The singer is Joe Melanotte.*

As he makes this announcement the women begin to scream their appreciation, some running from the corners of the room, others crawling on their knees over the bed, others still pulling themselves along like dogs with their backsides on the ground. They gather round the television set, with their plates of pasta, avidly staring at the screen and Joe Melanotte singing passionately, tightly squeezed into a strange striped smoking jacket and with hair like a horse's mane.

Assuntina has invited Mastorna to sit on the bed and he has obeyed. He, too, has his plate of spaghetti and is awkwardly curling them onto his fork, comforted in his wretchedness.

The fat lady, who has rolled up on the ground at Mastorna's feet like a huge cat, takes her eyes off the television screen and gives him a languid, maternal look.

She shrugs, a lazy, age-old gesture of acceptance, and starts to speak to him, cleaning his trousers with her hand and untying his shoe laces, as if to invite him to get into bed.

– *What can be done about it, Mummy's little boy? Life's like that. Today we're alive, tomorrow who knows. God is all-seeing, all-providing. We are in his blessed hands. So, handsome little boy, listen to this ignorant lady who could be your mother. Stay here. You've seen? Outside, no-one knows us, they're savages, and besides, it's cold, always winter.* (As if conceding a point.) *True, every now and then someone drops in, even here, they haven't forgotten us completely, but who understands the questions they ask? 'What do you want to do?' they say, 'where do you want to go?' What do we know! We want to stay here. You can see for yourself, we lack for nothing. ... A plate of spaghetti, a little music and our love, you poor darling, are yours for ever.*

In the middle of the huge room, a sort of metallic cage starts to shake and rattle, screech and click as an old lift descends. It has transparent sides and is pompous and baroque like a funeral carriage. In the lift there are three or four whores, half naked, plumed. The lift thuds to a stop: the door squeaks as it opens; smiling and waggling their asses, the whores do the rounds of the room, passing in front of the soldiers on the divan.

– *All my daughters. Good girls. Worth their weight in gold. Here we have a very exclusive clientele. Dolores, see her? She even speaks Romanian. An oil magnate, handsome fellow, beard down to here, grew love-sick for her, wanted to marry her.*

Suddenly she stops talking and gets up, her back to Mastorna, as if to prevent him seeing. Meanwhile the lights have dimmed: a trill of bells can be heard and down below, in the brothel, there is a flurry. Even the old lady at the cash desk has woken up and is shouting:

– *Out of the way, close the doors, don't look, darkness in the house!*

Leaning sideways, past the huge backside of the fat lady, Mastorna can just make out in the distance the arrival of two people who must be dignitaries of some kind, maybe a Minister, a Cardinal? But, without turning round, the fat lady clips him round the ear as you would a nosey child:

Mastorna (to Assunta):

– *Who are they?*

– *What's it to you?*

The girl climbs onto his lap and looks at him with a big baby deer's eyes, a playful smile on her lips. She traces his profile with her finger, his nose, his lips.

– *Do you like it here? Are you going to stay with us?*

Another body, nearby, moves under the sheets and Mastorna sees a face appear a few inches from his own, the proud, crying face of a beautiful girl, with tousled black hair like the snakes of the Gorgon. Her pain seems to bring out both her suffering and voluptuousness; she is staring at a photo she is gripping hard in both hands.

Assunta:

– *She's my sister. But she wasn't with us in the 500. She died when I was still a baby. She poisoned herself.*

She winks at Mastorna, as if announcing some imminent naughtiness.

– *Gemma, how come you poisoned yourself, eh? Tell this gentleman, why did you do it?*

The girl clamps her jaw shut, panting hard, her pitch-black, proud eyes orbiting in her head, and finally, with a choked voice, tormented and haughty:

– *For love! The love of this …* (but her dialect is so strong her words are incomprehensible).

Gemma cries, screams, bites the pillow, kisses the photo repeatedly; it shows a combat soldier with a shining black moustache.

On the television Joe Melanotte is continuing to sing his passionate song; beneath them, far away, in the brothel waiting room, the whores walk back and forth; the chosen one gets into the lift with the client and, clattering horribly, the lift rises and disappears beyond the ceiling.

Mastorna (murmuring low):

– *How can you live like this?*

Assunta shrugs.

– *What else can we do?*

She has lifted the sheets with both arms and, indicating to Mastorna something curled up under them, at the bottom of the bed, she says:

– *Johnny, show him your little tongue. Did you like the goat? Is your tummy full?*

These words, spoken very affectionately, like someone talking to an infant, are being addressed to a huge python, at least five inches thick, curled up in a cold, revolting heap.

– *Give your Assuntina a kiss.*

She sticks out her tongue, tempting the reptile, which sticks its own tongue out rapidly. Quick as a flash, the two tongues meet, lick.

Mastorna is disgusted and slowly brings his legs up closer to his chest; but he is too tired to get out of bed; he looks at the girl playing with the snake. His eyelids are heavy. Overcome with sleep, he falls into a deep darkness.

When he wakes up the large room is flooded by a thick penumbra. Everyone around him is asleep: Assuntina, granny, granddad. Only Gemma continues to stare at the photograph of the combat soldier.

A humble combat soldier attracts Mastorna's attention: down in the brothel waiting room, now almost deserted, there are just figures moving about slowly; one is the fat lady, the other an old pilgrim with an ornate cane. San Giuseppe? San Gennaro? The voice of the fat lady can be heard mumbling a prayer.

She kneels.

Fat lady (whispering to Mastorna):

– *He is our blessed Saint. You may ask of him anything you desire. Ask him about the award.*

The strange figure has somehow petrified. He is ancient, decrepit, and the fat lady speaks to him with exaggerated fervour:

> – *Blessed Saint, has this learned gentleman earned his award? Why on earth not? What has he done wrong? He is some Mummy's little boy, he has lived his life, like us, like everyone. What else should he have done? Move your eyes, blessed Saint, move your eyes.*

The bearded head of the saint. Eyes closed. Immobile. Wooden. Suddenly it opens its eyes and moves the pupils rapidly to the left.

With an exclamation of joy, the fat lady turns to Mastorna:

> – *A miracle! You will receive the award, Mummy's little boy. You've deserved it. The award! The award!*

In the large bed someone next to Mastorna suddenly sits up as if roused from a deep sleep. He throws back the blankets, jumps out of bed, pulls on a pair of trousers and with an agitated tone invites Mastorna to get dressed and follow him. It's Armandino.

> – *Hurry up, I'll come with you. Aren't you happy? You've won an award.*

Exterior. Street. City.
A large crowd is moving in procession towards a huge pavilion festively decorated with banners and flags. Dozens of enormous spotlights shine high up on the façade, which glitters and glistens.

Mastorna, jostled this way and that, stunned yet absurdly hopeful, allows himself to be dragged forward by Armandino, who cuts through the crowd shouting, cursing, pushing.

In front of the pavilion, a hundred or so policemen have linked arms, making a human chain to withstand the rush of the crowd, which makes its assault in waves. The award winners are greeted with bursts of applause as they arrive in lavishly festooned automobiles.

Powerful and clear, a loudspeaker announces the names and, presumably, merits of those who are arriving.

Valets in all their pomp, assistants in coat tails, sweating private secretaries are bustling about, running to open the car doors. They bow and accompany the award winners up an endlessly long red-carpeted staircase which winds into the pavilion, as music and sounds echo all around.

People frenetically hold out autograph books for Mastorna to sign.

With high-pitched screeches the fans want him to approach, to give them his autograph; they touch him, pull the bottom of his jacket, take off his tie.

Armandino protects him, slapping and punching the crowd left and right.

Out of long, fabulous, black automobiles shining like mirrors, solemn as coffins, come ladies bedecked from head to foot with jewels, accompanied by gentlemen in coat tails. Some of the men are dressed in rags, some of the women are nondescript and look frightened.

The loudspeaker continues to echo, blasting out name after name with, here and there, an explanatory sentence.

> – ... *and all those who are deserving, even if only for a crumb of good intentions. No matter when, even at the last minute.* (In a state of agitation as if the speaker can no longer repress his own feelings.) *At this very moment General Jim Holyday has arrived. With all our hearts we wish for him one of the awards. You all know that the good news is received only at the last moment, when the votes are counted. No-one knows the result in advance, but General Jim Holyday carries our hopes. We are all with him and for him. Welcome, General!*

A hurricane of applause breaks out everywhere, whilst a vivacious old man, carried away with emotion, starts to climb the staircase with uncertain steps and enters the light of the foyer.

A beautiful lady greets him at the top of the staircase with open arms, kisses his face, his bald head, and pushes his face, dry as a prune, for a moment into her warm milky cleavage.

In the midst of all this shouting, clapping, whistling, Mastorna sees the Pope, who he had already seen at the station, arriving in the procession of award winners.

But this time he is no longer sitting on the throne borne aloft by altar boys. He is walking along, in muddied white silk slippers, the Papal tiara a little crooked, with a tired, rather lost expression, not a trace of his former pomp and self-importance.

He is no longer escorted by a large court, no assistants with flabella, just three or four priests struggling to hold up the train of his Papal cloak, occasionally dropping it onto the ground into the dust and rubbish, as if weighed down by an utter lack of confidence …

Interior. Large award hall.
Still pulled along by Armandino, Mastorna enters the hall: a huge parterre for the audience, men and women of all ages and social class. Flags fly all around, and there are thousands of spotlights, ceiling and wall lights, chandeliers.

Streamers are being thrown from the crowded wings; there are shouts and screams, applause, the music of various orchestras, making a deafening din. Tables are laid and decorated with lit candles, where people are eating and drinking; in the dimness trays can be seen swaying back and forth, laden with food and drink.

At a seemingly unreachable distance, at the end of the hall, the stage is bathed in a white light. The MC, dressed in coat tails, is standing in front of a microphone, going through his routine of insipid lines.

> – … *we are all waiting with baited breath, and my own heart, I must say, beats faster, because I too may be the recipient of an award or a punishment. And what could be a worse punishment than not to receive an award? What better award than not to receive a punishment?*

He laughs and everyone laughs, clapping nervously.

> – *My own mother is up here on stage. She is nervous on my account … for herself. And your mothers, too, are nervous,*

> *your girlfriends, your sisters: because the names of the award-winners are written there in those envelopes, they are a secret, top secret.*

Onto the stage steps a wonderful looking lady, in a brocaded mink coat and complete set of jewellery, like a profane Virgin Mary. She smiles left and right, responding to the whirlwind of applause. An ascetic, smooth-skinned valet follows her. He's holding a huge coffer of envelopes. The beautiful, majestic woman smiles and her smile is instantaneously reproduced as a close-up on hundreds of television screens.

With a white hand she takes an envelope and gets ready with a graceful movement to open it.

But before she does, the MC indicates a giant screen behind the bouquets on stage, ready to be presented to the award winners, and, as if by magic, the screen lights up:

> *— As always, and as you know very well (perfection does not allow for innovation), we show scenes from the exemplary life of the award winners on this screen. This serves, if not as an example — what someone knows how to do, someone else may not be able to do — at least to justify the decision that has been taken.*

The beautiful lady smiles, in perfect agreement, and then deftly opens one of the envelopes.

Lady (reading):

> *— Nerina Dossi, aka Doris, housewife, from Castel delle Vigne.*

Lengthy applause drowns out the lady's voice, while a shabby and rather shy-looking woman gets up out of the front rows and climbs onto the stage, helped by the MC who immediately starts to clap his hands virtually in her face.

On the large screen there is a photo of the woman: a gigantic close-up showing her in an attitude of humility, her eyes averted, a wan smile playing over her lips, perhaps begging forgiveness.

A friendly-looking man with a coloured sash over his chest approaches the microphone and starts to speak:

> – Here you are amongst us, lily of the valley. We were expecting you. The honour you do us by joining our brave little community exceeds by a thousand cubits any worldly honour we might be able to bestow upon you. Like a luminous meteorite of goodness you passed over the world of work, of fear and crying, regaling us with the delights of joyfulness, your smiling face …

Prodded by Armandino, Mastorna has been taken into a corner of the huge hall to a table with mirrors and fierce lights.

Someone with greased, curly hair and a flashing moustache forces Mastorna down onto a seat like a barber's chair.

Immediately, girls dressed in manicure uniforms approach and wrap a large towel around his neck.

– How does he have to be made up?

Armandino:

– He's such a dear fellow. A great artist. A musician. A Maestro.

Man (jumpily):

– I see. But the motivation for the award? I have to know that.

Meanwhile one of the girls has already started to daub Mastorna's face with greasepaint while another is painting his eyes black. Mastorna looks about, increasingly disturbed and irritated.

Other people next to him are pushed onto chairs and quickly made up, as people babble suggestions, orders and counter-orders.

Up on stage, the award ceremony continues. The loudspeakers announce the name of another winner.

The giant screen shows his photo: an elderly little man with glasses and an arrogant air about him, pompously self-assured.

The man with the sash continues his speeches of unreserved praise:

> – ... *you were an example to your fellow citizens of a man of principle, a zealous, unstinting worker, of untarnished public and private rectitude ...*

The make-up artist with curly hair is becoming hysterical, because Armandino's generic description does not tell him how Mastorna should be made up.

> – *What kind of artist? Inspired, damned, Romantic, mystical? The public must see at once from the make-up I have given him, that the award is deserved.* (Turning to Mastorna:) *Why do you think you deserve this award they are about to give you?*

On stage the voice of the man with the sash continues to reverberate through the loudspeakers.

> – ... *who can look at you without feeling his heart beat with respect? Whose heart is not moved at the thought of your deeds?*

Around Mastorna the make-up artists, assistants, manicure girls and Armandino are discussing animatedly, each suggesting a different type of make-up; one lifts the line of his eyebrows, another combs his hair so a curl falls over an eye, someone else adds lipstick to his cheeks. Four, six, ten hands pull his face this way and that, pressing the corners of his mouth up, down, combing his hair, the parting in the middle, on the left, on the right, someone suddenly adds a false beard, then a goatee, then a moustache, fair, black, red.

> – *No, not like that. His expression is too hard.*
> – *Yes, that makes him look sweet!*
> – *Not humble enough!*
> – *Like that, he looks idiotic!*
> – *Too intellectual!*
> – *Nice!*
> – *Fickle!*
> – *Fool!*
> – *Fabulously handsome!*

- *Hypocrite!*
- *Coward!*
- *Thief!*
- *Mummy's boy!*
- *Hero!*
- *Shithead!*
- *That's no good, no good at all, too frightened!*

Then the loudspeaker slowly echoes his name. It's him they want, no doubt about it.

- *Giuseppe Mastorna. Cellist.*

Mastorna, face covered in greasepaint, lipstick and eye liner, exasperated by all these hands running amok, jumps up and, wiping his face with his towel, goes up to the stage, whilst the audience begins to clap deliriously. Fanfares, flags waving, balloons launched into the air.

The man with the sash comes towards him, reading from his prompter the customary litany of praises.

- *Come closer, chosen one of old planet Earth, excellent example of the hum-…*

He is about to say 'the human race' but as he opens his arms in welcome the pieces of paper he is using as a prompter fall to the ground. With difficulty he bends down to pick them up, panting, and continues his speech in a fluster.

> *… come closer, allow my unworthy hands … the sacred golden image … no, here it is, master of harmony, producer of sonorous enchantments, we were expecting you! To the timid sound of your instrument the leaves fluttered, men, burdened with sorrow, felt the call of Paradi-…*

Again he breaks off, looking for the right piece of paper.

The MC comes to his assistance, picking up the piece of paper with the continuation of the sentence, which he reads out:

> ... *Paradise, the expert music lover heard his aesthetic expectations realized. You honour us, Maestro, with your presence, you comfort us by accepting this tangible token of our unstinting admiration!*

On the giant screen at the back of the stage there is a photo which should be of Mastorna, but isn't. The photo shows someone squalid, bundled into overlarge coat tails, smiling stupidly, immobile, one hand raised in salute.

All the members of the panel of judges clap wholeheartedly, while the beautiful lady in the white mink coat with a sparkling crown of precious stones on her head walks towards Mastorna with the box containing the Award.

Mastorna (pointing to the photo):

> – *But that's not me!*

> – *I am pleased to place in your hands the tangible token of our estimation ...*

Mastorna's voice is hoarse with rage:

> – *That's not me! Can't you people tell it's the photo of someone else?*

But the man with the sash, the MC and all the members of the panel of judges are smiling with amusement as if Mastorna were a capricious child (nodding their heads energetically they seem to be telling him that the photograph is of none other than himself).

Below, Armandino, his chin resting on the apron of the stage, is pulling his usual faces, winking eloquently, as if to tell Mastorna not to bother with these details, to be less pedantic.

Armandino (in a low voice):

> – *What's it to you? Think nothing of it! Just take the Award. It's worth its weight in gold, even has artistic merits. Take it!*

Implacably, the beautiful lady flashes the whitest of teeth in an enormous smile and continues with her practised singer's voice …

> – … *the sacred golden image so many dream of. That you may be happy here with us for all eternity!*

So saying, she opens the box which is lined with silk and contains a gold-plated metallic token, which she is about to hand over to Mastorna.

But Mastorna does not take the Award. He looks at the trophy in silence, with a look of mockery and then, with a little tap of his hand, he knocks the box out of the hands of the lady who looks at him stonily, jaw dropped, eyes wide open. In the sudden silence that has descended on the entire hall, Mastorna begins to speak with a wavering voice:

> – *Eternal happiness? Here? With you? In this circus? In this noise and vulgarity? In this cretinism? I can do without your eternal happiness!*

Murmurs all around. In the silence there is a kind of choked hiccup that soon becomes a terrifying heart-rending wail.

It's coming from the audience, immersed in darkness.

> – *This is your afterlife? Authentic life? This is what we were supposed to be struggling for, after so many years of fear, anxiety, solitude, suffering? A stinting, bitter life, all just to get to this wretched ceremony? This is the kingdom of Heaven?* (Screaming with despair.) *It cannot be! With all my strength, all my passion, my intelligence, my heart, I proclaim: death cannot be this! We must not, cannot accept it!*

Humiliation, confusion, tiredness, disdain, fear, lead him to break down into tears which flood his eyes and fall down his cheeks, covered with greasepaint and eye liner.

In the hall some have started to clap, others are whistling, voices can be heard here and there, some encouraging, others disapproving, shocked.

- *He's right.*
- *Get him to stop.*
- *It's a scandal.*
- *At last someone who says what's what!*

Mastorna:

- *When we were children we went to Church, remember? They took us to Church ... they said prayers and confessed their sins ... men have built enormous cathedrals ... have suffered, hoped, been killed ... for what? For this charade? Answer me: all for this charade? Ever since I arrived everything has been chaotic, incomprehensible, worse than before, a ridiculous piece of tomfoolery without an ounce of sense. It makes me think back to our humanity with regret, our common sense, our human lives, for all their mistakes. A God who has invented this is a confused, clumsy God who needs our help, our advice.*

More applause and more whistles greet Mastorna's words. Comforted by the encouragement and galvanized by the heckling, he continues his speech with an increasingly aggressive tone.

- *What squalor. What poor imagination! So this is death in all its glory?*

A single voice from the darkness of the hall pipes up with a question:

- *What did you expect? What did you think it was going to be like?*

The question is greeted by the audience with some laughter, but then there is absolute silence as they wait for Mastorna to answer:

Mastorna tries to concentrate. It's painful, as if he is trying to remember something:

- *Yes, yes, what would I have wanted to happen?*

But it is as if his mind were blocked. Lost, desolate, he confesses:

> — *I don't know* ... (then, inspired). *But there must be something more than this ... something that isn't exactly like what we have already been through. It can't be just the same. The same ignorance, fear, vanity, shambles, as before. And no-one able to tell us what has happened, what we should do. We have the right to an explanation* at the very least.

Voice (oozing rhetorical pathos):

> — *He is right. What did we die for?*

Other voices:

> — *An explanation!*
> — *Give us an explanation!*
> — *Tell us once and for all what we are doing here!*

With a satisfied smile, following this success, Mastorna gestures to the crowd to be quiet, because he still has something to say. After looking with disdain at the members of the award panel, who are confabulating at the side of the stage, unsure of what to do, Mastorna resumes more calmly:

> — *I came here full of optimism and humility, ready to answer to whatever would be asked of me, willing to pay whatever debt I had to pay; in return I asked for a little clarity, unambiguous words, an accommodation, some indications to guide me. Instead of this they give me some kind of medal with a motivation that would make our lowliest and most frivolous Court laugh. They give me a stupid trophy for equally insignificant actions.* (Pointing to the photo on the giant screen.) *They can't even get my photo right. Are you pretending not to know me? Must I help you to remember me? Must it be I who tells you who I am and what I have done? Well, if it has to be me, what was the point of being spied on, observed from behind my back, for an entire lifetime? You* must *remember everything about me. Everything* must *be written in burning letters in your minds, your memories, and*

if not, if it isn't written, then you have been negligent and you, not I, deserve to be punished. Or perhaps this medal, which you give me for no reason, is a symbol of my whole life, a merry and incomprehensible 'he lived happily ever after' with which to wish me good riddance? In that case I refuse to accept such shameful recognition. I say no. Enough is enough. What is happening here is monstrous and criminal, a humiliation, an insult to my heart and my intelligence. I was led to believe in an illusory idea of justice, an award, a punishment, and now I realize that with these I have given my life an entirely imaginary sense that has prevented me from discovering its true sense. What should I do? What can I do? Cry over the disappointment, the bitterness, the pain? It would be too little, it would mean giving myself up to this disgusting mire that is trying to suffocate me. I spit on this absent, mad Court and scorn its silence.

The end of Mastorna's speech meets with utterly contrasting reactions; some applaud frenetically, cry with enthusiasm and approval, others heckle, curse Mastorna, demand his immediate arrest. Groups of sympathizers have moved to the foot of the stage acclaiming Mastorna as a liberator. Between the rival factions, insults and blows are exchanged; everywhere in the hall people are fighting and struggling. Shouts and whistles, a deafening noise. The members of the panel try to calm the furious. Someone motions to the orchestra to start playing: a dance tune strikes up and the tangle of people begins to divide into couples. Many start to dance, whilst the loudspeakers invite everyone to be calm and moderate.

One of the groups which had applauded loudest has climbed onto the stage and surrounded Mastorna; they toast him, hug him, hoist him in triumph …

… as a portly man dressed in a pinafore, with a cap on his head and filthy mackintosh thrown over his shoulder, pushes his way through the crowd; he is badly shaved, sweating, fat, a rugged moustache sprouting from under his nose, half a cigar stuck in his mouth, light-coloured eyes, possessed like a crazed animal. He speaks with a strong Emilian accent and, despite the corpulence, moves with epileptic haste and liveliness: he pulls Mastorna down from the shoulders of the throng of fans, and hugs him close to his bosom, repeatedly.

> – *Well done you old swindler! You really told them, this bunch of assholes with their bollocks full of incense! Come here, let me hug you. It's the first time I've ever kissed a man, but you deserve it!*

Mastorna recognizes the man with the cap who keeps hugging him and slapping him on the back as his old Philosophy teacher from school.

Mastorna (surprised, moved):

> – *Professor, Professor De Cercis!*
>
> – *Ah, so you remember your old chum De Cercis! But tell me this, have you forgotten your dialect, you old swindler you! You speak all posh like some other bastards. Shame on you!* (Talking to the others.) *Hey, he was no genius when he came to me for private lessons! This time you rumbled things straight away, didn't you? You realized nothing had changed, there are no answers to any questions? Remember what I said: 'A metre above the cap I'm wearing on my head ...'*
>
> – *... there's nothing at all, just air blowing about ...*

In a duet they continue:

> – *And if you want to stand on tiptoe to look for something you're likely just to catch cold.*

They both burst out laughing whilst the crowd of fans applauds wildly.

> – *They threw me out of all the schools in the Kingdom and to get by I gave private lessons to dimwits like you.*

More laughter and hugging. Then, more seriously, almost moved:

> — *Well done Mastorna! At first I was afraid; I really thought you had become an asshole like everyone else and would be pleased to get your medal.* (Then, suddenly turning to the thronging crowd and the members of the panel.) *Animals, cowards, Fascists! What are you still blathering on for about prizes and punishments? Do you know of any better prize than 'man to man' or better still 'woman to man'? Instead you see these fatheads, these irredeemable cretins, they never give up, you know, they come here every day, keep on asking, searching, hoping ...* (shouting at the audience) *you continue to jerk off waiting for a fuck that never comes ...*

The Professor's foul language, his violent, blasphemous oratory provokes a new reaction amongst the crowd. Screams, whistles, insults, shouts of 'Enough! Throw them out!' hail down from everywhere.

A compact squad comprising members of the panel, assistants and policemen, advances threateningly on Mastorna, De Cercis and their sympathizers.

Amid all this chaos, calm as you like, De Cercis takes Mastorna by the arm and leads him towards the wings of the stage, speaking to him with a calm and low voice, confidentially:

> — *We have to stick together, dear Mastorna. There aren't many of us, alas, but we've formed a band of people, a working party let's say, or pressure group, call it what you will, but as I say there aren't many of us in an ocean of buffoons and dupes. You've seen them, haven't you? They were expecting to be received by the Holy Mother of God in person and to sit on a puff of cloud for all eternity, angels singing them a lullaby. They wanted a phosphorescent halo they did.*

Backstage. Award hall.
They reach the backstage; clapping, some workmen, stagehands and electricians come towards De Cercis, and the Professor, as if

egged on by the applause to say something more, hurriedly delivers himself of some more words as if addressing a gathering:

> – *They say 'God doesn't pay on Saturdays'. But we, who are men, we want to be paid on Saturday too, because on Sunday we want to spend our hard-earned dough, buy our kids an ice-cream, go to the cinema, the theatre, purchase some books, go to the brothel. And if the person at the cash desk cheats, we're capable of taking him by the scruff of the neck and wrecking everything, because we're men, for goodness sake,* paying *and* getting paid *is a matter for men, respect what is* yours *and* demand what is *mine, provided what is yours you obtained honestly, without harming others, without trampling all over their rights, because in that case, you lousy Fascist scoundrel, I'll beat you to a pulp until you cough it up.*

The workers applaud loudly. De Cercis shakes hands left and right and, taking Mastorna by the arm, leads him away, speaking quietly:

> – *Good folk, they move me every time! How much work is left to be done! But we're getting there, you know? Every evening we go to Raoul's, that's where we have our meetings. There aren't many of us, as I say, but we have clear ideas. You remember Raoul's café? Remember Adelaide? She's here too, of course. Behind the counter, shoving her big tits under everyone's nose. Now that we're on the subject, don't talk about my wife in front of Adelaide. You understand, I haven't seen my wife since we separated, ten years ago. Wonderful woman, poor thing, she still teaches History of Religion, but in bed, damnation take it, she was like the Messiah, she never came.*

Opening a glass door, De Cercis takes Mastorna into an old provincial café.

Interior. Provincial café.
It's the old café where, as a boy, Mastorna went to play billiards. Nothing has changed since then: the misted windows from the steam and cold, the smoke-laden air, the cracking sound of the cues

as they strike the billiard balls, the red velvet divans with white, embroidered doilies, smeared with hair grease. On the walls there are paintings by the local artist and some distance away is the room of the respectable old ladies who play draughts or chess to while away the afternoon.

Further down, near the billiard tables, the room of the vitelloni,[5] the intellectuals, friends of De Cercis, echoing with shouting, laughing, loud raspberries.

There she is, Adelaide, behind the counter, serving coffees and washing glasses in the steam of the espresso machine; she is a lovely brunette, well-formed, powerful-looking, heavily perspiring, a hint of hair on her upper lip, white eyes like a lioness. Swift of hand and tongue, she could hold her own with the clients, retorting good-humouredly to their over-gallant, appreciative remarks.

De Cercis (shouting loud):

> – See who I've brought? Giuseppino Mastorna! Know where he was? At the drivelling nonsense of the Fair of Unending Dreams.

As Mastorna slowly advances inside the café, looking around tenderly, his oldest memories come back to him. De Cercis is still at the door, talking to the people who silently accompanied them to the café. As if to reward them for their solidarity, De Cercis resumes his speech (to the group outside):

> – We don't believe in the immortality of the soul, there is no actual proof, so I do without it, am not interested in it. On the other hand I do believe in the immortality of the body; what we call death, the decomposition of the body, is but a change of state, a metamorphosis, in which the body becomes something else, by an observable – albeit aesthetically far from pleasing – bio-chemical process.

The group outside claps.

De Cercis waves, closes the door and approaches Mastorna who is staring, fascinated, at Adelaide behind the counter, in the steam of the espresso machine.

> – *You fancied her too, didn't you, this devil woman? But just look at her moustache, sometimes I think I'm making love to Stalin!*

Then, out loud, he announces one of his familiar sacrilegious paradoxes:

> – *Truth is directly apprehended: you don't get there by climbing a staircase of mental concepts. And Adelaide, as far as apprehension is concerned, shakes me to the foundations, like an earthquake: therefore Adelaide is the truth.*

And, catlike, despite his large belly, he slips behind the counter and embraces Adelaide, sticks to her large body like a child to his mother, disappearing now and then in the whitish steam of the coffee machine.

Outside the group of admirers nods vigorously and claps, then falls silent, their noses pressed to the glass, eyes wide open, staring at the Professor.

A bald, pale type, his beard badly shaved, sitting with others behind one of the tables in the café, gives a slight nod to Mastorna, who goes over to him and shakes his hand.

> – *I'm glad to see you're one of us. You were just a kid. Do you remember me?*

The voice of De Cercis, still hugging Adelaide, booms out from behind Mastorna:

> – *Embrace him Mastorna, he is a brother. Remember that scandal when don Eugenio Terlizzi finally woke up and threw away his cassock? He's the dearest of them all, old Eugenio, the Unfrocked. Embrace him!*

The former priest offers Mastorna a cigarette and starts to speak, low, nervously:

> – *Undeniably many fervent materialists, who, albeit harbouring no doubts about the complete annihilation of the body at death, live an altruistic life of sacrifice and impersonal dedication to human progress, demonstrating true nobility, more so than a devout believer, whose morality requires the fear of Hellfire and the promise of Heaven.*

Voice of De Cercis:

> – *Well said Terlizzi! They are laughable, the people who want to be decorated for their actions: and the motivation, when all is said and done? 'They stuck to the rules.'*

And, with a singsong lilt, he shouts furiously:

> – *And because he was*
> *a blameless citizen*
> *and because he studied*
> *and because he voted*
> *and because he washed …*

The former priest and the others join in the chorus:

> – *and because he was married*
> *committed adultery*
> *schemed*
> *he is deserving of the recognition of society*
> *and at the end of his life repented.*

Voice of De Cercis (alone):

> – *now he has been rewarded.*

All together:

> – *The Oscar of the Eternal Father.*

Applause, laughing.

Voice of De Cercis:

– *I am a 'human man', I have only ever paid any attention to man, and to be a man already involves a great deal of effort in this world. What do we want from His Transcendence?*

The former priest:

– *If he is transcendent, let's leave him where he is, allow him to float above our heads ... we are too busy looking where we are putting our feet in order not to trip over.*

Someone else:

– *Life is a matter for adults, a professional affair, there is no time to joke or get strange ideas into our heads, even if they do sing well, yes, so well you almost swoon.*

Voice of De Cercis:

– *We have to go forward, quickly, without distractions, pointless questionings, wasting time; we know well enough the history of the clever sods who have bust their brains and often their hearts against the marble wall of metaphysics, and where did it get them? The idea that the only alternative to the 'human man' is ...*

All together:

– *... deceived man!*

Voice of De Cercis:

– *If God exists that's entirely his business: we don't have much to say about it, we have other things to do. I've never been a furious anti-cleric, when I yell, it's in the name of my young brothers, what on earth does it mean to spit heavenwards? They're the hysterical reactions of frightened dimwits, spewing out bile and disappointment. I prefer the terrible, courageous, imperturbability of Stendhal, envied by Nietzsche, for his: 'God only has one excuse, that he doesn't exist.' And I have more affection for – yet don't like – that crazed nihilist Stirner,[6] who laughed with glee: 'Digest the host and there's an* end to it. Amen!' As you can see I like to quote others, it's my profession, it would be shameful to quote myself. Having said this, dear sirs, I take my leave. Get ready Adelaide, remove the apron from your lily-white belly and let us go for a walk with Mastorna.*

He has opened the door to the café and stepped out, followed by Mastorna and Adelaide.

Exterior. The streets and squares of a provincial town.
Outside it is dark, foggy. The provincial town's streets and squares are deserted and silent.

The group of admirers is still there, immobile, waiting.

After a moment's hesitation De Cercis walks on, an arm laid heavily on Adelaide's shoulders.

Mastorna follows them and, some way back, the group of admirers also follows, a flock of sheep with no will of its own.

De Cercis seems to have lost some of his cockiness; he is no longer so sure of himself and doesn't know which direction to take.

De Cercis (rather quietly):

— Which way shall we go?

The deserted streets disappear into the fog. Only the sound of steps can be heard, echoing in the night, and the shuffling of the flock's feet.

— For me it was all so easy when I got here. I was immune: I didn't feel at a loss for a moment. It's all the same as before? That's fine with me.

He has stopped once more, unsure. He looks at Adelaide with apprehension. The woman, too, has stopped: she has closed her eyes and is yawning. De Cercis shakes her and appears to be afraid of something when he speaks:

— What are you doing? Wake up! Open your eyes.

Adelaide half raises her eyelids with immense difficulty; she seems drugged. With an effort she begins to walk again. Comforted, De Cercis holds her by the hips.

> – *Adelaide is a beautiful Heaven! Vast, maternal, when she opens her eyes, her arms, her thighs! That's the refuge! And I have no trouble in telling her my prayers. Isn't that so, Adelaide? Answer me, isn't that right?*

But the large woman has closed her eyes again; she is yawning continuously. She sits down, on the kerbside of a street with porticoes, reminiscent of Bologna.

De Cercis is trembling with fear: he bends over the woman, trying with all his might to wake her.

> – *Christ no, you can't fall asleep! Mastorna, help me, we can't leave her here.*

To the others:

> – *Hey, you lot, come closer, give us a hand.*

More and more desperate, he stammers and holds onto Mastorna.

> – *This is the only curse. This big sleep that takes hold of us all, sooner or later. But you have to stay awake. You mustn't fall asleep. See those cowards there? They fall like ripe apples, one after another!* (Shouting.) *Wake up!*

He goes over to the group of admirers and shakes them energetically, trying to lift them off the ground, but they have all fallen onto the pavement, here and there, and are sleeping, eyes closed, arms and legs contracted, like huge foetuses.

Pale with fear, De Cercis returns to Mastorna's side.

> – *Help me! Keep me awake, I beg you, help me pace up and down: I mustn't fall asleep! They tell a horrific story in this town. If you fall asleep, they say, they say that … Fascists come and take you, who else? They put you on a truck, sons of bitches, damn them, and nothing more is heard of you, no-*

> *one knows where they take you. But who believes these stupid stories?* (Shouting.) *I don't believe it!*

The empty porticoes and squares echo back his voice.

> — *Kiddies' stories. We're men, stop busting our balls with this nonsense. I don't believe it!*

De Cercis is down on his knees, he can't keep his eyes open any more for the sleep and he is muttering.

De Cercis (muttering something confused):

> — *I don't believe it! I don't believe in anything ... nothing ...*

His voice falls away, a hoarse whisper. De Cercis falls into deep sleep in the foetal position, like the others, next to Adelaide, and Mastorna finds himself alone, in that provincial town street, the outlines and architecture of which seem familiar, yet strangely disquieting. The doors are closed, all the windows shut. There is a noise like a truck approaching, then a squeaking of brakes.

A huge truck appears on the other side of the square; three or four people with the soiled coats of male nurses advance under the porticoes.

Someone, who appears to be their commander, points to the sleeping bodies and orders them to be loaded onto the truck.

Quickly they are loaded.

Two male nurses are lifting the heavy, sleeping bodies of De Cercis and Adelaide. Mastorna appears to want to intervene.

> — *Where are you taking them?*

The nurses move towards the truck with the Professor's body and one of them, without turning round, answers:

> — *You shouldn't be here. This is not your place. You cannot come with us, you are not like them. Perhaps you are worse: at least they had no doubts, they were coherent, to the last and they have a precise destination, a place reserved for them. We're taking them to the depots. They are huge dormitories where*

they will stay for many years. Occasionally someone wakes up, but what happens after that is none of our business.

The two nurses have reached the truck, laden with sleeping bodies; De Cercis and Adelaide are placed on the backs of the others and are immobile, like lifeless puppets.

– *But you, unable to deny and unable to believe, you really do seem worse than the others.*

Before getting onto the truck, he asks:

– *What's your name?*

– *Giuseppe Mastorna.* (With infantile dismay.) *Where should I go? There must be somewhere for me too. I can't be so different from the others that I have no destination, nowhere to seek. What do you do with people like me? Where are the others, the ones like me? Where do they go?*

But the face of the nurse is impenetrable, he shows no feeling whatsoever, neither sympathy nor condemnation. He looks at Mastorna lengthily with clear, inexpressive eyes.

Then he jumps up onto the truck, sits on the sleeping bodies and, from up there, launches an appeal.

– *Is there nobody out there who can help Mastorna?*

The echo reverberates along the empty streets and around the deserted squares.

Exterior. Streets of a provincial town (gravedigger).
The creaking of a door opening some way off and then, in the alleyway, a figure approaches, a man, buttoning his trousers, like someone waking from sleep.

The man finishes dressing in the middle of the road. He puts on a long, black coat full of buttons, then a top hat; he is carrying a whip. Despite the distance it is clear he is dressed as a gravedigger. He beckons to Mastorna to follow him.

The Journey of G. Mastorna by Federico Fellini

The truck has left with its load of sleeping bodies. Mastorna is alone in the square; he follows the cloaked figure who leads the way down a street, occasionally cracking the whip. Mastorna follows about ten paces behind.

Gravedigger (without stopping):

> – If you'd come to me earlier, I could have told you where to go. We're all heading that way, my dear sir. I've accompanied so many! It's the only safe place. It really exists! The only thing we know for sure is that when we die, that's where we go ...

The funeral march, the gravedigger ahead, Mastorna some distance behind, continues through deserted streets, the doors closed, the windows shuttered.

From behind the windows, some whispering can be heard here and there, occasionally a window opens slightly and shadows can

Fellini to Mastroianni: *"Marcello...you shouldn't play the cello like that, like it was just any old instrument."*

be seen, of people that appear to be looking furtively out into the street. Voices whisper remarks.

Voices (from behind the windows):

– *It's Maestro Mastorna ...*
– *He never thought he was going to die ...*
– *Was he a believer?*
– *So so.*
– *He was an atheist.*
– *So So. What did he do?*

Someone whispers an incomprehensible answer and there is a ripple of smothered laughter.

– *You don't say? ...*
– *And now where's he going?*
– *Where are they taking him?*

Exterior/Interior. Room (Street in a provincial town).
A window at head-height opens as Mastorna walks by and the voice of a woman can be heard rapidly, intensely, whispering his name:

– *Peppino ...*

Mastorna stops, approaches the window and behind the slightly open shutters, he sees a woman, her hair flowing over her naked shoulders, topless, full breasts, a fleshy, scented arm reaching out and grabbing him by the face, whilst a sad voice whispers with love:

– *I came all the same to your funeral, you know, even though your wife told everyone she would slap my face. Peppino, dearest, my life, my heart. ... I have been faithful to you. Never more, never again, with anyone.*

The beautiful woman reaches her naked arms through the window and pulls Mastorna towards her. She kisses his forehead, his eyes, his lips, his hands.

Behind her, Mastorna can make out the comfortable room of his clandestine affair, the flowery wallpaper, the window on the large wardrobe right in front of the bed, the huge unmade bed, and on the dressing table the dark lampshade to create some darkness and the mood for love.

Moved, Mastorna stands on tiptoe and embraces his beautiful lover with desperation and passion, her shoulders, her breasts, tormented by the memory of her perfume, her warmth.

– *Our room ...*

– *You remember? Nothing's changed, see, I've kept it exactly as it was, that last time, your dressing gown, pyjamas, slippers.*

Now the woman, in tears, lovingly pushes Mastorna away, with maternal concern.

– *No ... they can see us! You know how much I would like to, but we can't, there are eyes spying on us, you have to go. ... Goodbye my love, my darling ...*

The woman withdraws, sobbing. She closes the shutters and the light inside goes out.

Exterior. Street in a provincial town (gravedigger).
The gravedigger has stopped at the end of a street, where he is waiting three quarters turned round, cracking the whip, and then slowly beckoning Mastorna on.

Mastorna begins to walk and the whispering voices behind the windows resume.

– *Now where's he going?*

– *Where are they taking him?*

– *Where do you think? To the only place where he belongs.*

– *His only place ...*

– *The only reasonable place ...*

– *To the cemetery.*

The façades of the houses have become walls with recesses for the coffins of the dead.

Mastorna is walking between two high walls with coffins inserted into the recesses. The dark night has slowly become a fixed grey.

And in that atmosphere of eternal twilight Mastorna reaches the graveyard.

Interior. Cemetery.

The place is an architectural folly, with chapels in all styles, willy-nilly, sculptures everywhere, of all types, macabre and bizarre representations frozen in stone, grotesque and tormenting, clownish.

Exterior/interior. The Mastorna Chapel.

Inside the Mastorna family chapel: an abandoned, shabby little building. The rusty gate is ajar.

Mastorna goes in: the building has a low roof, stained with moisture, dust on the ground, dirt, the putrid remains of some chrysanthemums placed in a corner ages ago.

Many letters on the tombstone are missing: only ... EPP ... TORNA ... remain. The dates are illegible, the stone has crumbled from rainwater and time.

In a corner, a sodden broom. Mastorna picks it up and makes some efforts to clean the place up. But it is so desolate and abandoned that, after a while, he gives up.

He goes outside, leaning against one of the shabby chapel walls, looking around emptily, without recognition.

Exterior. Cemetery.

Thus he is able to watch the ceremonial visits to the nearby chapels.

The dead leave the chapels and sit outside, as hordes of relatives, all dressed in black, gather into a circle around them, as if they were having afternoon tea, bunches of chrysanthemums on the visitors' laps. Eyes lowered, lengthy silences, noses blown.

They look at the dead with sad smiles, shaking their heads disconsolately.

And the dead allow themselves to be looked at: nearly all of them look distracted, distant. Some mumble incomprehensible phrases in answer to questions from a relative. Some are still presentable: they look human.

Others are absurdly changed: just a pile of worm-eaten bones on a chair or dust the breeze disperses gently.

Some of the dead, from inside the tombs, try to see who is coming, a relative or friend who will come no more.

Mastorna looks on, a little envious, at the gatherings taking place in the nearby tombs. A melancholy bell tolls. Closing time.

The relatives kiss their dead on the forehead, touch their hands and leave, taking the chairs with them.

The dead are alone once more; they return to their chapels and close the doors. The light is fading, it is getting chilly.

And Mastorna? Is no-one going to visit him?

A sturdy-looking, elderly farming lady, dressed in black, a knotted handkerchief on her head, is walking along one of the cemetery pathways, pushing a bicycle.

Mastorna recognizes her and energetically yells:

– *Jole!*

The woman turns quickly and approaches, crying and blowing her nose.

Jole (tearfully):

– *Youngster! How bad I've been feeling! What a terrible accident! It was in all the papers. Let me look at you, touch you. May I hug you? I can still pick you up, you know? Do you really still remember me, your old nanny? Once you sent me your records, with your nice music. I brought some flowers from my orchard. At first I came every day, your chapel was the prettiest*

> *of all! I cleaned it, polished it all over. How much time has passed! I've grown old, as you can see?*
>
> – *Are you married, Jole?*

The woman blushes and laughs awkwardly as if ashamed.

> – *Who would marry an ugly old maid like me? No, I've always lived with your parents, they take care of me, treat me well. How long is it since you've seen your father and mother? Why don't you ever go to see them? I know you are very busy, but you shouldn't forget your father and mother! One terrible day they die, are no longer there, and you regret not spending any time with them. Now that you're here, why don't you go home? Just think how happy they would be. Be a good boy, let's go, I'll take you on my bicycle. I may be old but my legs are still good. Come on, get on the bike, I'll pedal.*

And Mastorna gets onto the handlebars of Jole's bike and she pedals slowly and surely, red in the face with joy, towards Mastorna's home.

Birthplace. Exterior. Road to Mastorna's home.
A quiet, out of the way road in a northern provincial town.

Small craft workshops alternating with houses. A few craftsmen are standing on the thresholds of their workshops. They nod to Mastorna deferentially as he passes.

Otherwise the road is deserted, silent, maybe it's the siesta, everything is neat and tidy, clean, as in the days of remembered childhood. A horse is tied to a doorway, bucking occasionally, without anger. Hooves on the roadway can be heard loud and clear.

Before getting to the façade of a dignified, historic building, Jole shouts at the top of her voice:

> – *Look who's here! Giuseppe has come home! Signora, signor Filippo!*

Mastorna has got down from the bike and Jole, all excitement, has disappeared through the gate, probably a tradesmen's entrance, leading to an orchard and then to the house proper.

Mastorna has stopped to look at the old doorway and, higher, the shuttered windows. In the house opposite someone is tapping against the glass of a window.

Mastorna turns; a girl at a second floor window is making signs, then she disappears only to reappear again; she opens the shutters and throws a piece of paper down into the road, crumpled into a ball.

Mastorna picks it up but doesn't look at it; he looks up, smiling, and calls the girl by name.

– *Margherita! Let me have a look at you! How beautiful you are!*

But the girl stays hidden behind the shutters.

– *It's not true. I'm not beautiful.*

Mastorna (delicately, under his breath):

– *Why don't you come down? Aren't you going to school today?*
– *My sisters have gone out, and I have to stay home, to help Mother.*
– *Let me see you.*

The window remains empty. Only a little of the girl's hair can be seen.

– *I'll show myself if you promise not to look. I'm ugly today.*

Slowly her face appears, a graceful, high-spirited, still infantile face, but in her eyes and smile, a woman's enchanting seductiveness. Immediately she covers her face with her fingers like a fan.

– *Don't look at me!*

Her eyes sparkle from behind her opened fingers.

Mastorna has an expression of melancholy and nostalgia on his face.

— *Your aunt was really nasty to me. She made me cry, she told my mother I'm a flirt and I won't let you study.*

A pause. The girl lowers her hand slowly.

— *See how ugly I am? My nose is red.* (Then shouting.) *No, don't be a fool! Get down, my sisters will be here any minute.*

Mastorna is climbing up the drainpipe of the house, using some iron spikes in the façade.

At the end of the road Margherita's sisters appear: two good-looking girls, older than her, wearing what looks like Venetian costume, throwing streamers, one of which falls at Mastorna's feet. They laugh together, whispering into each other's ear, girlish, silly.

Margherita has quickly closed the shutters and from behind the glass, before disappearing, she signals to Mastorna to open the crumpled piece of paper.

Margherita's sisters have reached the doorway and go in. They can be heard giggling on the other side of the door; then one of them sticks her head out and whispers to Mastorna:

— *At six o'clock we're going to Church to pray for the Virgin Mary, mother's not coming, Margherita will be there too.*

Smiling at these cherished memories, Mastorna now enters his home.

Interior. Mastorna's home.

The hallway, the staircase leading to the upper floors, the familiar, pleasant smells of days gone by. Mastorna slowly wanders through the house of his childhood: at the end of the corridor, his father's study, the door ajar. He can hear his father's voice and the tip-tapping of a typewriter.

— *Brunello Casati, Cesena, 400 kilos of coffee, 10 sacks of Japanese rice, 200 kilos of jam …*

Through the door, Mastorna sees the tall, authoritative figure of his father pacing back and forth as he dictates the orders for his business to an elderly lady at the typewriter. As if he has sensed

Mastorna's presence on the other side of the door, the man stops his pacing and with a harsh voice asks:

— *Who's there? Don't disturb me. I'm working.*

Mastorna feels an age-old fear and awe and creeps along the walls of the house to the foot of the stairs, then follows the staircase up.

— *… General Store Umberto Casalecchio, Forlì, 200 kilos of copper sulphate, 100 crates …*

And his mother? Where is she? Mastorna timidly approaches the door to the bedroom: medicine on the dressing table, an orange juice, the lampshade covered with a dark cloth to dampen the light. Voices:

— *Quiet, mother has just fallen asleep.*

— *How is she?*

— *Better.*

— *She ate the main course.*

— *How is mother today?*

— *Well. She got up, even went out into the garden.*

— *Today, how is she?*

— *Not so good. But she has eaten.*

— *Don't make mother angry.*

— *Don't make a noise.*

— *Don't upset your mother.*

— *Today, how is she feeling?*

— *Quite well. She's eaten almost everything.*

— *Do you want to see mother?*

Then, from below, his father's booming voice:

— *No, for goodness sake, no. It's a scandal! A musician! A penniless wretch! First get your degree and then do what you want! Heavens! Good Heavens! No, for the love of God. The head of the Bank told me he was willing to give you a job as soon as you graduate. A wonderful position others have to work years for and you ... you, crazed and reckless, you want to be an artist? Frin frin frin, with that daft instrument? As long as I live I shall never permit it. Never.*

Her head deep in two pillows in the penumbra of the bedroom, his mother slowly turns her entreating eyes to Mastorna:

– *You two will be the death of me! When your mother is no more, you'll finally notice her. Is there any more crème caramel?*

Mastorna's father has appeared, standing behind him. Tall, strong, waxed moustaches: with a harsh tone he says to Mastorna:

– *To be quite honest, we weren't expecting you. For some time now your mother and I have become accustomed to your silence, your failure to keep your promises, your altogether deplorable behaviour. However, we have arranged a party for you: in your honour. Everyone is here!*

Exterior. Orchard-garden.
Mastorna is taken downstairs to the orchard-garden, closed off by convent walls, overgrown with weeds and with three or four leafy trees.

Around large tables in a horseshoe, laid extravagantly as for Christmas, Mastorna's relatives are eating and drinking festively. Everyone is there: uncles, aunts, brothers and sisters-in-law, grandparents, great grandparents, and ancestors further back through the generations.

His father takes him to his seat at the centre of the table, next to his father and father's father.

Mastorna, still standing, shakes an uncle's hand, an aunt's, bends down to kiss his grandmother, moves along the table, receiving pats on the back as he goes, chortles and some disapproving or diffident looks, in a mixture of cries, laughing, winking, toasts loudly proposed, speeches made with exaggerated, overblown emotion, amid Christmas and Easter decorations, a tree, eggs, the crib, little girls dressed for Confirmation; a priest gets up to bless everyone with the aspergillum, someone starts to sing a Romantic – dreadfully sentimental – song. There is clapping, a woman shows everyone her newborn baby in a small carriage, ooohs and aaahs and ecstatic screams, and Mastorna is almost imprisoned by all these arms and legs, mouths uttering words, eyes crying, wide open in surprise, misty with alcohol, heavy with sleep, the eyes of relatives, his family, his ancestors.

All of a sudden his father gets to his feet and shouts:

– *It is shameful! His great-grandfather a magistrate, his grandfather a doctor, one uncle a schoolmaster, the other a bishop and him … a music man? A cellist? Frin frin frin …*

Everyone looks at Mastorna sternly.

Voices:

– *Happy New Year! Happy Easter! Happy Summer holidays! Happy birthday! Many happy returns! Try these cold compresses with lemon!*

Still in bed, her head sunk in the pillows, his mother is there in the orchard, slowly eating a huge slice of Christmas cake. With a joyless smile she asks Mastorna:

– *Are you Peppino? My Peppino?*

Mastorna nods and his mother asks him:

– *You're my child? My pet?*

And staring at him with feeling:

– *Do you love your mother?*

Father (looking at him threateningly):

– *And your father? Answer me! Do you love your father?*

Other voices:

— *And your aunt and uncle? Do you love them?*

— *Do you love your granny?*

— *When I married the second time, my bride was the cousin of a brother of your aunt. Do you love me?*

It is a deafening chorus of voices repeating the same words over and over: 'Do you love us? And us?'

Then a man, whose face he has seen for years in a portrait in the corridor (who knows who he is, maybe granddad's granddad, since he is wearing nineteenth-century clothes), begins to shout:

— *Let's see what you can do.*

Immediately the others join in.

— *Do it for your mother.*

— *Do it for your father, for Goodness sake!*

— *Do it for your grandmother!*

— *Do it for me, I beg of you!*

— *Do it for your aunt!*

— *Do it for your conductor!*

— *For the good name of the Conservatory!*

— *For your country!*

— *For the Duce!*

— *For Saint Filomena the Martyr!*

— *Then you don't love us!*

— *You don't love us!*

— *You don't love us!*

The faces, the voices, become oppressive, overwhelming, an obsession.

Exterior/interior. Greenhouse/shed.
Oppressed and bewildered, Mastorna takes refuge in a small shed at the end of the garden. It is used for storage and to grow plants.

In a jumble, covered in dust, it contains the objects of Mastorna's childhood, like an archive or museum of his memories: clothes, shoes, school uniforms, exercise books, toys, his school desk, skis, prams, his first doll, bangers, footballs, his student's beret, his military uniform ...

(A field of ashes)
NB: I don't have a clear notion of how this sequence should end, just a vague idea that doesn't really satisfy me. I hope to find something better. However, the general sense of the sequence is this: Mastorna is sucked back into his memories and becomes a prisoner of them. The pained, useless, memories of his life threaten and oppress him and he risks being suffocated and destroyed by them.

I imagined that in order for him to save himself from these obsessions and to get out of the dark cockpit of his memories, Mastorna lights a firebrand and sets everything on fire. The remains of his memories are burnt, higher and higher flames come from the pile of toys and clothes, the shed where Mastorna has taken refuge, which fills with smoke and flames, and the fire moves into the garden and then the house: from the gigantic pyre tormenting voices emerge, calling Mastorna, asking for help, repeating the absurd refrain: 'Do you love us? Wish us well?'

Repentant, ridiculously Mastorna would now like to put the fire out and crazily walks through the flames trying to extinguish them. But it is too late and he runs the risk of being burnt as the thick smoke swirls, until a hand reaches out and grabs him, pulls him to safety ...

(Exterior/interior. Ambulance)
... pushing him, clothes smouldering, face smeared with soot, screaming with pain and fear, into an ambulance which sets off, its siren blaring, towards the hospital.

Inside the ambulance, Mastorna, as if out of his mind with distress, continues to wail and scream. Bent over him, the hostess from the station (in the early part of the story) tries to calm him down, soothe him like a friend, lovingly.

Interior. Doctor's surgery.
When Mastorna opens his eyes, he finds himself on a small bed in a doctor's surgery: a large, well-built man in a white coat is talking to the hostess with a tone of satisfaction and approval.

Big doctor:

> – *Certainly, of course! Good, very good, excellent! You have made enormous progress. You burnt everything, eh? Nothing left over from the embalming? Miss, can you assure me of this? Total cancellation of all the sclerotic slavers of memory?*
>
> – *To utter nakedness!*
>
> – *Perfect! Excellent job! Memory is totalitarian, passive, tyrannical, enslaving, and prevents life from developing naturally. The other day, in a lecture to the lads, speaking of this cannibalism by the past, I compared memory to a kind of horrific, obtuse Saturn, devouring his own children: a sort of period of probation, under supervision, granted to the present; how much genuine suffering is associated with an event, which illegitimately maintains its ability to give offence, its aggressive nature, intact, so we cannot move forward, it stops us, destroys us. Good good, my work here is done. I wish the patient a speedy recovery, my sincerest compliments once again.*

The huge man leaves the room, the hostess closes the door and turns to look at Mastorna, smiles and winks.

> – *If you feel up to it, we can go down to the passport office. As soon as you have told us your destination ...*

Mastorna is now sitting up in bed; he gestures with utter disconsolation.

Mastorna (in dismay):

> – *Yet again?*

Hostess (continuing):

> – ... *your destination and, above all, after stating in good faith who you are, you will be free to leave.*
> – *So it just starts all over? The same questions you asked me at the station, a month ago, a year ago? How long has it been? You just carry on asking the same old questions. Now I hardly know who I am.*
> – *That's already a good answer.*

On the other side of the window there is a large park. Along the paths, lined with blooming flower beds, a crowd of people are walking slowly. Others are sitting on park benches with the vaguely peaceful air of patients convalescing.

> – *Who are they?*
> – *People like you, pending identification.*

Mastorna turns to the hostess as if to ask for an explanation but at that moment the door opens and several people enter the room, in dribs and drabs. They are men, women, dressed in plain clothes, and have a satisfied, drawing-room, look on their faces. The first of them asks:

> – *Have we come too late? Is it already over?*

Hostess:

> – *You're right on time. Take your seats.*

She indicates a row of seats behind the bed. Then, with quick, resolute, movements she lowers the black curtains over the windows. The room darkens suddenly. The seven or eight visitors have sat down: they are joking among themselves, offering each other cigarettes and chocolates. The hostess switches on a small desk lamp on the table. Still smiling, with her rather ironic, schoolmistressy tone, she says to Mastorna:

> – *These people have kindly offered to be, let us say, a jury. Relax, do not be alarmed. We are all here to help you. I imagine you*

> *already know some of them, am I right? This, I believe, is your former Colonel, this your teacher of religious education ... your harmony teacher from the Conservatory ... these two girls ...* (with a jokingly provocative voice) *... well, you remember them, don't you?*

Mastorna looks back and awkwardly acknowledges the greetings of the people behind him, as the hostess indicates them, one by one. Yes, it's true, the faces are all from his adolescence, his youth, his life. The two girls, obviously whores, young, buxom, with dyed blonde hair, heavily made up, respond to Mastorna's embarrassed nod haughtily.

Meanwhile, at the end of the room, in front of Mastorna and the spectators, the hostess has lowered a small screen from the ceiling and is now moving towards the table where she lifts a telephone receiver and says merrily:

> *– Ready in the back room? We can begin.*

A small beam of light comes from a small hole in the back wall, lighting up the screen: a projector can be heard whirring in the back room.

An idiotic, cunning-looking fellow sits down next to Mastorna and asks him:

> *– What's on?*
>
> *– My life.*
>
> *– What?*
>
> *– My life* (later, the sleazy, comical, sinister fellow demonstrates great skill in his scientific explanation of the first stills depicting the origin of life).

Quick, out of breath, another man arrives, fumbling in the half-dark towards Mastorna, until he is just a few inches away.

> *– My name is Succhieva. Pleased to meet you. Would you like a piano recital? It's not obligatory, as you prefer, but if I were*

> *in your place, I would accept. Music always helps, you know better than I do, it's a great ass-licker. Thank you. All the best.*

And slipping away quietly he goes over to a small piano against the wall, opens the lid, takes out a musical score and pulls it close to his eyes, reading:

> *– Dossier 52. Life of Giuseppe ... they write so badly in the office ... Mastorna.*

The spectators begin to clap, with genuine or feigned pleasure.

The teacher of religious education calls them immediately to order.

> *– I beg you, all of you, to remember that for the person concerned this is a solemn moment, he needs concentration and silence.*

The piano player meanwhile has rushed to the piano and is crouching behind it, bashing out some ditties, merry and sad, as in the days of silent movies.

Up on the screen a strange show begins: one image after another, at breakneck speed, almost impossible to take in. Occasionally one or another still is held for a moment, just enough time to make it recognizable, then the previous frenetic pace resumes. A whirlwind of shapeless images, a display of glittering, swirling lights. The pianist knocks out a fast-paced tune to accompany the pace of the flashing images.

Sitting on the edge of the bed, Mastorna, lost, full of dread, turns to the hostess whose eyes only can be seen in the light of the desk lamp on the table. She smiles to Mastorna with encouragement, then signals to him to be calm and patient, indicating the screen.

The dance of light has stopped and a dark, round object can be seen: the foetus of a child, four months after conception, in the placenta.

The two whores:

> *– Neat! You can recognize him already!*
> *– What a huge head! Darling! With hands in a fist!*

Another voice, by way of explanation:

> — *His organism as it forms, the circulation, the first nerve bundles, his arms and legs growing.*

A sense of chill, of utter desolation, takes Mastorna by the throat. He averts his eyes and stays in this pose, head in hands, until he feels a light pressure on his shoulder.

It's the hostess, winking, encouraging:

> — *You must watch. Know what we are looking for? One moment in your life (one is enough, you know), one moment in which you were authentic, spontaneously yourself. And you must help us find it.*

The images are flashing past, unrecognizable, incomprehensible, too quickly for anything to be made out clearly: a baby crying in its crib, a boy learning to walk, sleeping, running, sleeping, standing, in bed, standing, at his school desk, in bed once more.

Now the boy is seen from behind, in a meadow, a butterfly flits into the scene and flies around his head: the boy reaches a hand up and tries to grab it.

In the room where the film is being shown someone cries out:

> — *Stop! Let's see this scene again, more closely.*

The film stops, goes back, starts again at normal speed, from the moment the boy, sitting in the meadow, tries to grab the butterfly. The same voice as before, as if seeking consensus, says:

> — *This seems quite convincing.*

But, irritated and angry, someone else replies:

> — *At that age we're all spontaneous! Children are authenticity itself.*

A third voice:

— *We need this kind of moment, one of spontaneity and authenticity but with the awareness, the understanding, of an adult.*

Another voice (sighing, conciliatory):

— *You want too much, my dear fellows ...*

Second voice (piqued):

— *But that's what we're here for, otherwise let's call it a day or watch a decent film.*

Fourth voice:

— *That's an idea. A nice pornographic film.*

Laughter, calls for silence, then the voice of one of the whores (warbling with feeling):

— *See how handsome he is ... looks like a little angel!*

On the screen Mastorna is attending his first Confirmation service, then the images begin to flash by, one after another again: unconnected, incoherent, belched out from the abyss of time: Mastorna walking down the street turning to look at a passing woman: Mastorna on a diving board, reading a musical score rather sceptically, playing in the orchestra, cowering at the sight of the conductor, playing his heart out on the cello.

The voices and comments continue, nearly all of them negative.

— *Mechanical, passive, utterly absorbed by the others, let's move on, there's nothing of value here, he is not this. This is a robot, a mere performer and (you will all have noticed) just one of the flock.*

Now a love scene: a younger Mastorna, almost handsome, in a car with a beautiful girl: kissing her, caressing her, biting her lips, his fingers fumbling with her blouse, unbuttoning it.

Colonel's voice:

> – *Goodness me, not bad at all! Good technique and the girl appears to be enjoying it.*

Upset, almost ashamed, Mastorna takes his eyes off the screen and glances at the hostess, who is taking notes at the small table. Feeling Mastorna's eyes upon her she pulls a face as if to say, 'Good for you'.

But the same dissenting voice pipes up, ruining the atmosphere and the sympathy the spectators seemed to be feeling for Mastorna.

> – *Ridiculous, less and less authentic. Utterly given over to instinct; mechanical reactions one after another. Let's not waste time. Move forward.*

Under his breath Mastorna says:

> – *I realize I was always very sensual, naturally attracted to women. Isn't that authenticity? Everything else was a lie ...*

Dissenting voice:

> – *Not in the least. And that too is a lie.*

Bursting out hysterically:

> – *Can't you all see it? He's just copying the languid looks, the trembling nostrils, the techniques of a lover he's seen actors using at the cinema.*

The film continues speedily; in church, his wedding, standing with the orchestra to receive the applause of the audience, after the applause, furious shouts at someone or something, images flicking by rapidly, dizzying, unconnected.

Exhausted, worn down, discouraged by the nonsensical series of images, actions, postures, Mastorna takes his eyes off the screen and makes as if to get off the bed.

> – *Enough. Let me out of here. How absurd! What's the point of staying here to watch these leftovers of wasted time? You carry on, I'm leaving, this has nothing to do with me.*

The hostess suddenly lifts her head, her eyes misty, a victorious expression on her face.

– *Did you say* nothing to do with me? *What a magnificent answer. See how you have positively influenced the jury?*

The members of the jury are reaching out their hands to shake his, to congratulate him.

– *Well done. Excellent!*
– *We're making very good progress.*
– *'Nothing to do with him', his own life, he meant, not bad at all. You have no idea how close you are to success.*
– *Now all we need is one small document, a fragment, a trifle, nothing, and as far as we are concerned our job is done. You could leave right away.*
– *An authentic image, without cultural superstructure, free from instinct, unconditioned by feeling. … Stop, everyone look at that!*

The film slows down once more, goes back and resumes from where it had left off: Mastorna is middle-aged and is driving a car through a city centre. He has stopped at a red light. Cars everywhere. Lifeless expressions of those at the wheel. Inexpressive glances from driver to driver. Bored, waiting, Mastorna turns his head to the right. In the car next to his, on the back seat, there is a large dog, looking at him. Mastorna sticks his tongue out.

– *There!*
– *Not bad!*
– *Seems good.*
– *Again!*

The scene is repeated in slow motion.

Now the assembled spectators are unanimous, even the previous dissenter, who gets up and waves his arms through the beam of light from the projector, signalling to stop the film.

Dissenter (to Mastorna):

> — *Approved! Not one hundred per cent because (allow me to say) there was a slight (admittedly almost imperceptible) element of self-satisfaction in this gesture too. The mocking, joking face you pull when you see the animal is not entirely innocent. ... But beggars can't be choosers. Let's say this is the still we were looking for. Allow me to introduce myself, Filiberti, we were in the third year at primary school together, you don't remember, eh? Never mind, we didn't get on. Well, dear Mastorna, it was a pleasure to see you again, I wish you a pleasant journey. Ah, here's the proof!*

The man projecting the film has come into the room with a few frames of the film, from which he cuts three or four stills with a pair of scissors.

Dissenter:

> — *Now, if anyone stops you and asks you who you are, show him this and tell him: 'I'm someone who when he doesn't know what to do, sticks his tongue out at dogs in the back of a car'. And if you like you could also add that beautiful, highly religious phrase you pronounced a few moments ago: 'It has nothing to do with me'. Well done indeed, all the best, dear Mastorna; have a good journey. May I hug you?*

The dissenter opens his arms and hugs Mastorna, patting him affectionately on the back. He seems moved and the others, too, despite the celebrations and good spirits, have misty eyes. They are moved delicately, discreetly, without ulterior motive.

> — *Have a good trip!*
>
> — *Good luck!*
>
> — *Remember us!*

Particularly moved, the Colonel makes himself heard above the general commotion:

> — *Recruit Giuseppe Mastorna: attention! Forward march!*

Exterior. Road and park.
Outside it's a warm spring day. The hostess leads Mastorna towards a car in front of the park gate next to the road.

> – *Did you think you'd got rid of me? No, it's my duty to accompany you as far as the airport, even onto the runway.*

Before opening the car door she turns to Mastorna and says:

> – *I beg your pardon if I must ask you to undertake your journey with two others, you don't mind, do you? They are also going to the airport. Please, get in.*

Inside the car (parents).
Mastorna gets into the car, where a middle-aged couple is sitting. Mastorna nods and the couple smile kindly. Mastorna sits on the front folding seat, rather perplexed and troubled. The man and the woman are exact doubles of his parents, but their mannerisms and behaviour are utterly different: the man, identical to his father, does not have the strict, authoritarian bearing of his father, and the woman, identical to his mother, looks at him and smiles in a way that his mother never had.

The hostess gets into the driver's seat and starts the engine.

It's a pleasant day, with a few clouds moving slowly over an otherwise blue sky. The windows of the car are rolled down. As they drive, a scented spring air wafts into the car.

For the first time, Mastorna feels the beneficial effects of the aftermath of an immensely challenging enterprise brought to a successful conclusion. He is tired and does not feel the need to remember. His heart feels a slight, not unpleasant, agitation. In the back of the car, unperturbed, the man and the woman are looking at the countryside and the leafy trees going by. Mastorna says peacefully:

> – *Are you my father and mother?*

The man nods and smiles.

> – *Yes, this time that is how it has turned out.*

Continuing to drive the hostess looks at the three passengers in the rear view mirror and approves of this remark with a comic expression.

With a graceful voice, delicately playful, the woman says:

> – *But it could have been different, us your children, you our father.*

The man, with pleasant complicity, points to his wife and says:

> – *Or she my daughter and you her husband.*

The woman laughs and flirts a little with Mastorna, caressing the back of his head.

> – *Tell me, would you have liked me for your wife?*

And she kisses Mastorna fully on the mouth: Mastorna returns the kiss soberly. His father watches the scene with affection and sympathy.

> – *What a marvellous couple! If I were your son, I would be very handsome, I think, or else. …*

His father pauses, for effect, and smiles with a feigned look of astonishment, like someone who is about to say something utterly incredible:

> – *Why not? The combinations are infinite and you and I, dear Peppino, might have met in a café on Lindenstrasse in Berlin and become lovers!*

His mother bursts out laughing.

Hostess:

> – *Excellent, mental somersaults continue with the mental somersaults* (and then with an exaggerated, comic tone of knowingness)*: In the beginning they will be silly, naïve, excessive, but in the end you will find each other in the only authentic manner possible, by your own individual choice.*

Exterior and interior. Airport.
The windows of the modern airport come into view. Mastorna follows the hostess who picks her way unfailingly through hordes of passengers moving in every direction, past the ticket counters, the check-in areas, the waiting rooms and boarding gates. The noise of aeroplane engines at full throttle almost drowns out the loudspeakers with women's voices making the announcements warmly and suavely: the times of incoming and outgoing planes. The glass construction of the large airport mirrors unreal skies, diaphanous transparencies, floating clouds inching their way over the deepest blue.

– *Flight three. On the runway. Northbound. Sky clear.*

– *Flight six. No seats left.*

– *Flight nine. There is something not quite right for the passengers on flight nine. Try again later ...*

– *Flight thirteen: hurry ...*

Following the hostess through the crowds at the barriers, Mastorna sees his parents far off, swept away by another current of people. The man who had been his father removes his hat to respectfully bid farewell, and his mother's face also briefly appears: head slightly bowed, with a detached, courteous air. Mastorna stares at them until they are swallowed up by the crowd. He murmurs to himself, sweetly:

– *Goodbye ...*

Through the huge windows he can see the runways with gigantic aeroplanes taxiing into position.

Crowds of passengers are behaving rowdily, as in some working men's clubs, singing songs and waving their arms in celebration.

When a pilot appears, the crowds break into applause, they surround him, want to touch him, ask for autographs. His deep, masculine voice can be heard giving out flight information.

> — *It's very windy up there, many planes are having to change route. But everything is fine, all the same. Do not be alarmed. The only thing a man should worry about is not having to worry about anything.*

He bursts out laughing and the crowd applauds frenetically. The loudspeakers alternate announcements with military and jazz music.

Suddenly, in the midst of the crowd, some anxious, others celebrating and excited, with their luggage, parcels, merry faces or worried looks, in the midst of all this human tangle in waiting rooms, the long corridors leading to the boarding gates, or huddled together in front of the windows, Mastorna sees Armandino, stealthily walking along, smoking his eternal cigarette, hands thrust into the pockets of his grimy overcoat.

Mastorna (calling out):

> — *Armandino!*

But he doesn't appear to have heard and is heading for the bar, where he sits at a table, looking around with his wily eyes. Mastorna goes over to him, almost pleased to have come across this unhappy fellow traveller. He touches his shoulder. But Armandino doesn't turn round: he's trying to light his cigarette end.

> — *Armandino! What's up? Are you leaving too?*

Armandino puffs at his cigarette and continues to survey the scene with his eyes, as if he hasn't noticed Mastorna, can't see him.

The hostess arrives and bursts out laughing.

> — *I wonder how long it will take before you realize where you are. There's no point calling him, he can't hear or see you.*

Mastorna seems not to understand the hostess's words and moves round to sit in front of Armandino. He shakes his hand, then takes him by the shoulders and jostles him.

> — *Don't you recognize me? Remember me? Why are you here?*

The hostess snorts:

> – *He isn't here! He doesn't know he's in the airport. Or rather, for him, this isn't the airport. Shall we drink something?*

Puzzled, Mastorna continues to stare at Armandino. It seems impossible that, barely a foot away, he cannot hear or see him.

Hostess:

> – *Where did you run into him?*
> – *He wanted to give me a hand. In his own way, he wanted to help. Is there nothing I can do for him?*
> – *You're already doing it, I'd say.*

Armandino appears to give a start. He looks more attentively, turning his eyes from left to right, right to left. He has the expression of someone who has felt something, heard something, a voice, but so far off he might have been mistaken.

Mastorna (leaning forward):

> – *Armandino. Can you hear me? Can I do something for you?*

Armandino sniffles and goes back to his previous absent expression, or rather, the look of someone perpetually distracted by something, as if he were looking at an entirely different scene or countryside.

After a rapt silence, Mastorna begins to speak quietly, venting all the disappointment, hopes, contradictory feelings, distress and fear that have been torturing him.

> – *I'm happy to leave. Many times, during this journey, I thought I didn't want to leave any more. I could have stayed with Armandino or in De Cercis's café. Tiredness, nausea, dejection, made anywhere seem desirable. Everything seemed better than the vague, senseless, incomprehensible prospect of leaving. I don't think I've understood much of what has happened to me, but now I have only one wish: to go away, to leave. Anything is preferable to this chaos, this confusion, the boredom of this city of yours.*

The hostess has been listening to every word, now and then nodding her head approvingly in her customary exaggerated fashion. So exaggerated, it seems mocking, like she is making fun of him.

– *Well said, Maestro. What does the proverb say? 'When you wish to leave, they call your plane number and you have already left.'*

Raising her finger into the air, she invites Mastorna to listen to the loudspeaker:

– *Flight fifty-two. The sole passenger is kindly requested to come to runway number …*

A sudden noise drowns out the last few words of the announcement.

– *What number did she say?*
– *Like you, I couldn't make it out. But if you really want to go, we'll find your flight. Come on, let's go!*

She has got up and with determination is heading towards one of the gates leading to the runways. Mastorna begins to follow her but stops to look at Armandino one last time. He is lighting another cigarette from the butt of the previous one.

Exterior. Airport runways.
Outside it is evening. From the centre of the tarmac, runways stretch out in every direction, with planes of all shapes and sizes taxiing slowly. The planes are old and new, bi-planes, helicopters, some as large as ocean liners. On the steps leading up to the waiting planes, men and women are fighting to get on board, shouting and screaming. The noise of the engines makes the ground tremble, gusts of wind from the whirling propellers and howling turbo jets force the passengers to stop, their overcoats almost torn off their backs, their trousers flapping against their legs like crazed flags against flagpoles.

From the terraces of the airport, now in half-darkness, crowds are waving handkerchiefs, saying goodbye.

In front of Mastorna, a huge plane is heading into the wind, its enormous fuselage passing as it taxies towards a runway. All the windows are lit, six or seven metres above the tarmac. The outlines of the passengers can be seen at the windows, and voices can be heard, calling, someone crying out his pain in the darkness and chaos.

Mastorna walks on with difficulty, trying not to lose sight of the hostess ahead of him, in the jumble of passing planes. He turns anxiously to a steward at the top of one of the mobile staircases leading up to an awaiting plane, and shouts into the roar of the engines:

– *They called flight fifty-two. Which runway? Where's my plane? I'm the only passenger.*

The steward points vaguely to somewhere ahead.

Mastorna walks over the runways, lit in straight, parallel lines.

A large plane takes off, flying low overhead, its engines thundering.

Mastorna throws himself onto the tarmac, face down in some wet tufts of grass. The plane drones on, like a huge cloud passing with a deafening roar, followed by a hurricane wind.

Mastorna gets up, runs towards other lights. Beams of light from the taxiing planes slice through the darkness, lighting up the outline of a man running by the side of a runway, gesticulating wildly, but no-one can hear him.

At the end of the runway Mastorna encounters the hostess, waiting, almost invisible in the darkness.

Now the noise of the aeroplanes is more distant. The airport seems far away, a series of brightly twinkling lights and, opposite, where Mastorna is standing, the darkness of the countryside stretches away. There is a slight breeze. Slowly everything falls silent: only the scratching of the crickets can be heard. Wheezing, tired out, Mastorna mumbles:

– *Where's my plane? There are no runways here! How can a plane take off from here?*

Hostess:

– *What a lovely smell of hay!*

She breathes in the night air with pleasure. Mastorna become enraged (shouting):

– *You are part of this airport, you must know where my plane is, you're here to assist me, you're at my service. I order you to take me to the runway for departure. Why don't you answer? What ought I to think of all of you? All of you who pretend to help me but only make fun of me? A joke? Another joke, to go with all the others? Well then, it's no different from being alive: you wait and don't receive, seek and do not find. I suffered, hung on, endured, waited in line with the others, now I must have what is rightfully mine. I couldn't be any more respectful, devoted and patient than this, but you too must respect me. I have to leave, you understand? Tell me where my plane is.*

In the darkness, the beautiful hostess replies humbly:

– *You overestimate me. I am just an employee and have never had the slightest intention of making fun of you. I sincerely want to help you, but ...*

Mastorna waits anxiously.

– *But ... do you really have to be on this flight?*
– *It's absolutely necessary. It's my only hope.*
– *A hope is much less than a necessity: it's only a distraction.*

Then, with a tone which is half-ironic, half-compassionate, she asks:

– *Must you hope?*
– *Who can prevent us from hoping? What could we do, without hope?*

The hostess suddenly falls silent, pointing in the darkness to the fields of hay:

– *Did you hear that? Did you hear that cry of joy?*

— *No, I didn't hear anything.*

Rummaging through her pockets, the hostess takes out a strip of paper and puts on a pair of glasses, opening out the strip of paper close to her eyes, she reads:

— *'The formidable meaning of a thoughtless cry of joy could not be understood for as long as the long night of hope and expectation persisted.' Not bad, eh?*

But Mastorno stubbornly insists:

— *Your quotations are of no use to me. Now, more than ever, I need to hope.*

With a look of resignation, the hostess shrugs, then points upwards and with a mocking tone, says:

— *In that case, Maestro, here is your plane.*

Exterior. End of the runway (an aeroplane falling to pieces).
High up, in the darkness, a light has come on, lights, some intense, others feeble, swinging back and forth at a height of about twenty metres above ground, and the sound of engines and propellers can be heard. The light lowers and the shadow of a plane can be made out, a tiny, rickety aeroplane, hanging in the air, rising and falling uncontrollably. A rope ladder is thrown down from the belly of the plane.

The hostess invites Mastorna to climb the ladder.

— *Have no fear, Maestro, go ahead. Good luck!*

Mastorna grabs hold of the rope ladder and starts to climb, sprightly. The plane lifts, gains altitude. Mastorna, hanging onto the rope ladder, is slowly sucked into the plane.

Somewhere in the forest of lights below, the hostess becomes smaller and smaller, waving her right hand in a passionate farewell, then she is gone.

Interior. Aeroplane (an old crock).

Mastorna finds himself in a slender, uncomfortable fuselage, not much bigger than a trunk. It's an absurd plane, with a chassis that seems to be made of planks of wood nailed together or bound with string, like a toy plane made by little children playing. And yet, contrary to all the laws of common sense and physics, it is flying, hopping from cloud to cloud, almost like a real plane.

Nailed to the walls, and made out of the tops of wooden crates, there are small candle holders, with lit candles: the flames dance as the plane swoops and the air enters from all directions.

Lying face down on the floor, his hands thrust into the holes in the floor, Mastorna tries to creep forward toward the pilot's cockpit.

The plane swoops and rises, plummets and climbs, like a roller coaster.

Mastorna tries to get to his feet and hits his head on a beam, falls and rolls to the back of the fuselage but doesn't give up; he tries to move forward again, crawling on his knees, whilst the plane continues its crazy motion, bumping, falling and climbing nose up, almost vertical.

Once more Mastorna rolls to the back, hitting his head, but now angered, obstinately he tries to crawl forward again across the floor, now vertically in front of him, like a wall. Air is sucked into the holes of the fuselage. At the height of anger Mastorna yells:

– *Who is the nutcase flying this thing?*

Once again, the plane climbs and Mastorna falls back, is now upside down in a grotesque pose, like a discarded puppet.

– *Who is the pilot? Are you trying to frighten me? Where are we headed?*

There is an infantile laugh, a series of ringing sounds suffocated by cries of absolute joy.

Finally, Mastorna reaches the cockpit, which is tiny, not much larger than a crate of beer. There are no controls, levers or dials.

Sitting on the floor is the pilot, an old Chinese man with a thin moustache much wider than his face. He is sleeping. Peacefully. His mouth is curved into a delicate, ineffable smile. Unaware of his surroundings, he is perfectly calm.

The person actually flying the plane is a young Chinese girl sitting next to the man; she is no more than five or six years old, very pretty, shining eyes and dark hair cut into a short fringe. She turns and, seeing Mastorna, bursts out laughing. Then she takes the joystick, which is just the end of a broomstick, and shouts in fun as she pulls it towards herself.

The plane starts to climb and Mastorna rolls back down to the end of the fuselage.

— *Where are you taking me? Where are we going?*

Delighted laughter from the girl, who now pulls a piece of string and pushes the broom-handle away, sending the plane into a fearful loop.

Mastorna rolls forward, crashing into the cockpit. The small Chinese girl pulls his nose.

Mastorna (freeing himself angrily):

— *Where are we going, you mindless pest? Where are you taking me?*

The child points her finger against Mastorna's forehead.

— *We're going here.*

And she giggles convulsively.

— *... it's such fun, I'm going to wee myself, it's all so funny!*

Mastorna just manages to prevent himself from strangling her; he is bleeding from above the eye, one of the facial injuries he has received ricocheting around in the fuselage; he is sweating heavily, his face full of rage and fear.

— *Little halfwit! You want me to go crazy, but I'm stronger than you, I'm not going to give in.*

The Chinese girl puts a sweet into his mouth. Mastorna spits it out angrily.

— *Be a good girl, you damned pest, where are we going? Is it far?*

Suddenly the girl becomes serious:

— *Where do you want to go?*

Then she puts her finger on her nose:

— *... is this far?*

Mastorna breaks down; sighing, he sits on the floor, his eyes staring ahead as if focusing on a new idea, either comforting or simply absurd. A sense of emptiness and resignation. Under his breath he murmurs:

— *I'm tired, go wherever you like. I don't want to think any more. It'll be all right in the end. Thank you.*

The child turns to him suddenly and says with a serious voice:

— *We're arrived. It's important.*

In fact, the plane is no longer moving.

Mastorna looks out of the window: they have landed in a tiny field on the side of a mountain, at the top of a wooded valley.

Exterior. Mountain valley.
The valley is closed on all sides by high mountains. At the bottom of the grassy meadow there is a wooden hut with the word CUSTOMS under the roof. The chimney is smoking slightly. A woman seems to have a blanket wrapped around her shoulders as if to get warm. She walks forward briskly, waving her arms in welcome.

Mastorna turns up the collar of his overcoat and takes a few steps forward, towards the woman who continues to approach with uncertain steps, as if she were tripping up or were uncertain on her feet. Finally he recognizes her; it's the hostess, who falls into his arms, patting him on the back vigorously, excessively, as if she were drunk.

– *Fantastic. You made it! Did you enjoy the flight? Maestro?*

She looks at him with the unfocused eyes of someone who has had too much to drink.

– *A drink is called for. We have to celebrate this achievement. Warm me, I'm freezing.*

Mastorna is looking at her, surprised to see her in that state; the hostess sees his surprise and takes his hands, places them on her shoulders.

– *What's wrong? Are you afraid of touching a woman? Do you think you no longer deserve Paradri ... Padradi ...*

She hugs him close.

– *Hold me, embrace me, I'm cold. Or do you want to set out immediately? Now you have everything you need, you realize? You don't need anything any more. We've stopped fooling about with you. See? That's the path you should take.*

She points to a valley to Mastorna's left, with sheer cliffs.

– *That's where the pass is. What a lovely mouth you have! Will you give me a kiss before you leave? Come, I'll go with you. How do you feel?*

They have begun to walk towards the valley, taking the path that rises and disappears behind a vertical rock face.

It goes out of view beyond that face. Only the sky is visible on the other side. A closed, empty sky, colourless, immense, impenetrable, without depth or height, an infinitely long grey sheet seemingly meaning nothing, without either sense or reason to exist.

Mastorna looks at the emptiness, the milky immensity, fascinated and, at the same time, disappointed, unable to look away.

The hostess gives a drunken hiccup and laughs dully.

> – *Now, as your guide, I should tell you one more thing, but my head is spinning. Do you really want to leave immediately? I can come with you only up to there.*

And she points to a hut, not far in front of them.

> – *I'm dying of cold, let's go in and get warm. You can leave tomorrow. It's getting dark already. … Directions? Clues? We are strictly forbidden from giving any. Know why? Because we haven't got the faintest idea, not the foggiest. So what are you going to do? Do we have to say goodbye here? … If we spend the night together in the hut, perhaps I'll remember what I have to tell you, but it must be something rather silly, something that makes sense only to you, because, you see, I've forgotten it …*

Turning towards the hut she calls:

> – *Hey, you two, get something hot ready! The Maestro is spending the night with us.*

Interior. Hut.
It's a comfortable, wooden hut, well heated by a rudimentary stove, stoked to raging. There's a table, with some registers, and a makeshift bed with some blankets in the corner. From the ceiling an oil lamp is hanging, sizzling as the wick runs out. The two customs officers are wearing old-fashioned uniforms. They have made some hot punch and are now giving some to the hostess and Mastorna, next to each other on the bed. Silently they are drinking from the steaming mugs. Outside the window the light is fading. The pass and pathway can still be made out, the path rising steeply and then turning as if into the sky, now darkening. No-one speaks. Only the sizzling of the oil lamp can be heard and, now and then, the whistling of the wind. Mastorna begins to speak, quietly, as if confessing his feelings to himself.

– I'm surprised, disappointed, proud of myself, distressed, depressed, enthusiastic. I'm all of these things without understanding how I feel overall. I'm unable to give or deny a value, a definitive value, to come to a conclusion about myself, my life, I'm not sure of anything. I have no definitive convictions, not one, yet I feel good, at peace ...

The two customs officers, sitting on a bench, have taken out some musical instruments: a penny whistle, a small accordion, and they are playing tunes, some happy, some sad.

The hostess has stretched out on the bed and is singing quietly to herself. Mastorna looks at her, lies down next to her, caresses her hair.

– What did you want to tell me? Do you remember now?

The hostess looks at him with immense nostalgia.

– Is living really beautiful? Tell me, describe to me your houses, your cities, tell me about your sun ... your spring, tell me how you cry, how you love ...

She puts her hands behind his neck and pulls him closer.

– Now I remember what I wanted to tell you, some lines of poetry, written by one of you, who spent the night with me here a long time ago.

She smiles and quietly recites:

– 'Openly I dedicated my heart to the momentous, suffering earth. And I promised to love it faithfully, for as long as I lived, without fear, with its heavy burden of fatality, and not to contemn a single one of its enigmas, thus I made with the earth a mortal bond.'

The hostess moves her face closer to Mastorna's, she kisses him on the lips, lengthily. They stay in the warmth and half-darkness of the bed.

The oil lamp sputters and dies. The final notes of the customs officers' instruments are still in the air.

Now there is a deep silence. Only the whistling wind is audible.

In the depths of night Mastorna wakes unexpectedly, sits up in bed; there is moonlight inside the hut throwing long, black, unmoving shadows everywhere. He looks at the hostess's beautiful face as she sleeps peacefully. He places his hand close to her brow, stands up, looks at her once more, murmuring a goodbye without words.

In a corner, the two customs officers, wrapped in their cloaks, are sleeping, one leaning against the other, snoring loudly.

Mastorna takes a log, puts it into the stove and the dying flames leap back into life. Then he goes to the door, opens it, looks behind him one last time at everything he is about to leave behind, and steps out.

Exterior. Mountain valley.
It's a cold, but clear night with a starry sky. Deep silence. Mastorna walks towards the pass, unfalteringly, determined: he has already reached the path; in front of him, bathed in moonlight, the black spur of rock, the mountain, is like a gigantic sanctuary with the stars as its roof. Mastorna has stopped; he turns to look at the customs hut, clearly visible in the black meadow, illuminated from behind. Then he resumes his journey and no longer looks back.

Interior. Hut.
Day is breaking. The customs officers are getting up, stretching and yawning. The hostess is looking through the window at the mysterious pathway now covered with the mist of dawn, a look of terrible nostalgia in her eyes.

She stands up, goes into the kitchenette and starts to do something, makes some coffee. She takes a clean tablecloth out of a drawer and lays the table.

One of the customs officers:

– *Has he left?*

The hostess nods, continuing to lay the table.

The other customs officer:

> – Now what? How is it all going to end? What has Mastorna found on the other side of the path?

With the tone of someone telling a fairy story, the hostess says:

> – On the other side of the mountain Mastorna found a city. He was surprised to be walking in a city that looked just like Florence ... the streets were lit by the sun, the buildings, the shops, the florists ... the well-appointed shop windows, the traffic lights: it was Florence, but there was something different in the air, in the sunlight, in the faces of the people he met ... hard to say what the difference was ... it was as if the things, the people, were new ... seen for the first time ...

The hostess's voice can still be heard as we see a Florence street.

Exterior. A Florence street and square.
We see Mastorna walking, quicker and quicker, like someone afraid of being late for an appointment. But even hurrying, he looks at everything, enchanted by what he sees, the faces of people he meets, the dazzle of the shop windows, the flowers, the colour of the sky, the trees, the eyes of people who pass close by. They are familiar, everyday sights.

A baker's boy goes by on a bicycle.

A first floor window opens and an elderly man in pyjamas appears, arms folded, his eyes still sleepy.

A young man washes down the pavement in front of his shop.

A shop assistant arranging a bunch of roses in the window ... a traffic warden with a whistle in his mouth, the yellow and green tram rounding the bell and ringing its bell, laden with office workers, porters, housewives ...

A group of school children in uniform, with blue ribbons, crosses the road, in huddled conversation ...

A beggar asks for charity.

Two women with heavy shopping bags are nattering at the corner of the street ... everyday sights, the customary show, tawdry, meaningless; chaotic, but for Mastorna, this morning, utterly wonderful ...

... and Mastorna, in fact, repeats to himself over and over as he hurries on:

– *Wonderful ... wonderful.*

Exterior. Concert hall.

He has come to the entrance of a theatre and goes in, walking backwards as if to fill his eyes with the visions of the street. Like a drunk he repeats:

– *Wonderful ...*

Interior. Concert hall.

Mastorna reaches the auditorium breathless and walks down the aisle separating the expensive seats, which are covered with large white sheets.

The stage is lit diagonally by the sun's rays, filtering through the skylight.

In the orchestra pit there is the quiet intermittent sound of instruments being tuned; on the stand, the conductor is in shirt sleeves; he is turning over the pages of the score, jotting things down here and there with a pencil.

With the air of a late schoolboy, Mastorna tiptoes forward and takes his place in the orchestra pit. Rapidly, he removes the cello from its case.

His colleagues look at him with curiosity, one of them points into the wings and whispers:

– *Your wife is here.*

Mastorna turns and in the penumbra of the wings sees a woman, sitting calmly. Mastorna stares in disbelief, then waves and murmurs:

– *Luisa, I …*

But the woman, with the discretion of someone who doesn't want to disturb, motions to him not to move, to stay where he is.

Another member of the orchestra looks at him in surprise, with curiosity and whispers:

– *What kept you until now?*

Mastorna opens his mouth as if to reply but just then there are three sharp sounds from the conductor's stand.

The orchestra settles into silence and picks up the instruments. The trumpet, pipe and flute players bring these instruments to their lips.

Mastorna has raised the bow of his cello, ready for the first note.

The raised hand of the conductor holds the baton still, then it suddenly falls and the orchestra begins to play a solemn tune, grandiose, desperate, infinitely sweet, intoxicating.

Up in the roof, where the skylight is open onto the spring day, swallows fly in and swirl, chasing one another in the rays of the sun and the specks of dust, tinged with gold.

Translator's notes

1. Filthy Italian.
2. The Fulgor was the name of the cinema in Rimini where Fellini saw his first films, many of them comedies starring Charlie Chaplin, Laurel and Hardy and the Marx Brothers. A little later, he made a deal with the owner, who gave him free admission in return for some caricatures of the stars in the style of Nino Za which were hung in the foyer and about town to advertise the programme.
3. Before the setting of the sun, Creator of the world, we pray.
4. A famous TV quiz-show host and oftentimes presenter of the San Remo song festival.
5. The title of Fellini's first film to be distributed internationally. From the dialect word *vidlòn*, overgrown calves. Sometimes translated as 'spivs' or 'layabouts'.
6. Max Stirner, author of *The Ego and Its Own* (1844), a radical critique of Hegel and socialism, which earned a detailed reply (and rebuttal) from Marx.

Mastroianni to Fellini: *"If you could believe that I am Mastorna...I would automatically become Mastorna."*

Imagining *Mastorna*

> [S]cripts are blueprints, not finished works, and even to discuss one that was never filmed is to give it an identity of its own that was never intended.
>
> (Jonathan Rosenbaum)[1]

1 What would *Mastorna* have been like?

Like *8½*, Fellini's next film, *Giulietta degli spiriti* (1965) lavishly blended memories, dreams, fantasy and desire, this time with an increasingly explicit interest in analytical psychology and the esoteric. Unlike *8½*, it was poorly received. Critics complained of its excessive symbolism, protracted fantasy scenes, the reiterated childhood memory of the repression of sexuality by the Catholic Church, and the schematic visions of femininity, which gave the film an overblown baroque feel. It was considered self-indulgent and self-referential (fingers were pointed at the harem scene repeated from *8½* – as it would be again, in a final attempt to assuage feminist critics, in *La città delle donne*) as if the elements of *8½* which the critics had admired now disturbed them.

Fellini cited Jung's paper *Marriage as a Psychological Relationship* in an effort to explain the film and the inability of a man to fully explore his female side.[2] It was one of the very few times he invoked a specific work of theory to justify his cinema, over and above his well-publicized acknowledgement of a generic debt to Jung, a thinker who, as he saw it, validated his own sense of the enlivening forces of the irrational and magical. The critics were unimpressed and continued to see in *Giulietta* a sad epilogue to Gelsomina/

Cabiria, a failed, middle-aged Cinderella. He was even accused of a Puccini-like sadism in relation to feeling. Not since his solo debut, *Lo sceicco bianco*, had a full-length film by Fellini been treated so badly.

For his intended next film, *Il viaggo di G. Mastorna*, he said he wanted to get away from a 'stylized reality', studio sets and faces as 'masks'. Characteristically, this remark was couched as the desire to move on but it was at least a partial concession to the criticism meted out to *Giulietta*: 'Until now I have worked with prefabricated sets, costumes, faces, lighting. … A form of expressionism, all worked out to the tiniest detail, even for the lighting; now, however, the fabulous nature of the story, the haziness of it, the disquiet and mystery, should be suggested by the most everyday figurative things, obvious ones, natural.'[3] Specifically, about *Mastorna* he said: 'Lifelike, that's what this film must be.' Lifelike (unlike *Giulietta*), you might suppose, to disguise *Mastorna*'s lack of life, the fact that everything we see in the film, after the initial aeroplane scene, is dead. Indeed, had he made *Mastorna*, it might have turned out to be Fellini's most realistic film of the 1960s, perhaps even the last to attempt to capture the grain of life, the kind of surface texture he had learnt to produce in his neorealist days. In the light of his remarks and a declaration by Roberto Rossellini about his own filming techniques (given further on), it is tempting to imagine *Mastorna* as an imitation neorealist film.[4]

As it turned out, neither *Toby Dammit* (1968) nor *Satyricon* (1969), the works that actually followed *Giulietta*, showed any signs of Fellini backing down. They were unapologetic and uncompromising, visually aggressive to the point of unpleasantness, one highly satirical, pushed – Fellini said – to extremes, and the other disjointed, fragmented and grotesque, depicting a world in an advanced state of putrefaction. They did not reflect Fellini's declarations about the direction he intended to take for *Mastorna* which raises a doubt about how faithful Fellini would actually have been to his declarations and partial recantations of *Giulietta*. However, they cannot be dismissed as a palliative to critics, either: *Mastorna* was conceived as a continuation of Fellini's black and white films, particularly of *La dolce vita* and *8½*, made before his first full-length colour film. Stylistically it would have resembled them, rather than *Giulietta*.

The shooting of *Giulietta degli spiriti* had been divisive. Fellini had argued with his wife and three of his closest collaborators (none of whom – for different reasons – was to work on *Mastorna*). Although Giulietta Masina actively participated in Fellini's frequent seances (derided by his analyst, Ernst Bernhard) and was sympathetic to his exploration of the spirit world, for *Giulietta* she sided with the film's realistic component, the mid-life marital crisis, which she felt was being needlessly sacrificed to Fellini's intention to make a 'feminine' film (and feminine Guido).

Fellini's co-scriptwriter Ennio Flaiano walked away from the set, declaring that Fellini was now more interested in the dream world than in reality. It was an acrimonious, semi-public, rift. Flaiano had co-scripted every one of his films to date, with the sole exception of the half-film *Agenzia matrimoniale* (Marriage Agency, 1953), included in Zavattini's compilation *L'amore in città* (Love in the City). The reason for the falling out in 1965 was both footling and serious, as Flaiano himself said, with a drop of poison, in a letter to Fellini: 'Frivolous friendships come to an end over something trivial.'

Perhaps the trivial incident occurred in April 1964 when Fellini and his entourage flew first-class via New York to Los Angeles for the screening of *8½*. Flaiano found himself alone in economy. His boss claimed Rizzoli's people had mixed up the bookings and, for part of the journey, had sat with Flaiano, trying to sooth his ego, apparently, to no avail. When they arrived in New York, Flaiano bought himself a first-class ticket back to Rome.

It wasn't the first misunderstanding. Flaiano, a diarist, playwright, prolific screenwriter and prize-winning novelist, resented other writers being brought onto projects. Most of all, Pasolini rubbed him up the wrong way; his increasing success in films was something Flaiano didn't understand or accept. Unlike Pasolini, he was a droll, detached observer of his age, who never sought the limelight and perhaps, in relation to Fellini, felt undeservedly eclipsed. The resentment grew with every press conference in which Fellini, unfailingly, failed to mention the names of his fellow scriptwriters.[5]

So, for *Mastorna*, the scriptwriting team was changed; the familiar team of Flaiano and Tullio Pinelli was replaced by Dino Buzzati and Brunello Rondi. Rondi had helped in the scripts of *La dolce vita*,[6] *8½* and *Giulietta degli spiriti*, and would go on to collaborate on *Satyricon*, *Prova d'orchestra* and *La città delle donne*. A film-maker in his own right, he co-directed the late neorealist film *Una vita violenta* (A Violent Life), from the novel by Pasolini, in 1962. After this he specialized in films focusing on women's sexuality (some would call them erotic B movies), although he ended his career with a film on the young Mother Teresa of Calcutta.

It is impossible to say what Buzzati and Rondi contributed to *Mastorna*. Fellini referred to them as 'reagents' which suggests that he used them to discuss his ideas. To Fellini, Rondi voiced his concern about Buzzati's affinities with Kafka, a puzzling observation both because of Buzzati's renowned irritation with continuous comparisons of this kind, and because *Mastorna* had evident similarities with Kafka's *Amerika*,[7] a novel Fellini tried to put on screen for almost as long as *Mastorna*.[8] Rondi and Buzzati evidently didn't see eye to eye and it is known that Fellini worked with them separately, so it is possible that they never met.

The third argument was with Gianni Di Venanzo, Fellini's cinematographer for *8½* and *Giulietta* and frequently Director of Photography for Antonioni and Rosi. They accused each other of not understanding the difference between filming in black and white and colour. Until then, Fellini's only attempt at colour had been *Le tentazioni del dottor Antonio* – his contribution to De Sica's *Decameron '70* – where he'd had to abide by the decision of the other directors. For *Giulietta degli spiriti*, colour was essential to make the 'dazzling harlequinade' Fellini wanted to achieve: it was 'an integral part of the narrative texture' he told Costanzo Costantini.[9] Previously he had referred to filming in colour as 'breathing under water' so he evidently had misgivings and these contributed to the tensions on the set. In the end, *Giulietta* was praised, if at all, for its cinematography, which pushed colour photography into hitherto unknown areas. The praise was unlikely to have consoled the director.

Like Fellini, Di Venanzo was born in 1920. His death on 3 February 1966, just as *Mastorna* was beginning to take shape, was one of the reasons Fellini came to regard the project as hexed: 'accident-ridden' was the term he used. In addition to working with new scriptwriters, he now had to find a new cinematographer to shoot in black and white, which most directors and cinematographers had abandoned.

Dino De Laurentiis's doubts about *Mastorna* were less superstitious: could death be the subject of a box-office hit? Half-heartedly, he allowed himself to be persuaded to go through with the project by his brother Luigi, who hired the art director, Pier Luigi Pizzi. Pizzi suggested shooting the film in a kind of sepia grey with some colour added here and there, a new technique.[10] He had hundreds of costumes made in pale, ill-defined colours. Pizzi would have replaced Piero Gherardi, the fourth person Fellini had argued with on the set of *Giulietta degli spiriti*. Gherardi didn't like the way the film was shaping up and wasn't ready on 10 July, the date for the beginning of shooting. 'He has the habit of making everything elephantine,' Fellini complained, thinking mainly of *Giulietta* (rather than *La dolce vita* and *8½* for which Gherardi had won Academy Awards). The relationship was 'stagnating', Fellini said and the split was consensual. In 1966 Gherardi worked with Monicelli on *L'armata Brancaleone*, but a dream during that troubled year indicates that Fellini was far from happy with this new break.

It isn't clear what Fellini meant in his letter to De Laurentiis about 'how to use the scenery to avoid location costs and trips abroad' whilst getting away from artificial sets. In all likelihood it was the recreation of the numerous locations intended for the film in the De Laurentiis studios just outside Rome, which we are given a glimpse of in *A Director's Notebook*. The idea would have been to present contrasting architectural styles to create a phantasmagorical composite city. Fellini went to Cologne to photograph the Cathedral with Giuseppe Rotunno, who then moved on to other cities in Italy, either to be used for location shots or, like Cologne Cathedral, copied into the set in Pontina. In Tazio Secchiaroli's photos of Mastroianni's screen test (re-enacted later for *A Director's Notebook*), Rotunno is behind the camera. He was the cinematographer for *Toby Dammit* and seven of Fellini's next eight films, so he would certainly have been Fellini's choice for *Mastorna*. However, all his films with Fellini were in colour: for an idea of how he might have shot in black and white you have to go back to Visconti's *Rocco e i suoi fratelli* (1960). In the meantime, Rotunno had become a pioneer of Technicolor, 16 mm, 35 mm and 65 mm film. So it is not clear whether Pizzi's idea of sepia grey with light colouring would have been adopted, although it would have given the film a sort of hovering visual uncertainty, the inverse of the freeze frames drained of colour used in *Amarcord* to turn the film into the pages of an old photograph album. For *Giulietta*, Fellini had considered copying Antonioni, who had painted some frames of his first colour film, *Deserto rosso* (1964); his trees and grass, for example, were turned an unnatural white or grey. In the end, Fellini had limited himself to determining the colour of the film through the costumes and sets.

The crew would therefore have been Fellini (with Buzzati and Rondi on the script), Rotunno, Pizzi and, unquestionably, for the musical score, Nino Rota.

Fellini had a number of ideas about the cast, too. The automatic choice for Mastorna was Marcello Mastroianni.[11] For the gravedigger he wanted Totò, the legendary comic actor who, Fellini said, like Pulcinella, could only play himself, 'a modern and secular version of God's fool, an amazing marionette'. One of Fellini's sketches for Mastorna shows a thin bowler-hatted figure, half Jacques Tati, half Totò, struggling with luggage.[12] Another idea was the singer Mina, who he wanted to play the last of the Beatrice figures. In 1961 she had told Mario Soldati that her favourite reading was Walt Disney comics, a preference she shared with Fellini. Her frequent television appearances, beautiful voice and striking face, combined with a poised cabaret style, had made her an iconic figure. In 1965, the year of the *Mastorna* script, she was hosting the television series *Studio Uno* in Rome, which ran for twelve shows and featured guests from the film world, among them Totò, Marcello Mastroianni (who sang a song, out of tune, accompanied by a dog, Bobby), Ugo Tognazzi and Vittorio De Sica. Alberto Sordi and Lina Wertmuller were to write songs for her. So Mina was certainly no stranger to actors and directors and would have known several members of the cast Fellini had in mind. However, she turned him down, both for *Mastorna* and for *Satyricon*, citing her experience in 'thirteen forgettable squibs' as ample proof she couldn't act. Her memory of Fellini's wooing is intriguing: 'With that beautiful voice of his, like a nun's, gentle and ironic, for hours on end he tried to get me to change my mind. … He was one of the very few happy men I have ever met.'[13]

For the two customs officers Fellini wanted Franco Franchi and Ciccio Ingrassia, the short and the tall, fat and thin, a latter-day Laurel and Hardy comic duo who had inherited the audience of Totò from the 1950s and made a string of box-office hits over the following two decades, caricaturing aspects of the Italian character and way of life. They also parodied Bond movies, spaghetti westerns and so on.

They had appeared in the De Laurentiis/De Sica flop *Il giudizio universale* (The Last Judgement) in 1961, a surreal film on Naples without a single Neapolitan actor, which failed to repeat the recent success of *La ciociara*, with its very Neapolitan Sophia Loren. The film may have influenced Fellini and his aversion to an all-star cast (here Vittorio Gassman, Alberto Sordi, Fernandel, Paolo Stoppa, Renato Rascel, Silvana Mangano, Anouk Aimee, Jack Palance, Ernest Borgnine and others). The story bore some resemblance to *Mastorna*. It begins with a voice from the sky announcing, 'At six o'clock this evening the Last Judgement will begin', and ends after torrential rain that had seemed to announce the imminent end of the world, with one of the characters saying, 'Perhaps we only believe we are alive, but are dead'.

In 1965 Franchi and Ingrassia appeared in *2 marines e un generale* with Buster Keaton. In 1968 they were directed by Pasolini in an episode of *Capriccio all'italiana*, one of the few occasions in which the critics were appreciative. The two were practically inseparable, turning down roles in films that did not include the other half. Exceptions in the mid-1970s were Ciccio Ingrassia's solo appearances as the mad uncle in *Amarcord* and as a gay, self-flagellating political conspirator in Elio Petri's *Todo Modo*.

For the part of Armandino, Fellini had in mind Pietro De Vico, a fine character actor and, from 1961 to 1966, the star of a popular TV series, *Giovanna la nonna del Corsaro Nero*. He had also appeared in *Il giudizio universale*. In 1964 he made *I marziani hanno dodici mani* (Martians Have Twelve Hands), a science-fiction comedy produced by Rizzoli's Cineriz, with Franchi and Ingrassia as Martians who land in Rome intending to prepare the way for invasion.[14]

For the award ceremony Fellini thought of Wanda Osiris and Vittorio De Sica. Osiris was a singer and actress who became Italy's first gay icon. She was a living parody of a Hollywood diva with dark make-up, platinum blonde hair, huge feathery costumes, high heels and highfalutin nasal delivery, who loved to pick the most spectacular locations in Rome for her dramatic appearances, accompanied by hand-picked dancers, or what today would be called toy boys. She was devoutly Catholic.

As Master of Ceremonies, De Sica would certainly have been able to produce the unctuous obsequiousness required of the role, with the added irony of presenting one of the founders of Italian neorealism in a role as far from realism as possible. He would have been the fourth actor picked from *Il giudizio universale* (which De Sica directed) and the fourth to be a current television star (with Mina, Mastroianni and De Vico).

For the innumerable crowd scenes, Fellini wanted to hire extras of Slavic origin, who would give the multitudes a varied, indefinable ethnicity.

In addition to the cast and crew there are also some indications of how Fellini intended to shoot the film. To De Laurentiis in his original letter/draft estimating script he expressed what he thought were the principal features of Mastorna:

1) The basic idea: *death is also life* as they sang in that dream chorus with Pasolini.[15]

2) The feeling of sheer *adventure*.

3) The *photographic* style of the film: black and white, photography as an expression of death, of everything that is no more and is fixed into eternal, lifeless immobility.

He indicated that the film was to be one of suspense, and even quipped that it would out-Bond Bond.[16] If 007, rather than Hitchcock, was his model for suspense, the film was probably intended to have a fast pace, building up a sense of mystery through incongruities that are evident but marginal, such as the location and architecture of the motel where the passengers are taken after the emergency landing. Despite the seamless action the scenes might have been presented as self-contained (dis)locations: i.e. the motel is detached from the city, the night-club appears not to be part of the motel, and so on. The architecture of Rome would have been mixed with that of Naples, Venice and Rimini, so we might have seen the Colosseum, St. Mark's Square and the Fulgor cinema at the foot of Mount Vesuvius.

As Fellini hinted to De Laurentiis in his first draft of the script, the suspense may have been enhanced by a *Sunset Boulevard* type of narrator, his disembodied voice alternating with Mastorna on screen, creating a sense of being in two places and times at once. For the return of Mastorna to Florence, the narrator's voice-over would have been replaced by the last Beatrice figure, one of the few implicit cinematic instructions in the script, and this would have underlined Mastorna's return to life by relinquishing his narrative role.[17]

Fellini told Zanelli he wanted to make something that looked 'dismal and shabby, everyday and ordinary'[18] perhaps to counterpoint the mysterious or supernatural element of the film. Since its events would have been an uninterrupted series of visions, Fellini might have wanted to pin down the physical world as a form of resistance to the viewer's growing sense of unease. This is something he had experimented with, to some degree, in *8½*. For example, when Guido goes to the railway station to meet Carla, he is at first relieved that she hasn't come, but she has got out of the train from the wrong side and so is only visible when the train pulls out. The effect is that of a naturalized and disappointed 'vision', compared to other apparitions. However, in *8½*, Guido only rarely confuses mental images with physical reality (particularly in the case of the part ethereal, part flesh-and-blood, Claudia). Mastorna, on the other hand, is entirely unaware of the nature of the world around him, perhaps to the very last. One early example of this in *Mastorna* is the confusion of diegetic and nondiegetic elements when Mastorna is riding on the bus towards the motel. Mastorna sees the images of billboards enlivened, a succession of slightly different expressions of a child, which, taken together, are like a cartoon animation. What does the baby mean, why is the child addressing him? In *Mastorna*, the gradual accumulation of enigmas and increasingly inexplicable incongruities bites into the naturalism of the scenes until no effort at construing the real holds, as when, in the Naples scene, one of the daughters passionately kisses a python. The more naturalistic the scene and the finer the grain of the 'real', the more disturbing the effect of the snake-kiss would have been. Although the scene would be understood as part of Mastorna's imaginings, the alienating effects of his visions could be maintained by continuing to see the world through his eyes, as he grapples with, and tries to hold on to, the real. Fellini probably intended these incongruities to be not only grotesque but comic, as he told De Laurentiis in his letter. He repeated this intention to Zanelli, adding that Kafka, reading *The Metamorphosis* out loud to friends, was frequently seized by uncontrollable bouts of chuckling.

In 1966, Zanelli spoke to Brunello Rondi about his ongoing contribution to, and idea of, the film: 'I think that *Mastorna* will have a great deal of affinity with *8½*: real anxiety, the problem of death, a character with which the director identifies …' He and Fellini worked in Villa Giulia on Lake Bracciano. Rondi says Fellini was studying *The Egyptian Book of the Dead* and its stories of journeys into the afterlife, ancient Tibetan sources and rereading *The Divine Comedy*. 'What we were really trying to do was give a sense of hallucination to real things: make the afterlife look like this life, today, but where some essential things are lacking. Bergman? Maybe. I dare say …'[19] According to Rondi, Fellini wanted the atmosphere of the film to be that of a 'remote, disquieting distance'.

And Fellini described Mastorna 'watching but not seeing': a blank look, deep in thought, suggesting that he is somehow aware of a wrinkle in the Universe but can't put his finger on it. He attempts to understand rather than apprehend the world, turns it into an abstraction. This is very similar to Guido in *8½*, frequently shown with his face slightly turned away, deep in thought, barely aware of what is happening in front of him, as he is confronted by aspiring actors and actresses, his production manager and producer: a man on the retreat, whose inner promptings are perpetually held in check.

Fellini told Zanelli that his intention in the film was to show how Catholicism and transcendental philosophies preyed on the fear of death and imprisoned the mind, drawing attention away from the concrete world. This would have been a reversal of the distraction in Bosch's triptych of *The Temptation of Saint Anthony*, which he had used for his 1962 contribution to De Sica's *Boccaccio '70*.[20] The painting shows fish which are strikingly similar to the monster in the final scene of *La dolce vita*. In the right panel, Anthony is portrayed trying to look at the viewer, but his gaze is averted by sinful mankind. Both Marcello in *La dolce vita* and Guido in *8½* are often shot with a distracted glance and the lack of face to face contact[21] was something Fellini also wanted to show in *Mastorna*.

Throughout his film-making career, Fellini maintained certain techniques learnt from neorealism which other directors abandoned (while Pasolini preserved them along with some others): its loose narrative structure, the absence of a specific ending or resolution, the use of dialect and the overdubbing of dialogue to suit an actor's expression (which the neorealists had learnt in the Fascist period, when dubbing was compulsory). It is reasonable to suppose Fellini would have been true to them in *Mastorna*, too, which would, to some extent, have been a choral film, in episodes, with a large number of extras. The 'locations' might have been used to include several different dialects, or regional inflections. And the neorealist technique of dubbing might have been pushed to an extreme, as it was in *Satyricon*, by jerkily overdubbing the dialogue so the sound and the movement of the actor's lips are out of sync, giving a sense of estrangement. It would have indicated that the dialogues are interior monologues that may or may not need to be verbalized, disembodied voices. The dialogue might have had the semblance of telepathic exchanges.

In the case of *Mastorna*, one statement by Roberto Rossellini,[22] made at the time of *Roma, città aperta*, not specifically seeking to define neorealism, but nonetheless revealing of what Fellini's *maestro* was seeking in his films, is particularly appropriate. It described film-making in a way that suggests psychological urgency, technical virtuosity and a relentless investigation of the subject:

> I need a depth of perspective that perhaps only the cinema can give, and to see people and things from all sides, to be able to cut, leave out, dissolve and use interior monologue. Not, you understand, in the way of Joyce, more like Dos Passos. To put some things in and leave others out, to include what takes place around a given event, which may perhaps, however distantly, have given rise to it. I will be able to place the camera according to my abilities and the characters will be followed and obsessed by it: today's anguish comes precisely from this inability to escape the implacable eye of the camera.[23]

Whether or not Fellini would have sought to represent Mastorna's anguish through the implacable eye of the camera is impossible to know, but in his letter to De Laurentiis Fellini told him he intended 'to tell the story of the film lucidly but at an ever faster pace, without a moment's respite, right to the end', and this inexorable pace might have been enhanced by the camera hounding Mastorna at every turn, almost hunting him down.

In one reading of Fellini, *Mastorna* would have closed the series of black-and-white films interrupted by *Giulietta*, which Kezich regards as the beginning of a new cycle. Compatible with this view would be the appraisal of *La dolce vita* and *8½* as ushering out neorealism by introducing postmodernism to Italian cinema. Certainly, *Mastorna* is a script – and would probably have been a film – open to the full array of critical tools developed for postmodernism. If the view is correct, Fellini's next half-film, *Toby Dammit*, was a late colour addition to the first cycle, which, broadly speaking, took him from his neorealist beginnings to fully-fledged postmodernism. Based on a story by Edgar Allan Poe, *Never Bet the Devil Your Head* (a spoof on transcendentalism),[24] it appears to take the trajectory of Fellini's last films in black and white to a logical, and extreme, conclusion: the artist's death. Its kinship with *Mastorna* is unmistakable (in specific scenes, notably the very first shot of the threatening sky, the airport location, the award ceremony and, above all, the sense of a man assaulted by the world, his eyes blasted open by interrogatory spot-lights, seeking to disappear, to close his eyes).

But in another reading of Fellini, in which the hiatus between black and white and colour is discounted in favour of overall continuity, and Fellini is seen as a proto-postmodernist from the outset, *Mastorna* would have continued the exploration of heterotopy, parallel worlds and transit states that Fellini had always investigated and was to continue to take an interest in until his very last film, *La voce della luna* (The Voice of the Moon, 1990).[25]

2 Why didn't he make the film?

In Maite Carpio's documentary on the *Mastorna* project,[26] De Laurentiis says seraphically: 'Fellini didn't make the film before me, with me or after me. Why?' suggesting that the failure was entirely Fellini's. In his reconstruction of the Mastroianni screen test in *A Director's Notebook*, shot in 1968, Fellini suggests that he couldn't find Mastorna even in the actor he had chosen for the part. The re-enactment includes the following exchange:

> FF: Lower your head a little, a little more. Quiet back there! Lower your head. Stop. Give him some eye drops. How come your eyes are always red, Marcello, what have you been up to? And another thing, Marcello. Get his moustache to stay put, it's always falling off. Marcello, I wanted to say, you shouldn't play the cello like that, like it was just any old instrument.
>
> MM: I understand.
>
> FF: What is it Marcello? You seem a little jumpy.
>
> A voice off screen: Want a coffee, Marcé?

FF: Not now, I don't want it now, does he have to drink a coffee right now?

MM: I'm not jumpy. I just don't understand what you want, that's all. First like this, then like that …

FF: You should express …

MM: (talking to a make-up artist) Have you finished … do you mind!

FF: … growing terror, as if you suddenly realized …(to the crew) This light up here. Quiet back there a moment! No, without the hat, I don't like the hat, maybe we'll try the hat later … put it away. Marcello, once in a while look at the camera. I was saying … what you should try to do is express a feeling of growing bewilderment (Mastroianni looks annoyed), because this instrument represents your genius, the reason for your vocation.

Voice of FF (in English): A very tense, nervous test. Marcello felt my embarrassment. He was put off by my insecurity. Moustache, wigs, make-up, but I felt that Mastorna was not there, he was still hiding his face from me.

MM (now seemingly on his own, in English): All right, I understand. But when you made *La dolce vita*, wasn't I well cast, in *8½* wasn't I right?

FF (in English): Yes, I know Marcello, but those were other films, different characters.

MM: No, Federico, it's because now you have no faith. It's as if you are scared. If you could believe that I am Mastorna, (peeling off half a moustache) I would automatically become Mastorna.

In these exchanges – partly remembered, partly invented, certainly scripted – Fellini and Mastroianni blame each other for the failing of *Mastorna*. Specifically Fellini has Mastroianni accuse him of a kind of lack of faith, a failure to believe in him as an actor suitable for the part, and in himself, as a director.

One could ponder the reasons for such an elaborate reconstruction of the original screen test at the Luce Institute in Cinecittà. The documentary was made by NBC for an American audience and was sponsored by Burlington Industries, a chemical company, so it is at least possible that Fellini was scouting for backers for *Mastorna*. In the first part of the programme,[27] Fellini appears to change his mind about the future of the film. As the camera plays over the abandoned set in Pontina (aka Dinocittà), with the twin towers of a Gothic Cathedral incongruously towering over a field of grass, a two-dimensional three-storey façade of buildings on one side and scaffolding surrounding the carcass of a commercial aeroplane on the other, Fellini's voice begins to recount in heavily accented English:

> These strange lonely shapes were built for a film that I planned but I never made. It was called *The Voyage of Mastorna*. The settings have remained like this, useless and empty, in a studio near Rome. In this square a plane would have come down and out of it would have come the hero, a cellist. There, and from this square began his voyage through an absurd, nightmare landscape.

After a brief glimpse of Mastorna, Magritte-like with a bowler hat,[28] suitcase in one hand, cello case in the other, seen from behind in a gathering snow storm, the voice of an American interviewer cuts in and we see Fellini walking along, dark glasses folded into his jacket pocket:

> Off-screen interviewer: And so Mr Fellini, you never made *The Voyage of Mastorna*?
>
> FF: No. Not yet. But I will do it because it is the story that I prefer the most. I had prepared everything because the character materialize himself. (A woman outside a hut waves.) You know sometimes I have had the feeling to have met personally Mastorna. But every time he slips away again. Aha ciao Gasparino. May I introduce my step-girl,[29] Miss Marina Boratto?
>
> MB: How are you?
>
> Interviewer: Hello Miss Boratto, glad to meet you.
>
> FF: Ecco qua. [Here we are.] (They enter a shed.) This is the Mastorna cemetery, a kind of elephant graveyard of scenery and props. You see? Design of plane, tower, costume from the Roaring Twenties. Ha, it gives me a funny feeling, a kind of remorse, as if a million eyes were staring at me, waiting. (MB picks up a painting.) Ah, this is the square where the plane lands. I wanted something that would

give a very foreign feeling so I suggested a German square. For me a German atmosphere is always very foreign.

MB: E quella testa cos'è? [What's that head?]

FF (picking up a dummy's head): Here we have the head of a suicide because the film had a sequence where a group of people kill themselves by jumping out the window. This one went down head first.

(MB takes the head which is now split open and pokes at where the brain would be, laughing, then puts it down.)

FF: For the moment Mastorna has not arrived yet but everything is ready to receive him. We will see. Well meanwhile I have developed another project … another voyage. (Cut to the Colosseum at night, the traffic of Rome, prostitutes and transvestites … as the programme switches to anticipations of *Satyricon*.)

In a few short minutes, Fellini says he never made the film, he hasn't made it yet, he will make it, we'll see. One moment, the props shed is a cemetery and elephant's graveyard, the next everything is ready to receive Mastorna, yet Fellini feels remorse and a million eyes trained upon him: more than remorse, he seems to feel guilt and shame, as implied by Mastroianni's scripted accusation.

However, Fellini says nothing about the plot of the film, a strong indication that he believed he might still make it. The suicide scene is left unexplained, as a teaser, bait dangled before potential backers. Furthermore, at the time of making *A Director's Notebook*, Fellini was paying hundreds of millions of lire to buy back the rights from Alberto Grimaldi who had taken over the project from De Laurentiis; it is unlikely that he would have gone to such an expense merely to shelve the film for good.

Mastroianni's involvement with *Mastorna* in 1966/67 was symptomatic of Fellini's uncertainties, reservations and fears. When he first tried to make the film in 1966 Mastroianni was playing Rudolph Valentino in the stage musical *Ciao Rudi!* which was panned by the critics but played to packed houses every night. Since he was unavailable, Fellini pretended not to have always had him in mind for the part. But as the film took shape, Fellini insisted and

Fellini: *"A very tense, nervous test. Marcello felt my embarrassment. He was put off by my insecurity. Moustache, wigs, make-up, but I felt that Mastorna was not there..."*

Mastroianni paid a hefty penalty of 100 million lire to buy his way out of the musical. Then, in September 1966, with Mastroianni on board, Fellini told De Laurentiis he no longer felt able or willing to make the film. Threatened and cajoled by De Laurentiis, the project was resurrected and was up and running again in February 1967, by which time Mastroianni had signed with Visconti to make *Puccini* (also never completed).

Fellini's reaction to losing his chosen actor was equivocal at best. He flew to London to look for another lead, allowing De Laurentiis to assume he was following up on his latest suggestion: Laurence Olivier. But there is no record of him meeting Olivier on that occasion and he came back from London empty-handed. The search, such as it was, went on. To keep De Laurentiis happy (and quiet), Fellini told him he had signed Enrico Maria Salerno, who had narrowly missed being chosen for Marcello (or Enrico?) in *La dolce vita*. The producer didn't think Salerno was a big enough attraction. Names were bandied about: Giorgio Strehler? He would have jumped at the chance. Oskar Werner or Gregory Peck? Too short notice. Invited over by De Laurentiis, Paul Newman met Fellini to talk about the role.[30]

In March 1967, an overjoyed Ugo Tognazzi signed a contract to play the lead. Until the last minute, Fellini hoped he would turn it down: could Tognazzi look sufficiently possessed, controlled by spirits, neurotic? Whether it was Fellini's deeper reservations about even Mastroianni, or his evident difficulties with replacing him, one of the reasons Fellini didn't make the film was his lack of satisfaction with the leading actor.

Another reason was the feeling that the film was jinxed. In Carpio's documentary, Fellini's friend and biographer Tullio Kezich says: '*8½* is about a director who is unable to make a film; what Fellini feared in 1963 came true three years later with *Mastorna*, a film he couldn't make. Fellini was something of a shaman and *8½* was, in some way, premonitory.'

This seems bizarre if it is intended as an explanation of Fellini's failure to make *Mastorna*; *8½* was certainly a film about a director going through a creative crisis, resolved (in Fellini's case) by turning the crisis into the film. However, during the writing of *Mastorna* there is no evidence that Fellini was troubled by his creativity. If trouble there had been in his recent professional life it was the poor reception of *Giulietta degli spiriti* and the arguments with colleagues on the set. More to the point was Kezich's further remark that Fellini was an extremely superstitious man who interpreted events, accidents, even trivial details, as good or, more often, bad omens. He heeded dreams. In June 1966 Fellini confided to his diary/dream book:

> Doubts. Mortifying sense of impotence. Will I manage to make this film? Gherardi left three months ago, Norman just the other day.[31] I'm alone. I don't understand the *I Ching* and when I think I can see some kind of interpretation, the answer is always the same: Wait. The time has not yet come.

The bad omens had begun with the food poisoning the evening he had met Buzzati and his wife. With Buzzati he had visited two clairvoyants, Gustavo Adolfo Rol and Pasqualina Pezzolla, the latter of whom had drawn Fellini aside and told him Buzzati was seriously ill (which was true: Buzzati was under treatment for the disease that would kill him seven years later). At a crucial moment, when Fellini was still making up his mind, Rol, unable to bring himself to warn him face to face, put a piece of paper into his pocket, with the words: 'Don't make this film' which Fellini discovered a few days later, and interpreted almost as an anonymous message from the beyond. Fellini voiced his fears to De Laurentiis, who called him a big baby for believing in the paranormal.

On 13 September, Fellini dreamt he met Gherardi outside the Verano cemetery in Rome and the two talked about the film, Fellini imagining that they could work together again. The following night he had a premonitory dream:

> Impulsively, I decide to leave and rapidly, chaotically, pack my bags. In a black night-gown Giulietta looks at me in dismay. I hurry to the station. The train leaves at 8.30. I booked an hour earlier. I get to the station at 8.30 on the dot and the train is already pulling out. What should I do? Run? Take the train? Let it go? I make a huge leap and land on the footplate. The train is hurtling along, uncontrollably

racing towards the darkest night. The door won't open and all the windows are hermetically sealed. Nobody has seen me, no-one can help me. Hanging on, I can no longer get off the train because I'd break my neck, but I can't continue the journey like this either, I'm falling.

Help![32]

For 8.30 read *8½*. Not exactly out of the blue, later that day, Fellini put pen to paper:

> Dear Dino,
>
> I have to tell you something that has been building up inside me for some time and now has come to a head. It is a serious decision which I don't want to over-dramatize but it is the only honest response to my spirit, tired out now by repeated, fruitless attempts to placate, for reasons of friendship alone, deeper and truer states of mind. I cannot start the film because I cannot make it, due to everything that has happened. Don't misunderstand me: I have no doubts about the film, but the long series of contradictory events associated with the film itself, the atmosphere of opposition and stagnation that has accompanied its birth and the progress of preparations for it, have led me to fall out of love with the film and have exhausted me. In these circumstances I cannot make my film ...[33]

Upon receiving this letter, De Laurentiis jumped out of *8½* at Fellini, threatening him with ruin. The legal shadowboxing went on for some time until the two arranged to meet in the grounds of the sumptuous Villa Borghese. Their respective entourages of friends and lawyers were left sitting in their cars, watching the two men walking up and down, arm in arm, discussing the question with animation. Then De Laurentiis and Fellini embraced and returned to their cars, instructing the lawyers to work out the details. The film would go ahead. This was followed in April 1967 by what De Laurentiis immediately assumed was another trick of Fellini's to get out of the film. He was taken to hospital after collapsing at home, further confirmation, to Fellini's mind, that he was being warned off *Mastorna*. The newspapers began to worry that he was dying. At some point he said: 'This film will kill me.' If he had intended to make a film exemplifying Bernhard's exhortation to live one's death in full consciousness, he didn't want to be the literal example. Cancer was suspected and Sanarelli-Schwarzmann syndrome was misdiagnosed as pleurisy until an old school friend, a doctor from Rimini, put the hospital right. Just in time, the treatment was changed from antibiotics to cortisone, with an immediate improvement in the patient's condition.

During his convalescence he began to write a memoir that would turn into *Amarcord*, perhaps repaying a debt to the town that had saved his life, recycling some of the material of *Mastorna*. Petronius's fragmented memoir, *Satyricon*, also began to come into his thoughts. Ideas from *Mastorna* would be used for practically every one of Fellini's subsequent films. He referred to the unmade film as a shipwrecked vessel he would regularly plunder for treasure. Fellini could neither get away from it nor face it, and so decided to dismantle it and sprinkle the parts over the rest of his work, to make it, as it were, behind his own back.

After his convalescence, the ownership of the film changed hands, a godsend for Fellini, and proof of the existence of San Gennaro for the self-professed unbeliever, but very Neapolitan, De Laurentiis. The former Naples lawyer Alberto Grimaldi, a producer of spaghetti westerns, paid De Laurentiis 435 million lire for the rights, a little less than De Laurentiis had wanted from Fellini. As part of the deal Tognazzi's contract was transferred to Grimaldi.

Having slipped out of Dino's clutches, Fellini now had no reason not to make the film, yet, when everything was ready, the crew on call, the set half-completed and the costumes made, Fellini pulled out. He had signed with De Laurentiis to make a science-fiction film only to work on *Mastorna*; now, having signed with Grimaldi to make *Mastorna* he suggested doing something from Boccaccio or *Orlando Furioso*, or maybe a story about the Merovinghian dynasty, ideas cheekily recycled from De Laurentiis's distressed suggestions to Fellini. What about *Satyricon*? The saintly Grimaldi obliged and so *Satyricon* and not *Mastorna* became Fellini's next film.[34]

3 Fellini's other scripts

Fellini had written three other scripts which never became films: *Moraldo va in città* (Moraldo Goes to Town, 1954), written in collaboration with Flaiano and Pinelli, an adaptation of a novel by Mario Tobino (*Le libere donne di Magliano,* The Free Women of Magliano, 1956) and *Viaggio con Anita* (Journey with Anita, 1956/57), written with Pinelli.[35] During these years, between *La strada* (1954) and *Le notti di Cabiria* (Nights of Cabiria, 1957) he made *Il bidone* (The Swindle, 1955).

Moraldo is the 'Fellini character' played by Franco Interlenghi in *I vitelloni*. As he says goodbye to Guido at the end of the film, Interlenghi's voice is replaced by Fellini's.

When Giulietta Masina injured herself making *La strada* in January 1954, Fellini began thinking of a sequel to *I vitelloni*. The co-writers were the usual team of Pinelli and Flaiano. The script, published in episodes in *Cinema* from August to December 1954, became a film-in-progress for three years but never made it to the screen. Soon, publishing a script would sound the death bell to any Fellini project.

***

3.1 Moraldo arrives in Rome and (like Marcello Rubini) tries his hand at journalism, but (unlike Marcello) without success. At the newspaper he meets a drunk writer of children's stories and a penniless street artist. The duo teach him the metropolitan art of social scavenging, so different to the sober and responsible life of provincial townspeople he had grown up to believe in. The writer, appropriately named Gattone, is a parasite who eats at restaurants without paying and later moves in with Moraldo, despite the fact that the rent is overdue and the landlady is about to demand payment in kind. Gattone steals as Moraldo looks for work in the newspaper industry and then turns to decorating shop windows. Girls won't go near Moraldo because of his poverty. The days pass in solitude and humiliation, and the nights in the company of scrounging friends. Moraldo is thrown out onto the streets by his landlady and is taken

Imagining *Mastorna*

in by a mature, married woman, who runs a magazine and expects him to fulfil her slightest whim. Moraldo trades his dignity for food and a place to stay, finds a girlfriend, and begins to feel better about life. At a party given by his mistress, Moraldo bumps into Gattone again and is humiliated by his former friend's freedom and scathing wit, compared to his own state of virtual slavery. He is shamed into returning to the street, where he hooks up with a petty thief and con artist. He falls in love with a clerk, Andreina, who sets about ordering his existence, to the point that he finds himself living the kind of provincial town life from which he had tried to escape. He hates his office job and craves freedom, tells Andreina he will only make her unhappy yet is deeply affected by the death of Gattone, alone and penniless. Wouldn't he be risking the same if he tried to get free? Moraldo's father comes to town on business (as Marcello's does in *La dolce vita*) and, understanding his son's predicament, invites him back home. But Moraldo is too proud and free-spirited to accept. The following day he takes part in an orgy arranged by the street artist where he meets his former mistress with a new gigolo. Everything in the city is corrupt and decaying. He leaves just before dawn and walks through the city alone, his eyes averted, then sleeps in a field until evening. An acquaintance sees him and although he too is penniless, offers to help. It isn't much but it changes his outlook on life:

> The lights around seem brighter than before, cheerful … the faces he encounters, the people who walk beside him, seem less hostile. A girl goes by with beautiful, shoulder-length, dark hair; she smiles at him.[36]
>
> A shirtless boy up ahead pedals and whistles a tune … Two lovers come toward him, strolling slowly, arm in arm. A baby cries, women's voices go back and forth. Life, with its inexhaustible, unpredictable, possibilities, its unexpected meetings, its people, chance, adventure …
>
> Moraldo walks briskly among the crowd, smiling.[37]

The ending was adapted for the final shot of *Le notti di Cabiria*. Numerous elements of the script anticipate *La dolce vita*, but the characters of Moraldo and Marcello are substantially different. Moraldo's spirit is unvanquished, whereas Marcello, at the end of *La dolce vita*, turns away uncomprehendingly from an uncorrupted version of himself.[38] This script and the film Fellini made in its place are perhaps the last examples of Fellini's optimism in the teeth of misadventure.

***

3.2 *Le libere donne di Magliano* was based on the 1953 novel of the same name by Mario Tobino. Tobino was Director of the women's wing of the psychiatric department at Maggiano Hospital, Lucca; the novel is a reworking of his diaries from 1949 to 1951.

Tobino explained: 'It was my duty to say that even in Mental Hospitals there is an order, that madness has its laws, norms and mysteries, like anybody's life.'[39] With Pinelli, Fellini visited Tobino and the hospital at the end of 1955, and was astonished that the women were treated with humanity and without recourse to psychoanalysis or any form of theorizing. He was struck, above all, by the women, segregated in cells, naked, who sought to destroy anything they touched and were warmed only by seaweed, which they seemed to accept. One woman, deaf, dumb and blind from birth, seemed to consider his presence beneficial and became agitated when he left. Fellini must have wondered what sensations he had provoked and how. In February 1957 *Cahiers du Cinéma* published Fellini's account of the film, evidently spoken into a dictaphone. In March the script was ready but was probably burned by Fellini during one of his destructive bouts of frustration and anger. No copies remain.

The novel is the account of the doctor's loving care for his patients, in which he is partly assisted by his Catholic faith. Its narrative structure was congenial to Fellini since it is broken down into a number of episodes and has neither beginning nor end. The paragraphs are lyrical portraits of patients which, when added up, amount to a description of the loss of conscious memory and identity. The effect is choral rather than individual, although many patients are memorable and are described essentially physically: 'Sbisà has beautiful black eyes that shine with melancholy and endurance, the latter, strangely, making her appear happy.' The patients appear to be pursuing an ideal akin to the divine. The treatments are pragmatic and their descriptions unsentimental. Tobino's novel shows how even the so-called sane are in precarious balance, a balance that is maintained by closure rather than openness, and the alienation of the patients is seen as but one form of alienation in the world.

Fellini thought of Montgomery Clift for the part of the doctor. Clift was not interested, although later – after his car accident and facial plastic surgery – he was Huston's Freud. The sequel to Tobino's novel, *Per le antiche scale* (Down the Ancient Staircase, 1972) was made into a film in 1975 by Mauro Bolognini, starring Marcello Mastroianni and Marthe Keller.

***

3.3 Before *Mastorna*, Fellini's most substantial script for an unfinished project was *Viaggio con Anita* aka *Viaggio d'amore*, written with Tullio Pinelli and based on the journey of the director to Rimini in May 1956 when Fellini's father died. It is thought to be largely autobiographical. The script was ready in autumn 1957, when Sophia Loren phoned insistently for the part of Anita. De Laurentiis arranged for Fellini to meet Gregory Peck in Los Angeles to discuss the role. Peck was enthusiastic, Fellini less so. Mario Monicelli's 1975 film of the same title, starring Giancarlo Giannini and Goldie Hawn, is a very loose adaptation of Fellini's script.

Where *Moraldo* and *Mastorna* have the flavour of Kafka's *Amerika*, *Viaggio con Anita* is Joycean in its epiphanies and crystallizations of consciousness. The protagonist is an earlier version of Guido (and has the same name). Close to forty, self-confident, irreverent, this Guido is a well-known writer and intellectual, who manages to avoid smugness but not boredom, and is prone to sudden changes of mood, from a zest for life to extreme melancholy. His mood swings are a mystery to others and to himself.

He is unhappy with his bourgeois lifestyle and his seven-year marriage. When he learns that his father in Rimini is ill, he jumps into his Cadillac, picks up his lover, Anita, and heads for home. During the journey they stop off in Monterchi to see Piero della

Francesca's fresco *Madonna del parto*.[40] Guido's aesthetic pleasure before the painting is contrasted with Anita's voracious appetite and instinctive love of life. They stay overnight with the custodian of the church. On the evening of San Giovanni, Guido witnesses – and Anita takes part in – a ritual, in which the women roll around naked in the dewy grass. Later, Anita loses control of herself and dances erotically first in front of the men, then for Guido alone. He sees her more as an apparition than a real person and begins to fear she can never be his.

When they resume the journey, they are stopped by workmen who are about to blow up the side of a mountain. Again, Anita seems to invite the admiring looks of the men, and this time Guido is jealous and angry. As they enter a cloud of dust caused by the explosion Guido orders Anita out of the car. When the cloud disperses his mind recovers a little lucidity. He returns for Anita who is sitting on a wall, untroubled.

A little later he tells her the purpose of the journey. Anita shows a degree of sympathy and understanding Guido didn't expect. In Rimini, he drops her off in a hotel and goes home where he is greeted by his sister and mother. His father is very ill. When he is allowed in, he sees the frail man as if for the first time. The other people in the house treat him with deference because of his celebrity status.

His mother urges him to go to his hotel but instead he wanders through the town, which hasn't changed at all. He looks around in dismay but his reverie is interrupted by a taxi-driver who has been sent to tell him his father has died. He returns home and is immediately involved in the preparations for the funeral which he takes charge of, but passively, estranged, like a man with no will. He is surprised by the shows of grief since he is unable to express any. At the end of the evening he discovers his eyes brimming with tears. When he tries to tell Anita what has happened she rebukes him, as if he is unable to distinguish between what has happened and something he might have written: 'You're talking as if it were a story.'

As Guido goes through the motions of arranging the funeral and burial he meets old friends (one is called Titta) and is both appalled and envious; they haven't changed, they live quiet provincial lives but they have a kind of bonding he lacks. For the whole day he forgets about Anita; his mother asks him about his wife, suspecting the truth. When they finally have a moment together, he tells Anita he had never got on with his father, had left home when he was seventeen to seek fame and fortune. Anita sides with the family and loyalty: these are the things that give life meaning and purpose.

They walk along the seafront and come to a large building that looms out of the darkness at them. It is Guido's primary school. This breaks down Guido's last resistance and he opens up completely to Anita and himself. He has discovered something about himself, although he doesn't quite know what. The world he had left behind continues to live on, despite the fact that he has left it. It is an extraordinary, lively world, rich in feeling, the kind of feelings Guido had forgotten. His own life appears shallow and meaningless in comparison. He feels the strong urge to return to the kind of life his father lived and which had been mapped out for him.

In a side street Guido sees a twenty-year-old photo of Gradisca, the local beauty back then. The memory of his first attempts to make love to a woman fills him with excitement and Anita has to fend him off.

They walk further inland and come to a deserted piazza. Guido reads off the plaque: 'Piazza dei martiri' and he tells Anita about the martyrs, three partisans who had been killed there, all of them under twenty, acquaintances of his. He had spent some days with them in the Perticara mountains, serving in the Resistance. It was a time of bright hopes and everyone became a little bigger, better and more generous as a result. Now there is just silence and the martyrs have been forgotten.

A farmer on a bicycle pedals over the piazza and disappears like a ghost. Dawn is breaking.

Guido and Anita find themselves in front of the Cathedral where Guido's father has been taken for the following day's funeral. Like a headstrong child, Guido wants to see his father one last time. The doors are locked but Guido knows a secret entrance. Along the sides of the fifteenth-century church are a series of windows with twisted Gothic columns and decorative marble. They walk past some alcoves which were children's play areas and were also used by pigeons who settled there to die. In the last window, quite high up, there is a tiny door leading to the apse. Guido scrambles up and sits on the window sill. He impatiently urges Anita to follow him and she, too, steps on the jutting parts of the building to reach the ledge. They sit on the window sill side by side, next to the pigeon feathers and droppings. The door has been walled up.

The funeral seems like a summer pageant. A large crowd has gathered in front of the Cathedral. A swarm of photographers has arrived from Bologna. There is a band. Boys jabber. The crowd is dressed in black but look like traders on market day. Inside the Cathedral the service is going on but no one seems to be paying any attention to it; people are talking in the pews, benches are moved around loudly. It's chaotic. As the funeral service ends and the coffin is carried out of the Cathedral, Guido's mother finally breaks down into sobbing. Guido has to hold her on her feet. As if hallucinating, the world reduced to fragments, he sees the coffin passing over the heads of the crowd, followed by orphans, nuns and friends.

The horses that will draw the hearse paw at the ground almost joyfully. It is a warm and soft day. The bells peal rather cheerfully. As the procession advances, people at home close their shutters.

Guido supports his mother and follows the coffin as if in a dream. As he looks round he is surprised that what should appear terrifying is soft and gentle. He sees a woman crying and thinks she must have been another of his father's loves. He cannot make her out but she looks like an older version of Anita.

The cemetery is on the Rome road. Guido arrives by Cadillac.

Next morning he gets up early and says his hasty goodbyes. His mother and sister, from the garden, watch him drive off.

The seaside hotel is strangely quiet and empty. The lobby is deserted. A waitress in the small dining room is laying tables. Two small boys come down the stairs with model sailboats and buckets. Guido rushes past them. The door to Anita's room is open. The bed is unmade but there is no sign of her.

Terrified, Guido turns around and finds a chambermaid standing in front of him. She hands him an envelope. 'She left you this,' she says. He opens the quickly scrawled note and reads: 'Guido, you are the only man I love, please believe me. But our love cannot work. I would have preferred to tell you this face to face but who can ever win an argument with you? You would have persuaded me otherwise so I have slipped away. I love you so much. Your Anita.'

Guido is at a loss, hurt and filled with blind rage. It is like death. He slams the door shut and, alone in the room, rereads the letter. Then he crumples it and throws it away, tears welling in his eyes. He falls on his knees by Anita's bed and rocks back and forth, alternating insults with beseeching. He is a quivering, formless mass of despair.

Guido, suddenly older, gets into his car and heads for Rome at a snail's pace, staring into the distance. The buildings he will perhaps never see again go by. He passes the cemetery and at the gates brakes abruptly and goes in. The sunlight is strong and cheerful; the flowers have grown high; some bricklayers in the corner look like they might burst into song any moment.

Someone is at his father's tomb. A kneeling woman: Anita. He is amazed and overjoyed. He approaches slowly as a train runs by, covering the sound of his footsteps. Anita is bent over the tomb. The headstone has a photo of his father, looking rather overbearing. When Guido finally calls out to her she looks afraid at first. She turns to him, her face stained with tears. She dries her eyes and says hello. They speak amicably as if nothing has happened. Anita is full of life and beauty as before. But she is determined to leave him. Now that chance and piety have brought them both to that spot, she explains as best she can. Her words are artless but truthful, as well he knows. He realizes that his love for her is not just a blind, sensual craving, but has something to do with the simple life he has rediscovered during this stay. Yet he also knows he has a wife and a role to play in society related to its culture and art, its conscience and consciousness; the timeless world must be left behind.

The bells cheerfully ring noon. A skylark flies down between Guido and Anita, chirping merrily, then flits off. Guido and Anita walk from the cemetery; he gets into his car and drives away, his eyes glued to the rear-view mirror and Anita waving goodbye so gently and lovingly that his sadness is tempered by joy.

***

Although written before both *La dolce vita* and *8½*, *Viaggio con Anita* is a bridge between the two films. With the former it shares the difficult relationship between father and son, the scene of dumping the girl from the car and then returning for her, and the visceral longing for a woman who is out of reach (instinctive rather than cerebral, earthy rather than cultured, comfortable with her body, everything that they, the men, aren't). As an anticipation of *8½* it shows Guido with many of the inner conflicts of his namesake: estranged from his wife, his profession and his past, partially disembodied, introverted, with a sense of inferiority in relation to feminine spontaneity, he is guilt-ridden, joylessly creative, resentful and uncomprehending of the admiration of others.

The earlier Guido's inability to mourn is reminiscent of Meursault, the Outsider. He never countenances Meursault's radical honesty, choosing instead to act the part, without feeling it, to mechanically go through the motions of a successful life, as if ousted from his own existence, and at times, it appears, from his own skin (a situation experienced by Marcello, confronted by Guido Anselmi and literalized in *Mastorna*). He becomes reconciled with the memory of his father by imagining himself into his body, and by thinking of his father's infidelities. Yet they also make him feel uncomfortable, and his mother's tolerance and willingness, now that he is dead, to overlook his failings, are like a sponge wiping out years of incomprehension and pain and, with them, the reality of their relationship. His parents have been hypocrites and he, too, is a hypocrite: the guilt pushes Anita further away.

The final scene of the script ends like *Moraldo* and *Cabiria* with a smile in the face of life's hardships. The choral ending of *8½* presents a fuller form of reconciliation with life and art, albeit one that relies on a magical inspiration that leaves life in precarious turmoil.

Viaggio con Anita anticipates *Mastorna* and *Amarcord* (Gradisca/Titta), in the return to Rimini and the pacifying and disquieting memories of childhood. The scripts of *Moraldo* and *Anita* together explore the consequences of cutting the umbilical cord, a theme which continues into *La dolce vita, 8½* and beyond. The script shows a world where memory, guilt and desire are beginning to vie with reality for the attention of the protagonist: Anita is sometimes experienced more as a vision than a woman in flesh and blood, Guido's father comes back to life in his mother's dream and, through the narration of that dream, to him; the entire town seems to be evoked out of memory rather than perceived by the eyes and its drowsy lack of progress is complicit in this blurring of the past and present. The funeral service is a dream-like experience in which everything is knocked askew: for others it is like a party. More than ever, the outside world fails to reflect back Guido's inner feelings; he is characterized by distance, discord and dichotomy, struggling for intimacy, harmony and wholeness.

The Guido of *Viaggio con Anita* is an earlier version of Mastorna, who similarly conjures the world before him, only to be assailed by guilt and thoughts of hypocrisy and falsehood. The self-accusations are fostered not by his father's death but by an even more dramatic event, his own demise, urging a summation. For Guido, authenticity is denied, a predicament Mastorna inherits.

4 *Mastorna*, Capra's *It's a Wonderful Life* and authenticity

4.1 When Mastorna returns to Florence after his out-of-body experience, he greets everything he sees with a childlike gasp: 'Wonderful,' he says repeatedly, as if his eyes have been cleaned and he has acquired entirely new vision. Fellini explicitly likens him to George Bailey from Frank Capra's 1949 Christmas favourite *It's a Wonderful Life*.[41] George had walked through the streets of Bedford Falls wishing the buildings a Happy Christmas in the same vein of overwhelming gratitude at being alive. George is the unwilling heir to his father's business, the dreamer who is not allowed to dream, the traveller who never leaves, Moraldo (or the Guido of *Viaggio con Anita*) who stays in Rimini, you might say. Through no fault of his own, he becomes the victim of Scrooge/Potter's greed and dishonesty and is driven to suicide – or the verge of it – by failure, bad moral luck, the bankruptcy of his ambitions. He earns his second chance when his moral luck comes good and his life of self-sacrifice and devotion to a cause is vindicated. Mastorna has no such attachment to a moral cause, to his father's beliefs or to the community where he was born. Two of the questions posed by the script are how and why Mastorna earns his reprieve.

4.2 In *It's A Wonderful Life*, during the high-school reunion, class of '28, George and Mary get acquainted in a Charleston competition. Some way off, a jealous rival throws a switch splitting the dance floor in two and revealing a swimming pool underneath. After a little tomfoolery George and Mary fall into the pool and are followed by everyone else, not in neat, choreographed Busby Berkeley style but by jumping in chaotically and joyously in a moment of group folly and freedom from inhibition.

The corresponding scene in *Mastorna* is a collective 'suicide'. The suicides throw themselves down from balconies and their brains are splattered all over the tarmac; then, cartoon-style, they pick themselves up and go through the whole thing again: suicide as entertainment. One of the props we see in *A Director's Notebook* was intended for this scene. Although it may appear to be treated in a Disney-like unreal fashion, unfit for such a weighty subject, from this sublimely ridiculous moment on, things begins to change. Mastorna no longer rails against the injustice of his death and begins to notice the injustices around him. He loses his self-pity and starts to inhabit the strange realm he finds himself in. He lives his death, as it were, instead of refusing it. The scene is not intended, I think, to abolish the body. That would open the door to the suspicion of Cartesian dualism or, worse still, some sleight of hand: if you shed your body and revisit the important moments of your life without one, hardly surprisingly the fallout of being a bodily entity – guilt and shame, for example – disappears.[42] Fellini counters this by having Mastorna, as soon as the penny drops, protest that he is a body, with appetites, a statement that is given the approval of the teacher of religious education, as if to dismiss too simplistic a view of the Catholic Church as against the body *tout court*. Mastorna is not a floating spirit in a physical world; he interacts with the apparent physical world, which is actually no less mental than he is. He is, however, unable to 'dream' his own death (but can imagine a form of death for De Cercis and his friends). The trajectory of Marcello–Guido–Giuseppe goes from 'I'm getting everything wrong in life' (the famed Trevi fountain scene in *La dolce vita*), through Guido's confession in *8½*: 'I wanted to make a film to bury everything that is dead in us. But I haven't been able to bury anything …', to Mastorna experiencing and overcoming a living death. After starting off on the wrong track, self-pitying and self-absorbed, guilt-ridden and cloyingly attached to life, Mastorna finally rectifies Marcello's mistakes and fulfils Guido's ambition. Dead, he learns to bury the past, commemorate it and be free of it.

4.3 When George Bailey finds himself in Pottersville, the same thoughts go through his head as pass through Mastorna's in the motel and the railway station: has he drunk something? Is he dreaming?[43] What kind of a trick is it? Hypnosis, magic? Like Mastorna, for as long as he holds onto his previous experience of life, he gets nowhere. Pottersville is a brutalized, cheapened, vulgarized version of Bedford Falls, as Mastorna's parallel universe is full of gaudy, neon-blazed, crowded night-clubs and drifting, faceless masses, life without individuality. The transition from one world to the next is also similar; George's last moments in Bedford Falls are characterized by brutality: he is punched by an enraged husband, shouted at by a man whose tree he has run into, told to get out of the way by a passing truck; in each of these circumstances he has contributed to the rage of the man he faces. A moment later, in Pottersville, he is similarly hounded and abused, this time with less reason. The two parallel worlds slightly overlap. As they do in *Mastorna*. Before the plane crash the announcement about the emergency landing is worded strangely: they are going to land in an airfield for this 'eventuality'. Mastorna has already slipped into another world (or this blip is caused by the other world approaching), and the slippage is perpetuated by Fellini for the spectator's benefit: we may suspect what has happened and our perspective gradually shifts as the evidence builds up and we realize (before the protagonist) that Mastorna is viewing a dead world.

4.4 In the Savings and Loan office in Capra's film the camera just catches sight of a sign: 'The only thing you can take with you is what you've given away' (a wink at Capra's earlier film also starring James Stewart and Lionel Barrymore, *You Can't Take It With You*). It's certainly true of George's life of self-sacrifice and generosity, driven by a sense of duty towards others; and, in the final scene, he gets back what he gave away with interest. It comes to be true of Mastorna, too, in his life after death: he needs to give away his memories in order to recover them. George is saved by his loyalty to the past, to his father's dedication and to his view of business as service to a community, for which he is repaid. Mastorna is saved by cutting things out of himself.

4.5 The *Mastorna* portion of *A Director's Notebook* resembles Capra's film in the wind that suddenly begins to stir and becomes blustery when George is temporarily granted his wish to be un-born and the blizzard in which George sees his non-life flash before him. This is how Mastorna is introduced, after a characteristic Fellinian wind of change, in a snowstorm. As he remembers his unmade film and finally puts part of it on screen, Fellini recalls this moment from *It's a Wonderful Life*.[44]

4.6 Capra imagines a sliding-doors, control experiment, parallel life, a what-if? which is shown by Clarence to George so he can recover his real attachments and keep faith with what is authentic in him and his life. What if George had never been born? His brother would have drowned, his wife never married; the people his brother saved would have died, Bedford Falls would be a morally bankrupt, lurid drinking and gambling den owned and run by one man. Without people like George, people like Potter would take over. The finale of the Capra film is a vindication of the sacrifices made by George Bailey and the world he has created.[45]

Fellini has a different question: what if George jumps off the bridge and no guardian angel comes to the rescue? If he meets an untimely and unhappy death, what do we make of his sense of duty and respect for his father's vision of life, his self-sacrifice, the postponement of his own ambitions, his entire battle for selfhood? Without his moral luck, what do we make of him? Unlike George Bailey, Mastorna/Fellini did leave Bedford Falls. He was given an oppressive Catholic upbringing, had a strict father who disapproved of his artistic choice in life, was conditioned by sexual taboos and the Fascist vision of life as something to be lived collectively, not individually. He marries, has a lover, pursues an artistic career and becomes successful. But it turns out that he too needs to be saved, from the consequences of the conditioning and upbringing from which he has only apparently freed himself. The scars of the battle for selfhood still need to be healed. *The Journey of G. Mastorna* is apparently the story of his salvation and healing.

Even in 1965, the idea of a man who skips beyond life, unaware of what has happened, was by no means original. In Buzzati's children's story of 1938,[46] Domenico Molo dies and is put in the realm of judgements and punishments. As he watches others come before the law, plead their cases and receive their sentences, he understands what is truly important in life and so is allowed to return to it. At one level at least, this is also the storyline of *Mastorna*. Lubitsch had produced an ironic version of the process of judgement in 1943, with *Heaven Can Wait*, in which the dapper Henry Van Cleve tries to talk his way into Hell. Flann O'Brien's *The Third Policeman*, written around 1940 but published only posthumously in 1967, shares with *Mastorna* the disquieting comedy of the surreal. There have been many examples since, of course, some tinged with horror, such as *Sixth Sense* and *The Others*, some with hyper-realism, as in Giuseppe Tornatore's *Una pura formalità* (A Mere Formality, 1994). The storyline evidently lends itself to numerous genres, which Fellini used to modulate the tone of a seemingly unremitting descent into the circles of Hell.

Initially, the world presents itself to Mastorna as hostile or indifferent, supercharged with moral accusation and peopled by faceless multitudes. He is upbraided for a love affair dating back years, as if it were yesterday (and, in the strange time scheme of *Mastorna*, it may have been yesterday). After another infidelity, he begins to confess guilty feelings about his wife to a traffic warden long before he discovers the sad truth. At the railway station, where he learns that truth, the timetable and announcements are incomprehensible, excluding him from an ordered, logical world. One of the series of hostesses, or manifestations of the same Muse, tells him that if the signs were meant for him, he would understand them, as if the jumble and confusion were the result of accessing an abundance of subjectivities. After his discovery, Mastorna conjures up the wily Armandino, an entirely inefficient Mr Fix-it who others do not see, but whose refusal to be sucked into the world of the dead is Mastorna's first vain effort of resistance. Armandino distracts him from the request of (quest for) authenticity, which he then takes most of the rest of the script to get round to finally addressing. The Neapolitan lady with the shrine to the dead has a pair of strange daughters who want him to stay, one of whom seems vulnerable and the other threatening, half-repulsive, half-seductive, a harpy, a siren. The hostesses – Muses and Beatrice figures – snigger behind his back. His failure to understand his situation raises smiles, rouses the interest of con artists and provokes bureaucratic irritation. The award ceremony is a cheap and vulgar affair, a reality show *ante litteram*, in which his make-up depersonalizes him to the point of, precisely, making him up, turning him into anybody; and, in fact, the photograph and citation could be anyone's (Mastorna is later to relive this depersonalization in a completely different manner when he meets his parents on the return journey to the airport). The accusations become more explicit. He is told he is 'unable to deny and unable to believe', a limbo itself. People whisper his guilt from behind closed doors and shutters. The universe is intransigent and intractable, seemingly deployed for others, who obey different rules, are judged by inscrutable procedures and behave as if what matters always takes place elsewhere. There is the strong sense of an adverse destiny, a plot written by someone else. Yet, many of the people Mastorna meets are well-intentioned, understanding and sympathetic. The stranger who accompanies him to the station seeks some spark of understanding in him that he doesn't find. Politely, without forcing the issue, he withdraws. The Station Master tells him that he must state his destination and make a choice. Put like this, without a sense of what the possibilities are, and what the choice really is, the decision cannot be made and the demand is absurd. Yet, it turns out to be true (and his words echo those of Claudia to Guido in *8½* after thrice accusing him of being incapable of love). The bureaucratic babble is pointing him in the right direction. He does need to make a decision, to call judgement upon himself and shed his sense of guilt and shame, the residues of his upbringing and Catholic education. In the crucial judgement scene, the film of his life is projected at such speed that he can't make head or tail of it; the sheer pace empties his life of significance. It belittles him; yet again, the procedure appears scornfully inapt and inept. It's also a parodic version of the film of George Bailey's life shown to the apprentice guardian angel Clarence.[47] The judges who decide Mastorna's fate are somewhat less conscientious, ransacking his life for a moment of authenticity. Apparently, they are arbitrarily appointed, the trial is peremptory and the decision-making process flippant. It's a cosmic joke being played at Mastorna's expense, yet the search for authenticity is Mastorna's true search.

Authenticity was, of course, a major concern of neorealism. Whether inflected as an unmediated relationship between the camera and the social world, partly unscripted, with non-professional actors and shot on location, or as a focused analysis of the conditions of the working class in post-war Italy, with increasingly famous stars and evident directorial guidance, neorealism sought to distance itself from the posturing, rhetorically insincere, star-studded cast of the Fascist regime which had had but one scriptwriter, leading actor and director. Fellini may even have taken the era of Fascism, which coincided roughly with his first twenty years of life, as inauthenticity personified. After the fall of Fascism, he saw inauthenticity in the pomp and ceremony attendant on another supreme leader, the Pope. As he and Italy moved away from neorealism in the late 1950s, turning the camera inward, Fellini continued his preoccupation with authenticity, now in relation not only to the means of representing external reality but as an investigation of the inner life and conscience of his protagonists, the new pressures on Cabiria's final smile which withstands corruption and swallows down ignominy. Marcello believes that he sees authenticity fleetingly and bathes with it in the Trevi Fountain; Guido is nostalgic for it whilst moving – like Mastorna – in a world of ghosts, visions and his own and other people's make-believe. In *Mastorna* it comes to be the only passport on – or back – to somewhere else, an escape from Purgatory.

After his judgement, Mastorna rides with his parents in a car towards the airport. He barely recognizes them, younger, refreshed, his own uncertain age. He makes no accusations. The past has dropped away. They are on a similar journey, and exchange roles, his parents becoming his children, his mother his wife, his father a friend (even, in the letter to Dino De Laurentiis, a lover). The cards are shuffled and redealt. Determinism, the choices that have been made for him, genetics and upbringing melt away, the synaptic connections break and reform. Mastorna's individuality dissolves and, far from resenting it, he rejoices. It's a weight off his shoulders, the same weight he shrugs off when, for once in his life, he manages to 'be true to himself' and sticks his tongue out at a dog in the back of a car, his one authentic moment in life.

The gesture is, of course, incommensurate with the solemnity of the judgement that he has sought and which is being passed on him; as the sole example of authenticity in his life, it is frivolous, a characteristically Fellinian commingling of adolescence and adulthood. The gesture is inoffensive, petulant, mocking and self-mocking, a release, an unbuttoning that establishes empathy with its 'victim'. It communicates, as it were, dog to dog. It may hint that deep down he would like to raise a middle finger to the world (the Church, pompous intellectuals, the pretentious and phoney, anyone who seeks to condition the lives and sensations of others) but it's an innocuous version of anger and disgust, an uncorrupted grain of consciousness.

Authenticity should not be construed merely as spontaneity, however. Fellini is at pains to point this out in the script. The scene is an addition to the first draft, where the moment of authenticity is still the boy trying to grab a butterfly. In a letter to his lifelong friend and co-scriptwriter Tullio Pinelli, Fellini wrote: 'what we invented is all authentic.'[48] To Adorno's 'jargon of authenticity', Fellini opposes the role of the artist as benevolent creator. Authenticity does not preclude – may even require – invention and craftsmanship. It may also include the familiar connotations of truthfulness to origins, commitment and devotion, the kind of religious attitude to life Fellini describes to De Laurentiis when discussing musicianship. In which case Mastorna falls well short of the demanding profile; but the speck of unselfconsciousness – the one moment when Mastorna is not projecting his image on the world – is enough to warrant his reprieve.

By now we have discovered that the world Mastorna encounters is tailor-made for him, actually made by him, a Solaris space station where his senses of guilt manifest themselves and accuse him; the obstacles he faces are self-made. The weird, projected, guilt-ridden world he finds himself in proves less hostile but perhaps more deeply guileful and menacing than it had at first appeared. Even Armandino, the embodiment of the art of living by expedient (as perfected by many in post-war Italy, Fellini among them), in his misguided, selfish and lonely way, tries to help. When they meet again in the airport, Mastorna is charitable although, by this time, his level of consciousness has moved on and the two occupy different, no longer overlapping, worlds. The Neapolitan woman who fishes him out of the air as he plays at suicide is trapped in a limbo, unable to let go of memories of her husband and family. She creates shrines to her own past and her snake-charming daughter tries to seduce him into staying in their limbo. De Cercis takes Mastorna back to the days and scenes of *I vitelloni*; he's a friend but he, too, is fossilized inside a political battle that doesn't allow him to shake the dust from off his feet (and De Cercis is given one of the most harrowing scenes in the script as his men are thrown lifeless into trucks and carted away, a memory of the Nazi occupation during the war). It's only when Mastorna confronts his parents, and his relatives begin to make impossible claims upon him, that he begins to want to throw off the shackles of the past and his mind begins to conjure useful images, such as the park, and the judges he has been looking for. The suspense Fellini had in mind is in the topsy-turvy world in which Mastorna gradually sheds the role of rebel, objector, victim not because he is shown to have been hypocritical, false, unfeeling, blasé (all of which may be true) but because he stops persecuting himself for these and other failings. As he progresses through Purgatory he steels himself against blandishments, learns to sympathize with those whose impossible claims are symptomatic of their own desolation, purges himself of false attachments and shrugs off nostalgia and the burden of the past. At the same time, he drops his previous sense of victimization, his self-pity and rancorous shrieking at injustice. Like other Fellini films, *Mastorna* is about toxicity and decontamination.

4.7 Fellini told Charlotte Chandler: 'I have always been fascinated by the experience of near-death. I believe in that moment some people learn the secrets of life and death. The price of that knowledge is death, but before the body dies, the truth is imparted to the consciousness of those who die in such a way that there is a lapse of time between their absolute death and their last moment of life, something like a coma. This was what I envisioned for G. Mastorna.'[49]

To take advantage of this new knowledge, you have to come out of the coma, or else, as for Zampanò, your wisdom comes too late. George Bailey on the bridge and Mastorna, in the aftermath of a fatal/near-fatal accident, appear to gain such a consciousness without having to pay the full price for it. They cheat death. George is saved by a supernatural agency, or, we may prefer to imagine him close to drowning, seeing his non-life rushing before his eyes and finding in himself the strength to go on (and Clarence, in this view, is the metaphor for a just if not benevolent universe). He extends his life long enough to get his moral luck, the recognition of the entire community for which he has worked all his life, the reward for his dedication and self-sacrifice; as we can see Mastorna in a coma, much like Fellini imagined him – almost, you might say, *experienced* him during his illness – pulling back from the brink and finding a new faith in life, without guilt and shame. In both cases, wrongs can be righted.

George and Mastorna are, of course, opposites: George is faithful to his wife and community, a man who has given up his personal ambitions to embrace the ideals of his father in a world that is rapidly losing those ideals and, with them, all sense of community. He's an old-fashioned type of man, a paragon of public service. Mastorna is unfaithful, childless, someone who has chosen his career in the teeth of his father's wishes, and has little or no sense of a community; he has an artistic vocation (the butt of jokes throughout the script, 'frin frin'). George, we are inclined to believe, has had a nurturing upbringing that stifles his Romantic dreams but serves him well at most moments of need, until he's pushed over the limit by the depravity and rapaciousness of Potter and his cronies. Mastorna is a more solitary figure, whose upbringing contains elements of poison from external persuasion, the duty to conform (which includes the duty to be hypocritical, unfeeling, blasé and most of the other easy-ways-to-deal that Mastorna discovers in himself), and pressures that debilitate rather than strengthen resolve. In Fellini's world, George Bailey would have succumbed to Potter. Both protagonists stand in resistance and opposition to the ubiquitous, all-seeing, all-controlling, dehumanizing powers that be. In Mastorna's case, this resistance is a grain of authenticity, an irreducible, incoercible speck (or spark) of human spirit.

4.8 The transcending power of authenticity is described by Stephen Mulhall in relation to Heidegger's *Being and Time*, where it appears as a form of freedom from contingency, a recognition of unbelonging:

> In the objectlessness of anxiety, particular objects and persons fade away and the worldliness of our Being announces itself as such, that is, as more or other than any particular worldly situation in which we find ourselves. Hence, anxiety discloses that in inauthenticity we identify ourselves with the particularity of our situation – treat it as if a necessity or fate, regarding what we do

as simply what is done, beyond any question; and anxiety thereby discloses authenticity as a recognition of ourselves as not identical with any particular worldly situation, as essentially not coincident with what we presently are, as always transcending our present articulation and so as uncanny, our worldliness precluding our ever being fully at home in any particular world.[50]

5 Does *Mastorna* have a happy ending?

Notoriously, Fellini didn't care much for pretty endings. His *Satyricon* finishes mid-sentence. His episodic films appear to be have been excerpted from something longer that could be continued almost ad infinitum. Fellini's art seeks a form of continuity (and continuity with our lives) that eschews happy endings and neat structuring. Even Cabiria's flickering then broad smile is an act of resistance that may, one day, be overcome. Fellini told De Laurentiis in his initial letter that, properly speaking, *Mastorna* has no ending. On the face of it, he changed his mind. As the script stands, *Mastorna* has a very clear concluding episode and final scene: the hero returns to his life and sees the sun streaming in through the rooftop; he is happy to be home, and will set his life to rights by living the lesson of authenticity he has learned.[51] The end of the film is the beginning of his new life.

After his long conversations with Fellini in 1966, Dario Zanelli comes to this conclusion about the ending of *Mastorna*:

> Free of former conditioning and prejudices, after the obstacles of limbo, Hell, Purgatory, all the places he has visited on his journey in the afterlife, the musician Giuseppe Mastorna finds himself finally in a 'wonderful' Florence, the city of beauty sublimated by art, and there he celebrates, in the splendour of a surprise ending, as a symphony is played by a full orchestra, the serenity he had so tirelessly and exhaustingly sought, the harmonious happiness of a 'new life'. All the more appreciated, all the more to be cherished, because it is close to the ideal of a full, free and pure life on earth.[52]

Ermanno Cavazzoni believes that for his ending Fellini 'instinctively turns to the myth of Er in Plato's *Republic*' (the word 'instinctively' is intended to remove any suspicion of intellectualism in Fellini):

> The finale is birth to the world, luminous and clear as in certain days of happiness; Purgatory is before life, not after; it is not a place of arrival but a pre-birth experience inside the chaos of possibilities, with all the malaise of indecision.
>
> ... It is as if Fellini had instinctively returned to the great myth of Er (Plato: *The Republic*, X), of the soul that lives before birth in the flatlands of Hades and must choose, with immense risk and suffering, who to be; then it bathes in the Lethe, where all this suffering and the memory of the Underworld are obliterated, and so the soul, unburdened and pure falls from the heavens like a falling star (Plato says rises) and begins its life on earth; perhaps it continues to be reborn forever. Or for ten thousand years, says Plato, until it is returned to undifferentiated nothingness.[53]

This is actually a corrected version of the Er myth, purged of the meting out of the punishments and rewards which make the parable a forerunner of Christianity. By attributing this revised myth to Fellini, Cavazzoni[54] pinpoints one of the challenging aspects of the *Mastorna* script: you can only earn rebirth – learn to wish for your own birth – through experience, yet experience prevents it (or, as David Foster Wallace puts it: 'the horrific struggle to establish a human self results in a self whose humanity is inseparable from that horrific struggle'[55]). In Plato's story of reincarnation the dead pay for their sins and then choose their new lives – whereupon they are made to forget everything, including the choice they have made, by bathing in the waters of the Lethe.[56] Zanelli and Cavazzoni offer two slightly different takes on the same happy ending, both apparently borne out by Fellini's own exposition: Mastorna learns to rid himself of false, inauthentic, attachments to life and so can return (Zanelli), or be born (Cavazzoni), to it. The Mastorna who walks through the streets of his home town with a spring in his step is a man who is conscious of the 'horrific struggle' of life, but is no longer completely shaped by it. George Bailey is shown the world from which his own beneficial presence has been sucked out, and it's a world that has become brutally corrupted, obsessed with money, neurotically unfulfilled. Through his absence it urges him to return. What Mastorna sees, and fights for, is a world to be born into, from which his own corruption, obsessions and neuroses can, through authenticity, be banished.

I don't intend to challenge this interpretation, merely to suggest another possibility, which I will put, later on, in the form of 'directing' the last scene of the script, the way it could have been filmed to suggest an ambiguity implicit in the Fellini script. But first, we need to look a little more closely at the other film Fellini didn't make in 1965/66: the adaptation of Fredric Brown's *What Mad Universe*.

He read the novel[57] and quickly changed his mind about going ahead with the film for which he had been given a sizable advance on a fee of $250,000. However, some of the book remained with him: to Zanelli, in 1966, he declared his intention, with *Mastorna*, to make 'a science-fiction detective story'.[58] He described the next full-length film he actually made, his *Satyricon*, as a 'science-fiction film set in the past', and critics saw in it 'Flash Gordon Technicolor'.

The hero of *What Mad Universe* (neither What *a* Mad Universe nor What Mad Universe? but a title hovering between the two) is one Keith Winton, an editor of comic books. One day he's resting in the garden of a friend's house in New Jersey when a stray rocket falls not ten feet away. Momentarily stunned, Winton comes to his senses without apparent injury and notes with mild surprise that the tree he had been sitting under has moved and become a row of poplars. He doesn't appear to be able to locate the house he was staying at and decides to drive in to New York. At a gas station someone pays with bills that don't have the face of George Washington, or any face, on them, merely the words 'One hundred credits'. It must be the concussion, he thinks. But the weirdness continues until he is forced to the realization that the world, and not his mind, has been knocked askew. He has been transported by rocket to a parallel world where the New York he moves around in is not his New York. It seems to be a projection of the fantasies (including sexual fantasies, the astronauts mostly being pin-ups) of Winton's comic-book readers, a universe created, as it were, by the presumed reader of the novel (you and me, in a form of double or mutual reader-writer projection). Winton also suspects that the world he perceives is, somehow, partly a creation of his own.[59] When he walks into his office he finds himself sitting at his desk. The story of the novel then becomes Winton's attempt to return to his New York or, if you prefer, to shed his – our – comic-book fantasy world.[60]

Winton and Mastorna both find themselves in nearly duplicated worlds of continuous glitches, onto which they project their thoughts only to receive them back.

At the end of the *Mastorna* script the voice-over of the hostess tells us that:

> On the other side of the mountain Mastorna found a city. He was surprised to be walking in a city that looked just like Florence ... the streets were lit by the sun, the buildings, the shops, the florists ... the well-appointed shop windows, the traffic lights: it was Florence, but there was something different in the air, in the sunlight, in the faces of the people he met ... hard to say what the difference was ... it was as if the things, the people, were new ... seen for the first time.[61]

This is the George Bailey – or rewritten Er myth – moment of rebirth in which everything seems new, familiar yet subtly different, more vivid and vibrant, filled with the new life of the observer. It may even be the Keith Winton moment when he gets back to his New York.[62] Unless, of course, it's a fiction, more specifically, a science fiction, with the attendant psychological and metaphysical probing of that genre.[63] Since Mary Shelley, this includes investigating the relations between the creator and created, the nature of selfhood, gender, embodiment, inclusion/exclusion in a human society, the impact of technology and science, the role and manipulation of memory, free-will and determinism, existence and essence (as Sartre would have it), the world as projection and fictive apparatus, all themes explored by *Mastorna*.

Which brings us to the final shot:

> Up in the roof, where the skylight is open onto the spring day, swallows fly in and swirl, chasing one another in the rays of the sun and the specks of dust, tinged with gold.

We know from his description of the studio of his psychoanalyst, Ernst Bernhard, that this image of speckled dust was dear to Fellini.[64] And we know that the description goes on to give us the first scene of *8½*, with Fellini/Guido floating in mid-air before the umbilical rope around his ankle is yanked and he falls back into the sea. This, in turn, recalled the opening of *La dolce vita* with Marcello in a helicopter hauling a statue of Christ. And *Mastorna* would have begun with the protagonist in the clouds, about to fall to earth. This aerial perspective is half other-wordly, at the borderline between the human and transcendent (life and death), where a man either falls to earth or escapes its confines. Now, when he comes to fictionalizing the scene from Bernhard's studio, Fellini moves it to the theatre, and adds the swallows that rather miraculously appear. Mastorna is below, playing in the orchestra with the other musicians, feeling a sense of belonging for the first time in what, to him, must have seemed like years. A naturalistic interpretation might lead us to think that in fact no more than a day has passed, since here he is, keeping his appointment, which was for the day after the accident. On the brink of death he has seen his life speeding in front of his eyes and imagined the story we have read. Then he has pulled back from the brink, cheated death without the help of a guardian angel, and learnt the value of authenticity unassisted, since even his assistants were imagined.

Mastorna would then be a nightmare (or a coma) from which he wakes.[65] Or we might think he has returned to Florence, to his home, his wife and his orchestra, after a terrifying out-of-body experience sometimes called death, from which he has gained a reprieve, through the wisdom he has gained, as Zanelli and Cavazzoni see it and Buzzati originally wrote it. In this view the 'something different in the air' is not at all sinister. He sees everyone new, as if for the first time, because he has new eyes, not because what he is seeing is new.

However, we could countenance a mocking alternative to this vision of regeneration: the delusion/sham continues, only worse than before; the next parallel world Mastorna finds himself in is a patched-up version of the first, perfectly counterfeited, a sublime and ridiculous cosmic forgery, in which his newfound love of life will last for as long as the theatrical illusion persists and the sophisticated machinery and props go on working, or longer, if he is able to accept the make-believe world as his only reality and ignore the glitches as they begin to crop up, as surely they will, one after another. He would then live out a life dedicated to authenticity in a world that is entirely fake.[66] It is the moral trajectory of many Fellini characters: the soul, but not the world, can be saved.

The swallows that appear among the rafters of the theatre where Mastorna is rehearsing recall a famous scene by Dreyer, a film-maker Fellini revered. The image is sacred and profane, poised between the visionary and a last glimpse of the world. After the trial, during which she has not recanted her holy visions, Joan of Arc looks up from the stake and sees birds flying overhead, their wings caught in the sunlight.[67]

I imagine the last sequence of *Mastorna* like this: the camera is below ground-level, in the orchestra pit; a side-view of Mastorna shows him playing the cello, looking up ecstatically toward the roof. Above him, swallows entering the building are caught in a stream of sunlight. The camera cranes up to the level of the roof beams where one of the swallows is swooping and diving, then returning to the rafters, flying through the sunlight. Zoom from the side. As the camera moves in to a close-up, the bird's wings are shown in slower and slower motion. The orchestra disappears, the music becomes fainter, then falls to silence. The speckled dust, previously swirling in the sunlight, hovers motionless in the air. The bird's wings slow to immobility. It is a freeze frame, a photograph. Or it is a series of identical frames, the camera is still rolling and the bird has come to a stop, impossibly, in mid-air.[68]

Notes

1. In *Discovering Orson Welles* (Berkeley: University of California Press, 2007), 38.
2. Jung wrote: 'For the contained this is only a confirmation of the insecurity she has always felt so painfully; she discovers that in the rooms which apparently belonged to her there dwell other, unwished-for guests. The hope of security

vanishes, and this disappointment drives her in on herself, unless by desperate and violent efforts she can succeed in forcing her partner to capitulate, and in extorting a confession that his longing for unity was nothing but a childish or morbid fantasy. If these tactics do not succeed, her acceptance of failure may do her a real good, by forcing her to recognize that the security she was so desperately seeking in the other is to be found in herself. In this way she finds herself and discovers in her own simpler nature all those complexities which the container had sought for in vain.' The essay appears in volume 17 of *The Collected Works of C.G. Jung* (Princeton: Princeton University Press, 1954).
3. Dario Zanelli, *L'inferno immaginario di Federico Fellini* (Rimini: Guaraldi, 1995).
4. Fellini had already blended genres – neorealism and horror – in *Agenzia matrimoniale* (1953), in which a woman discovers that the person she is introduced to by the marriage agency is a werewolf. So poor is she that the inconvenience doesn't dissuade her. In Fellini's words: 'Given this opportunity by Zavattini, I decided to make a short film in the strictest neorealist manner possible, using a story that could not be imagined, by any stretch of the imagination, to be true, or even neo-true. I thought: What would James Whale or Tod Browning do if they had to shoot a neorealist *Frankenstein* or *Dracula*? That's how *Agenzia matrimoniale* was made.' Quoted by Fabrizio Borin in his contribution to *Ripensare il neorealismo: cinema, letteratura, mondo*, edited by Antonio Vitti (Pesaro: Metauro, 2008), 43–61, here 60.
5. It was an old and familiar story. As far back as 24 April 1955, Flaiano had accused Fellini of holding a press conference on *Il bidone* (The Swindle) without informing him or Pinelli (who also complained, in a separate letter, the following day).
6. In his book on *La dolce vita*, Tullio Kezich says Rondi was the 'scriptwriter on set', whilst Flaiano and Pinelli had completed their work by the time of shooting: *Noi che abbiamo fatto* La dolce vita (Palermo: Sellerio editore, 2009), 151. This suggests that Fellini did indeed often improvise the shooting script on the set. However, Kezich is wrong about Pinelli. On 20 July 1959, half way through shooting, Fellini wrote to Pinelli asking him to 'find a moment' for Paolina, the waitress Marcello fails to understand on the beach in the final scene of *La dolce vita*. So Pinelli's work was not done by the time shooting began. Evidently Fellini had an idea of the character – Paolina – and wanted to include her in the film but delegated to Pinelli (and perhaps, on other occasions, to Flaiano) the details. Rondi was probably used to write the dialogue for scenes that had already taken shape in Fellini's mind.
7. *Amerika*, subtitled, *The Man who Disappeared*, exhibits a similarly personal city architecture, with the Statue of Liberty holding a sword and a bridge connecting New York to Boston. As Michael Hoffman points out in the introduction to his new translation, many of the episodes in the novel are deformed replicas of one another, the frequent repetitions spelling doom in a spiralling descent through the circles of Hell. Fellini may or may not have known of Kafka's projected happy ending, in which, according to Brod, the hero (like Mastorna) was '... to find again a profession, a standby, his freedom,

even his old home ... as if by some celestial witchery.' Quoted by Michael Hoffman: Franz Kafka, *Amerika* (New York: New Directions, 2002, x).
8. He is pretending to be making an attempt in *Intervista* (1987), for example.
9. *Conversations with Fellini*, edited by Costanzo Costantini (San Diego: Harcourt Brace & Company, 1995), 70–71.
10. In 1991 Kieslowski shot *La Double Vie de Veronique* with a sepia overlay to create a monochromatic, dreamlike atmosphere and sense of otherworldliness. According to Stefania Rimini (in her notes accompanying the Italian version of the film, in Feltrinelli's *Le nuvole* series), the film was originally intended to be the story of the return to life from the hereafter.
11. In his letter to De Laurentiis, with the first draft of the script, Fellini refers to the main character as M. except for one slip of the pen, where he's called Marcello. See note 28.
12. Costantini (1995), 76. In these drawings, the set is depicted as a mixture of houses and factories billowing black smoke, with Cologne Cathedral in the background.
13. From 20 March 1998, in an article in *Liberal*, the weekly magazine of the Foundation and political think-tank of the same name, founded by Ferdinando Adornato.
14. In 1954, Flaiano had written a satirical story *Un marziano a Roma* (A Martian in Rome), which may, in part, have been a hostile portrait of Orson Welles and his life in Rome in 1948–53. The story takes the form of a diary. It records the salient events of the Martian's stay in the capital: he is invited to meet the Pope but turns out to be one of the least prominent guests on the list, is championed by the Communist Party, which asks him to judge a beauty pageant and is offered a bit part in a film by Rossellini on the condition that his planet comes up with some of the funding. After a while the visitor is obliged to charge a small City Council fee for the guided tour of his spaceship. Newspapers throw his photos away. After less than three months on Earth he has had enough but is unable to leave: his spacecraft has been seized by the judicial authorities following a suit brought by angry hotel owners. Flaiano's Martian quickly tires of Rome whilst the extraterrestrials of the film are corrupted by the city, give up their invasion plans and renounce their planet in favour of the dolce vita.
15. Probably a reference to Pasolini's *Il vangelo secondo Matteo* – The Gospel According to St. Matthew (1964).
16. Fellini told Costantini that 'Bond films represent cinema in its most direct and explicit essentials ... I believe them to be the most reliable and serious document of the times in which we live: this continual blurring of the border between political activity and police activity, the ferocity of power struggles, insectlike in their ruthlessness.' Ibid., 200.
17. The script includes no shooting details. Each scene (a total of fifty-three) is identified by the word 'Interior' or 'Exterior' and a generic location, sometimes with a time of day or night. However, camera placements are implied by words such as 'above', 'outside', 'below', since these do not always refer to the location of Mastorna. For example, after the accident, when Mastorna is still

inside the plane, the script specifies: 'Above, one of the plane's hatches begins to open'.

18. The word used by Paul Rayment to describe a similar afterlife is *puny*: 'Is this what it is like to be translated to what at present he can only call *the other side*? Is that what has happened to him; is that what happens to everyone? 'Gingerly he settles into an armchair. If this does not amount to a big moment, a Copernican moment, then what does? The greatest of all secrets may just have unveiled itself to him. There is a second world that exists side by side with the first, unsuspected. One chugs along in the first for a certain length of time; then the angel of death arrives in the person of Wayne Blight or someone like him. For an instant, for an aeon, time stops; one tumbles down a dark hole. Then, hey presto, one emerges into a second world, *identical with the first*, where time resumes and the action proceeds [...] whether he is wrong or right, whether what in the most hesitant of spirits he calls *the other side* is truth or delusion, the first epithet that occurs to him, typed out letter by letter behind his eyelids by the celestial typewriter, is *puny* [...] if death is a mere hiccup in time after which life goes on as before, why all the fuss?' J.M. Coetzee, *Slow Man* (London: Secker & Warburg, 2005), 122–23.

19. On 11 January 1969, Fellini and Bergman announced that they would be working together on a film to be called *Love Duet*. Akira Kurosawa had already pulled out of the project. Fellini intended to contribute *La città delle donne*, which was rejected by Universal due to Fellini's insistence on casting Mastroianni. It would take Fellini another eleven years to make the film. Fellini turned to another of Zapponi's ideas, *La donna sconosciuta* (The Unknown Woman) about a man who lives with his mother until he decides to marry a young girl. When the girl leaves him without explanation, he tries to find out everything about her and ends up dressing as her, 'Frankenstein's monster, prey to a delirious love' Fellini concluded, as if to hide the sexual ambiguity of the character (perhaps the bisexuality in *Satyricon* made him feel less vulnerable, without an alter ego of approximately the same age). Universal was not interested in this script either and Bergman made the film on his own, *The Touch*, from a script called *White Walls*, a flop.

20. The film was made to protest censorship. During the 1950s Italian cinema censorship – or Madame Anastasia as it was not so affectionately known – was particularly active and aggressive. It took a variety of forms from vetting a script to banning a finished film, or requiring light to severe cuts. The availability of public funding, lifeblood for the industry, was a form of undeclared censorship, often more effective than the official censor. The declared motives included the protection of minors and the safeguarding of public morality. In addition to state censors the Catholic Centre for Cinematography controlled 5,449 parish cinemas (1956), more than half the total, and its opinion was therefore fundamental for the commercial success of a film. The Prime Minister's office was consulted on films *in camera caritatis*. Among foreign films banned by the censor in Italy were Eisenstein's *Alexander Nevsky* (1938), Hitchcock's *Rope* (1948), *La Ronde* by Max Ophuls (1950) and several films by Claude Autant-Lara. Rossellini's *Paisà* and Visconti's *Senso* were both cut.

Many directors, championed by the Communist Party, protested against the censorship laws dating back to 1923 and the nascent Fascist regime. Producers favoured a form of voluntary censorship along the lines of the American Hays Code. The new co-operatives created in the 1950s (for example by Fellini and Lattuada to make *Luci del varietà*) failed after their products were not authorized for export. In 1951, an influential Ministerial under-secretary, Giulio Andreotti, later Prime Minister in a succession of governments, criticized De Sica's *Umberto D* for giving a false and negative view of Italy. As a result distributors withdrew the film, the Cannes Film Festival was instructed not to give it recognition, and few people actually saw it. The industry undoubtedly took note and the proponents of the narrow definition of neorealism, as a form of documentary (associated with Zavattini rather than Rossellini), point to this moment as the effective end of the movement.

In 1952, De Santis incurred the disapproval of the Prime Minister for *Roma ore 11* (Rome, 11 a.m.) and the panel of judges at Cannes – where the film was received favourably – was persuaded by the Director General of Entertainment to withhold a prize. Scripted in part by Zavattini, it told the true story of the collapse of a staircase in Rome on 15 January 1951, under the weight of 200 women replying to a succinctly worded job advertisement: 'Young, single, intelligent, hard-working, good shorthand, excellent opportunity, modest salary.' The film investigated the material and psychological needs of young women at a time of high unemployment. Many of the casualties of the accident did not receive hospital treatment because they were unable to pay the medical costs of 2,300 lire a day.

In 1954, in an atmosphere of imitation McCarthyism, improbable lists of film directors enrolled with the Communist Party were published. The Interior Minister, Mario Scelba, banned the import of Soviet films. The censor saw Communist sympathies in neorealism *tout court* and exercised a strong, preventive watch over the movement. The Christian Democrats removed Luigi Chiarini and other left-wing intellectuals from Cinecittà and the Venice Film Festival was similarly purged. In the late 1950s there were episodes of fervent Catholics tearing down posters of Botticelli's *Venere*.

21. D.A. Miller says that in *8½* on several occasions 'the camera too lets itself be caught in a similarly blank-eyed act of man-watching'; Miller, *8½* (London: BFI/Palgrave Macmillan, 2008), 56. According to Céline Menghi, the monstrous fish at the end of *La dolce vita* recalls a real event, the murder in 1953 of Wilma Montesi, whose body was found on the beach in Torvaianica. The murder became a source of political intrigue, since the Foreign Minister's son, Piero Piccioni, was tried for the murder and part of the ruling Christian Democrat Party pressed for a guilty verdict. The suspect's alibi for 9 April was provided by his girlfriend, Alida Valli. It was the first political scandal of the post-war era to nearly topple a government. Menghi cites the fish as an example of Lacan's dictum: 'The Thing regards us', suggesting, among other connotations, that the scrutiny of the fish puts its viewers to shame. Menghi's article appears in the biannual Freudian journal *La psicoanalisi* (Rome: Astrolabio, 2008, issue 43–44), 62–70.

22. Fellini worked with Rossellini on two of the masterpieces of neorealism, *Roma, città aperta* and *Paisà*, for which he directed the last episode. *Il miracolo* (The Miracle, 1948), from Rossellini's *Amore*, was written as a vehicle for Anna Magnani, at her request, by Fellini, who also co-starred (fair-haired and with a goatee). In the episode, a demented peasant girl mistakes a wayfarer for Saint Joseph. The wayfarer gets her drunk, makes love to her and disappears, leaving her pregnant. She believes the fruit of her womb is divine. Led in procession through the village, as she thinks for the veneration of her future child, she is scorned and derided. Catholics were quick to see a parody of the Immaculate Conception, but criticized the director rather than the relatively unknown scriptwriter.

Rossellini further alienated Catholics by his affair with Ingrid Bergman and the birth, out of wedlock, of their son on 2 February 1950. The couple married in Mexico on May 24, a union never recognized by the Catholic Church. The five films he made with Bergman represent a significant evolution in neorealism, with psychological introspection characterized by the camera lingering on the face of the female protagonist, a continuation of an experimental technique begun with Anna Magnani in the Cocteau episode *La voce umana* (The Human Voice) from *Amore*. Orson Welles criticized the latter and parodied the former in the stage production *The Unthinking Lobster*, possibly out of resentment. He suspected Rossellini of stealing from him footage of a film on the circus. Fellini, too, had a falling out with Rossellini. After a private screening of his first film, *Lo sceicco bianco*, Rossellini praised the film to the small invited audience but, eyeball to eyeball with Fellini, criticized its editing and narrative coherence (as did others after the film's release), suggesting that the debut director call him the following day for advice. Fellini never really forgave him and confided to his assistant director Moraldo Rossi: 'Rossellini is a genius, but only for his own work.'

Later, Fellini explained the debt he owed to Rossellini in terms that indicated his own view of neorealism: 'From Rossellini I believe I learned – in lessons on his part and an apprenticeship on mine that he never translated into words, never expressed, never made schematic – how to walk a tightrope in the toughest, most adverse, circumstances, which at the same time he naturally turned to his advantage, transforming them into feeling, emotional values, a point of view. This is what Rossellini did: he lived the life of a film as an adventure simultaneously to be lived and narrated. His abandonment to reality, unfailingly attentive, limpid, fervent, his ability to locate himself at the impalpable, unmistakable point between the indifference of detachment and the embarrassment of adherence, enabled him to capture, to fix reality in all its spatial declinations, to look at things simultaneously from the outside and the inside, to *photograph the air around things,* to reveal what cannot be grasped, what is arcane and magical, in life. Isn't this neorealism?' Federico Fellini, *Fare un film* (Turin: Einaudi, 1980), 45–46. *Mastorna* ends with an image of the 'air around things', discussed in detail in the main text and other notes.

23. Quoted by Mario Guidorizzi in *Cinema italiano d'autore*, Part I (Verona: Cierre edizioni, 2006), 40.

The remark could be contrasted with what Zavattini told Pasquale Festa Campanile in an interview in 1951, presenting neorealism as form of documentary:

'Let's take a character, say Umberto D. Of course the character was taken from reality, it didn't start out as an intellectual exercise. I think that instead of telling the story of Umberto D. we should tell the story of a real person who has retired, with him as the protagonist. That doesn't mean that, right from the start, the cinema forgoes the ability to tell a story in a way that moves an audience. But I'd say even more. The kind of cinema I'm interested in doesn't tell the story of something that happened, of a real event, with the actual people involved playing themselves. No, I think the cinema should show what *is happening*. The camera should look at what is in front of it.' Cesare Zavattini, *Opere*, edited by Valentina Fortichiari and Mino Argentieri (Milan: Bompiani, 2002), 705.

24. In true Hitchcock manner, Fellini told a dinner party that in Siena, the location of the famous *palio* horse race, there is a clock at a height of about 400 feet, in the Mangia Tower. It contains the stone statue of a man leaning out, watching the race below. Fellini imagined the hour hand slicing off the spectator's head which would then fall into the streets below and be kicked back and forth by the galloping horses' hooves.

25. Cristina Degli-Esposti discusses Foucault's notion of heterotopy briefly in her introduction to *Postmodernism in the Cinema* (New York: Berghahn Books, 1998), 8–9, and more extensively elsewhere, as referenced. Foucault's use of the term dates from 1966 and, put briefly, signifies a space in which a number of possible orders have been gathered together, a notion that seems to be literalized in Mastorna's collections of cities, religions, ethnicities, typical Italian figures – bureaucrat, Neapolitan mamma, con artist, musician – pasts and futures, in a single place.

26. The 2003 documentary *Mysterious Journey of Fellini* is part of the DVD produced by Umbrella Entertainment, *Fellini's Magic* (2006).

27. The programme begins with languid guitar music, the director's name and the title of the documentary on an otherwise blank screen.

Then a distant view of buildings standing in a field of tall grass. A bright summer's day. The buildings are incongruous: on the right, clearly visible, are the twin steeples of a Gothic Cathedral, in the middle what appears to be a tower, and, on the left, there is some kind of horizontal structure, surrounded by scaffolding. The camera moves at Andy Warhol pace.

Cut to practically two-dimensional three-storey buildings in a continuous line, a façade with windows. Then move to a small white hut with the sign CUSTODE (janitor) which has slipped from one of its hinges above the door and hangs down obliquely. The camera moves past the hut to the nose of a large passenger plane.

The camera pans over the side of the fuselage and then returns to the black nose of the otherwise white plane.

A voice is heard off-screen, Fellini describing the set and the film he never made, as the camera continues to take in the scenery: a riderless horse ambles away, a young man pokes his head out of a psychedelically painted Citroen 2CV, from which the driver's door has been removed. To the right there is another car, wheel-less, its bodywork painted black and yellow. A woman is sitting beside it. She has heavily made-up eyes, a striped t-shirt and a chain necklace. Next to her is a man with small John Lennon-type glasses, only dark. Apparently, he is playing the increasingly melancholic music we hear on the guitar.

The camera returns to the Citroen where another woman is approaching, carrying a large bag in her right hand. Four young people approach from the fields, dressed like hippies. Fellini's voice resumes: 'A little while ago I came back to see all this again. It was more beautiful now, falling down and covered with weeds. Somebody has found shelter in these crazy ruins.' Two Beatles look-alikes, from the Yellow Submarine period, approach.

FF: 'Hello good morning. Are you living here at the moment?'

Beatle: 'Ja. That's right. Frankly I was a bit surprised to find the Cologne Cathedral standing here. But I like the idea of camping here with my companions.'

FF: 'You know this was a film set?'

Beatle: 'Ja.'

Bearded bespectacled Guru-looking man: 'We've been celebrating a marriage here this morning. With an orchestra of grasshoppers.'

FF: 'Ah yeah? And where are these newlyweds?' Cut to a man and a woman walking through a field arm in arm.

Guru: 'Over there.'

Different voice (American accent): 'This is not your woman but the woman who stays with you. This is not your man but the man who stays with you.'

This voice belongs to another bearded man, older, he too with a chain necklace: 'Promise that you will stay together for as long as your feelings for each other last.'

FF: 'And how long do you plan to be here?'

Guru: 'It's not possible to leave now even if we wanted to. The automobile has no wheels, we had to sell them.'

Blonde woman laughs.

Man with chain necklace: 'I composed a poem on the ruins of your film.'

FF: 'What is it called?'

Necklace: 'Mastorna Blues ha ha.'

I live in a city that's called Mastorna
That a fool's dream laid out here in a field.
A city that's useless, where nobody wants to live
And nobody likes to work and hates to die.
All the houses are sealed with doors of wood
That no one intends to open.
And there's an aeroplane nailed down that's not
Going to take off.

Mastorna, city that's sad and beautiful.
Of that beauty I love above all other
Since all it stands for is Folly.
I want to die here in Mastorna.
And here to be buried in that cardboard church
Where no priest ever enters.' (Poem by Bernardino Zapponi)

The hippies look into the skies. Sound of aeroplane flying low. Wind in the sand and through the hair of the blonde woman, made up rather like a clown. Cut to inside the passenger compartment of the aeroplane. An empty, coffin-like, shell.

Voice of hostess: 'Attention please. Due to technical difficulties, we have been forced to make an emergency landing. The voice repeats 'Emergency landing' four more times, petering out.

Snow falls. Silhouette of a man in a bowler hat, his back turned.

FF: 'This is Mastorna, the hero of my film, a cellist.'

28. In terms of imagining *Mastorna*, an unresolved question is what painting or painter Fellini would have chosen to focus on. In the script for *Viaggio con Anita* it was Piero della Francesca, in *La dolce vita* Raphael and Bosch, in *Giulietta degli spiriti* Klimt, in *Fellini Satyricon* Pieter Breughel's *Tower of Babel* and *Triumph of Death* (updated by De Chirico, according to Gian Luigi Rondi). The fact that the only images we have of *Mastorna* by Fellini include Magritte's trade-mark bowler hat might suggest that the surrealist would have provided the painterly surface and inspiration for *Mastorna*. In both *Man with a Bowler Hat* and *The Son of Man* the face of the man is entirely obscured, respectively by a bird and an apple. This is, as it were, the way Fellini saw Mastorna, without a face. In a radio interview with Jean Neyens in 1965, Magritte explained: 'There is an interest in that which is hidden and which the visible does not show us. This interest can take the form of a quite intense feeling, a sort of conflict, one might say, between the visible that is hidden and the visible that is present.' In 1965, the New York Museum of Modern Art dedicated a retrospective to Magritte who died in 1967, the year Fellini abandoned the film. In the original screen test for the role of Mastorna, photographed by Tazio Secchiaroli, Mastroianni is seen wearing a variety of hats, including a bowler.

29. Perhaps this is a mishearing. Marina Boratto appeared in *Satyricon* and her mother in several films by Fellini.

30. The penchant for big American stars was not peculiar to De Laurentiis: incredibly, Angelo Rizzoli contacted Katharine Hepburn for the role of Giulietta. This insistence on box-office names might have made commercial sense but Fellini was wary of it. Besides, there had been numerous flops with prestigious international casts. Fellini didn't make a fuss over such things; he preferred to quietly ignore his producers and, in the case of Rizzoli, after the Hepburn gaffe, didn't make another film with him.

31. Piero Gherardi, costume and set designer, and Alessandro von Norman, production assistant.

32. This and the previous quotation are from *Il libro dei sogni*, Federico Fellini (Milan: Rizzoli, 2007), 501, for the transcription of Fellini's handwritten diary entry.
33. Tullio Kezich, *Federico Fellini* (Milan: Feltrinelli, 2002), 265.
34. Fellini told Charlotte Chandler: 'I had long kept secret the story of *The Voyage of G. Mastorna*, the film which I had thought to make during several decades of my life. It was conceived early in my career, and I would build on it in my mind, even as I worked on other films. I would never tell the producers much of the idea, which didn't help in getting money for it.

    'Once, it seemed it was going to happen. We got as far as building the sets. Then I fell ill. I hovered near death for a time. It was in that state that I came even nearer to *G. Mastorna*. When I recovered, I couldn't tell what parts of my memories were true and what parts were not. Now I can tell the idea I had for him because I have accepted it is a film I will never make, but I do not have the fortitude left to persuade anyone to produce it. Some of my associates have whispered to each other that Fellini doesn't make the film because he has grown superstitious about it. "Fellini has identified with G. Mastorna", they say, "and he's afraid he will die if he completes the film."

    'The real reason is that I myself have cannibalized *G. Mastorna* while Mastorna waited in the wings. I have borrowed bits and pieces from the idea for all my films since […] I planned to utilize certain autobiographical aspects of my own inner life, to draw from my real feelings rather than my real experiences, as I had previously done. My identification with Mastorna has always been intimate, as it was with Guido in *8½*. When I was directing Mastroianni as Guido, sometimes I felt like I was ordering myself around.

    'For a long time, I refused to talk about the story of G. Mastorna. I believed that if I told the story before I gave it life, I would rob it of its magic […] The original inspiration for the story came from my visit to the Cologne Cathedral, where I heard about a medieval monk who could fly at will – but not his own will […] I believed it would have been my best film if I could have made it, and now since I know I will not be doing it, I can go on believing it would have been my best film. Alive in my own mind, it will never disappoint me.' Charlotte Chandler, *I, Fellini* (London: Bloomsbury, 1996), 289–91.
35. Translations of *Moraldo va in città* and *Viaggio con Anita* ara available in John C. Stubbs, ed., *Moraldo in the City and A Journey with Anita* (Champaign: University of Illinois Press, 1983). Reference is made to them in John C. Stubbs, *Federico Fellini as Auteur: Seven Aspects of his Films* (Carbondale: Southern Illinois University Press, 2006). Like *Mastorna*, the scripts are lengthy present-tense narratives.
36. This description is similar to Gianna, Guido's wife, in *Viaggio con Anita*.
37. Fellini, Pinelli and Flaiano, *Moraldo va in città*, in *Cinema* (1954), 744.
38. Marguerite Waller suggests that his inability to connect with Paola, the waitress, on the beach is based on his perception of her as a figure from Raphael's paintings, a sexual and aesthetic object, and not 'a dislocated, homesick young woman who needs to acquire an empowering skill, not fatuous compliments,

if she is to find a place in modern Italian society different from the dependent and battered women who otherwise inhabit Marcello's world.' See 'Whose Dolce Vita is This Anyway? The Language of Fellini's Cinema', in Burke and Waller, *Federico Fellini, Contemporary Perspectives* (Toronto: Toronto University Press, 2002), 112. Marcello had promised to teach her to type.

39. Quoted by Tullio Kezich in his biography of Fellini, *Federico Fellini* (Milan: Feltrinelli, 2002), 173.
40. This fresco was the focus of Tarkovsky's *Nostalghia* (1983).
41. Fellini's fondness for American films of the era was also shown in his 1984 TV advertisement for Martini, which is based on the fairground moving-backdrop scene in Max Ophuls's *Letter from an Unknown Woman* (1948).
42. Capra was also aware of the predicament, naming his guardian angel Odbody.
43. Robert Conway, the hero of Capra's earlier romantic, science-fiction film *Lost Horizon* (1937), also wonders whether he is dreaming in the paradise-on-earth he has been taken to. And like Mastorna he finds that everything in Shangri-La speaks to him: 'All the beautiful things I see – these cherry blossoms, you, all are somehow familiar. I've been kidnapped and brought here against my will. A crime, a very great crime, yet I accept it amiably …'
44. Capra also used a blizzard scene in *Lost Horizon*, for the difficult journey to Shangri-La, as did Pietro Germi in his 1950 neorealist film *Il cammino della speranza* (The Road to Hope), co-scripted with Fellini and Pinelli. In Germi's film the snowstorm leads to a tragic death.
45. For a feminist reading of the rescue of George Bailey, see Kaja Silverman, *Male Subjectivity at the Margins* (New York and London: Routledge, 1992), section 2, 'Historical Trauma and Male Subjectivity'. Her analysis of the Dominant Fiction and Lacanian symbolic order is relevant to the issues raised by *Mastorna*.
46. The story is available in Dino Buzzati, *I sette messaggeri* (The Seven Messengers) (Milan: Oscar Mondadori, 1984), re-titled *Il sacrilegio* (The Sacrilege).
47. Or the News on the March opening of *Citizen Kane*, a film that might have given Capra some ideas for *It's a Wonderful Life*. Thatcher, for example, is another Scrooge figure, whom Kane meets in a snowfall at Christmas time.
48. Federico Fellini, *Ciò che abbiamo inventato è tutto autentico, lettere a Tullio Pinelli* (Everything we invented is completely authentic – Letters to Tullio Pinelli) (Venice: Marsilio, 2008).
49. Ibid., 289. A similar remark can be found in A. Arpa: 'I have always believed that some people learn the secrets of life and death, but only a few moments before bodily death: the truth comes to the person who is dying at the last moment of life: a sort of conscience.' A. Arpa, *L'arpa di Fellini* (Rome: Edizioni dell'Oleandro, 2001), 71. *Coscienza* in Italian means both conscience and consciousness.
50. Stephen Mulhall, *The Wounded Animal, J.M. Coetzee and the Difficulty of Reality in Literature and Philosophy* (Princeton and Oxford: Princeton University Press, 2009), 102.
51. In his letter to De Laurentiis Fellini talks about the overall tone of the film and the ending, as he conceived it at that moment:

'I'd like to say something, probably encouraging. Although it's difficult to understand from this brief sketch, I think the tone of the film, its rhythm, its episodes, should be very comic.

In this timeless dimension of feeling and thought, M.'s reactions are often so out of proportion, so unsuitable and unfitting that they become downright laughable.

I expect you'd like to know how this oddball story ends.

So would I.

I imagine M. with his last Beatrice on a mountain path which climbs upward. At a bend an infinite sky stretches out before them. He has got past the last frontier. The guide can no longer accompany him. He must continue the journey alone.

He has passed all the tests, freed himself of his preconceptions, thrown away his erroneous interpretations of life, rid himself of the nostalgia of feelings, the blackmail of sentiment.

His heart is firm and at peace, he can continue the journey alone, around the next bend where the adventures he will encounter will be part of his and no other life.

The guide, the last Beatrice, knows nothing about what awaits him but smiles at him comfortingly and confidently.

She takes her leave, kissing him on the cheek.

M. can see the path up which he has come and the valleys and woods below, even the cities he has been through, the regions, the entire world, and no longer feels any nostalgia.

Before him the white path turns sharply towards the immense, empty sky.

At this moment, disenchanted and clear-minded, when M. is about to take his first step away from everyone and everything, including his fellow journeymen and women, something unexpected happens deep down in his heart. It cannot be expressed; it isn't a clear memory, he doesn't think of a loved one, it isn't exactly a feeling, but these things and others together.

It's the sense, the scent, of what his humanity has been, his life as a man, expressed in a single heart beat. The colours of the changing seasons, the intense expression in a woman's glance, the shadow at the foot of a tree, the vague memory of a long-forgotten tune, all in one ineffable moment.

M.'s steps slow to a stop. He cannot go on.

What happens next?

In all sincerity, I don't know yet.'

52. Dario Zanelli (1995), 95.
53. Federico Fellini, *Il viaggio di G. Mastorna*, edited by Ermanno Cavazzoni (Macerata: Quodlibet Compagnia Extra, 2008), 229.
54. Cavazzoni may have been thinking of Fellini's remarks in a letter to an admirer, Georges Simenon, written after the release of *Il Casanova*, but referring to the period beginning with *Toby Dammit* (1968), in which Fellini says that he has begun to see himself 'as an accountant, a provincial playboy who believes he has had a life but hasn't even been born, has travelled the world without existing, and gone through life like a wandering spirit'.

55. David Foster Wallace, *Consider the Lobster* (London: Abacus, 2005), 64, in the essay entitled 'Some Remarks on Kafka's Funniness'. To come full circle, Wallace's remark is reminiscent of Adorno's criticism of Heidegger in *The Jargon of Authenticity*, as summarized in the Foreword to the English edition by Trent Schroyer: 'For Adorno, Heidegger's existentialism is a new Platonism which implies that authenticity comes in the complete disposal of the person over himself – as if there were no determination emerging from the objectivity of history' (Oxford: Routledge, 1973), xvi. *Mastorna* has common ground with Adorno's critique of how subjectivity is formed, and deformed, by the objective configuration of institutions.

56. One of the headings in Fellini's outline of the script to De Laurentiis was HOTEL OF FORGETTING. The uncompleted scene of the burning of memories seems to have this function in the script. The headings and brief summaries Fellini sent to De Laurentiis were as follows:

THE PROMISED LAND
In a region called 'the promised land' M. is tempted to stay forever. It is Paradise, a list of all the most puerile, pathetic and dunderheaded aspirations. Sickly sweet, the reunion with parents, with lost friends.
    Everyone comforts M., toasts him, all in thrall to a mindless, ecstatic happiness: 'At last! At last!'
    M. meets his mother, very young, beautiful, as she was when he was born: she takes him to his room as a child, undresses him, and M. feels that he is going back in time. They sleep naked in the same bed and she gives him her nipple to suck, she kisses him and suffocates him with tenderness and love.

POSSIBLE DEPARTURES
Huge airport of glass, like Brussels, a beautiful female voice making announcements like a seasoned actress. The old spirits await the new in the terminals, on the runway aprons, out on terraces. They wave ecstatically. As in Dante, they ask the new arrivals about the living. M. sees (and follows) a group of pretty nuns arriving, confident of what will befall them. After a few moments, Jesus comes to pick them up and takes them in person to a blue bus that is waiting for them.
    'Why them?'
    'They're nuns.'
    There is a huge ship he hopes to be able to get on. It is the ship of definitive separation, white, metaphysical, full of women from the Red Cross. The false guide from the afterlife invites him aboard. On the bridge he meets the fabled captain (his orchestra conductor, handsome, like a dancer, with his fabulous-looking wife). 'What are you waiting for?' the false guide says and adds: 'Detachment, freedom, transfiguration.' But with an excuse M. returns to land and then, with some nostalgia and remorse, watches the white ship set sail amid organ music and flying seagulls.
    The quay is windy, swept by torrential rain; it's the dead of night. M. and the others are waiting for a ship to arrive but out on the stormy sea there is only

a launch. On board a woman is signalling to M. to come aboard. M. dives in. The woman is the new Beatrice (the lighthouse. Disappointment? Used only for an advertising hoarding?).

THE LANDSCAPE OF FEELINGS, SENSATION AND THOUGHT
During his journey M. goes through all the regions that represent the ways he is a man. The region of sensation, essentially sensual, the first woman who attracted him, a boy, from newspapers and advertising hoardings. He meets the first of them, a drawing (maybe on a wall), now come to life, life-size, at the home of a school friend. The hypnotic eroticism of puberty, a child's sexual fantasies, women from fairy tales, the beautiful Andromeda lashed to the cliff, Titian's Venus, cartoon characters.

The Region of thought with its cultural leaders; the fantastic Classical world of secondary school, the pagan world, Greek gods, Homer's heroes.

His guide in this world is his old schoolmaster, a materialist, follower of Carducci, atheist.

SOMEWHERE TO STAY?
A police officer with a strange, incomprehensible arm-band, greets M. as he pops out (as if from an underground passageway) among the crowds of this new city (recognizable here and there, with old advertising slogans, like the ancient one with the old men enjoying Talmone chocolate).

In order to set M. on his way the officer wants to know who he is, his function. But M. doesn't know or, rather, he continues to say he's a cellist and is due to play a concert in Boboli. The officer makes some calls, gets advice, takes him to various neat and tidy, out-of-the-way places, where, he says, M. may belong.

They are 'housing projects', like some of the EUR area of Rome, with hundreds of identical flats, or, worse, the American-style district of Casal Palocco. Lots of little gardens, all the same, lots of family cars, all the same, lots of sprinklers, all at the same angle, TV antennae, all at the same height.

Library, theatre, cinema, modern church, sterilized, efficient brothel with girls in overalls in the window. A tidy public park where they give open-air concerts every Saturday: isn't this the right place for M.?

M. even rents a room, settles in, tries to fit in; he does what everyone else does, goes to Saturday afternoon concerts, but is nauseated by it all, repulsed.

ANCESTORS
M. continues to want to return home. By whatever means. They point him towards a terrible, deserted landscape, watched over by invisible monsters and they tell him: if you feel up to it, that's the way home. M. agrees to use the compass of real nostalgia and *sincere* orientation to find his way on his journey.

Unexpectedly he reaches his father's house (which he has never seen before) where he meets his parents – at some uncertain, abstract age – and a baby sister ('She grows each evening, she's already almost a woman'). Father and mother, as if at an old people's home, play cards and – pale – wait. But now the time has come to slaughter the 'fat cow'. It's an old-style banquet attended by a number of mysterious characters M. has never met before: his ancestors. A nightmare dinner follows, which is dominated by the head of the family, the oldest ancestor, who is venerated by the others but treats them all as slaves and traumatizes Marcello. They think M. is a traitor, someone who has gone astray. During the toast, they upbraid and warn him. In the end, after the wishy-washy pity of his mother and two old aunts, he is kicked out of the house.

HIS WIFE
A real attempt to face the unresolved situation he left behind: a will, a legacy for his lover ... At some point, in a huge procession through an area of town he doesn't know, but could be Tokyo, he sees his wife. He follows her and speaks to her but realizes she cannot see or hear him. He follows her home. It is the house he lived in at the time of his death but everything seems indistinct, misty. The man sitting with his wife at table over dinner has a face he cannot make out even when he goes up close, just a few inches away. The man is just an obscure, disquieting figure. The phone rings. How he would like to answer it!
    (Comic sequence: M. tries to communicate with his wife but at every signal, noise, knock, his wife takes fright and avoids him.)

THE HOTEL OF FORGETTING
Shortly after dying, M. starts to want to return to life and this desire is like a constant stabbing pain. Therefore the people he meets take him for a madman, for someone who is sick. They send him to a ghostly 'clinic for forgetting', on an icy mountain slope, which functions just like a clinic, with nurses and scientific apparatus, where the staff do their utmost (during a brief pause in his journey) to cure him of his 'base nostalgia for the world'. They get him to leave the photos of his wife and children (we can easily invent the details) in an 'archive' and prescribe a programme of rehabilitation and detoxification from earthly humours. Vestal virgins of forgetfulness, like the nurses dressed in blue, try to make him forget his life and use his energies for something more worthwhile, a higher aim. In a remote cell they show him a fantastic old man who 'has forgotten everything' (but he discovers a kind of living fossil, a religious relic, with round eyes, an abstract manner, who cares for nothing and no-one).

PROOF OF AUTHENTICITY
One day someone tries to lend M. a hand in a concrete way.
    In order to continue his journey and get past the remaining frontiers, he needs a document of authentic identity. The new guide takes M. to a projection room where a friend of his may have some material from which to take the identity card that seems so indispensable.
    The room goes dark and on a screen various episodes from M.'s life are shown.
    The cinema is now full of people: judges, controllers, functionaries, customs officers, who whisper amongst themselves as each image comes onto the screen. But M. cannot hear what they are saying.

The images go by without rhyme or reason, flash past senselessly; it is barely possible to see what M. is doing. As each new image comes onto the screen, behind him the audience murmurs what seems like disapproval.

Among all the images flashing by they are looking for one, just one, an action, gesture or look, that proves the authenticity of M. It must be one moment in which M. was truly himself.

It must be found or M. will suffer true death, total annihilation, unchallengeable, final, definitive, for eternity.

Finally, out of the blue, without beginning or end, the judges discern an incoherent image in which M. appears to be relatively authentic.

(For example as a boy in a meadow reaching out to try to capture a butterfly.)

The lights come on. Behind M., the judges and controllers seem undecided but in the end, albeit not entirely convinced, they accept the slide and glue it into a booklet like a passport: now M. can resume his journey.

OBSESSION WITH MEMORY
The persistence of memories which return again and again with agonizing nostalgia, memories as a weighing up of one's past, as a connection with life, pursuing, driving him on, never letting up; memories prevent M. from making progress on his journey.

Not the memories but the ideas of the memories. Terrifying, mummified monstrosities, kept stored up jealously for years, dripping with sentimentality and self-satisfaction. When he sees these images, these 'memories' of his life, M. screams with terror.

How many years have gone by since M. started this journey?

Now he is in a grassy meadow on a mountain slope, a light breeze blowing, which seems to carry off these ideas and free his mind and heart. Somewhere higher up (or elsewhere? They often have to remind him that in this dimension there is no up and down, no higher and lower, but M. fails to grasp this notion because of the strict moralistic idealism he has from his upbringing and cannot let go), higher up, I was saying, the wind is stronger and M. reaches a place where it is blowing with great violence.

'What else do I need to get rid of?' says M. in the hurricane.

'Your heart, your human heart which won't allow you to get free.' And there before him is the 'Clinic of Forgetting'. This is where he will be given the hardest test of all. M. must stay dry-eyed (a group of observers is placed close to his eyes, ready to spot the slightest tear) as he watches the people he has loved most in life destroyed, massacred, tortured and dismembered.

57. The Italian translation was *Assurdo universo*, published by Mondadori in the Urania series.
58. This commercially acceptable description may have been prompted by Elio Petri's *La decima vittima* (The Tenth Victim, 1965), starring Marcello Mastroianni and Ursula Andress, as well as by *What Mad Universe*.
59. *What Mad Universe* also probes the outer/inner dichotomy and the feeling that the world is projected by the mind of the apparent observer, when the

protagonist hears a voice addressing him by name: 'Keith stumbled out from against the building to the narrow open area of sidewalk between the crowd at the curb and the crowd at the back of the sidewalk. He tried to keep pace with the car and the thing that floated above it, the basketball-sized sphere. He had the strangest feeling that it was that *thing* that had spoken to him.

'If so, it had called him by name and no-one else had heard it. Now that he thought of it, that voice hadn't seemed to come from outside at all; it had been inside his head.' Fredric Brown, *What Mad Universe* (New York: Bantam Books, 1949), 82.

60. On the aeroplane, before the accident, Mastorna is watching a Laurel and Hardy film, in which they are trying to climb the sides of a giant bathtub. The film was *Brats* (1930), where the two actors play both themselves and their children and for which two identical sets were created but to a different scale, another parallel world.

61. The voice-over comes from Mastorna's last Beatrice who, the previous evening, replicant-style, had asked him: 'Is living really beautiful? Tell me, describe to me your houses, your cities, tell me about your sun ... your spring, tell me how you cry, how you love ...' Mastorna is returned to life to experience these things and tell himself what they are like, in other words, to live *knowingly*. During the judgement scene, when his life is projected onto a screen, he is accused of being 'mechanical, a robot', without a shred of real life. Judith Barad concludes her remarks in her contribution to *The Philosophy of Neo-Noir* (edited by Mark T. Conard, University Press of Kentucky, Paperback edition, 2009, 33) in a way that also describes Mastorna's experience: '... many people allow themselves to be programmed by their families, their societies. *Blade Runner* and Sartre urge us to escape this programming and become authentically human.' Fellini's intended 'dismal and shabby' world for *Mastorna* is a forerunner of the decadent future-world of *Blade Runner*.

In the *Mastorna* script, the *Truman Show* air of contrivance begins almost immediately: the pilot of the plane appears to act like a film star waving to adoring fans. A little later, details of Mastorna's life are used as part of a cabaret act, although it is not clear whether the routine prompts Mastorna's memory or whether it functions, à la *Blade Runner*, as a memory implant, foisting artificial memories on him. Fellini suggests that elements of Mastorna's recollections have been created by external agents for the purpose of rendering him more pliable and compliant.

62. When Winton returns he cooks up a convenient story to tell friends to explain away his adventures. They were illusory, merely the after-effects of the explosion, he says, unconvinced by his own words (a *Total Recall* type of inner/outer world conundrum).

63. In addition to anticipating *Solaris* and, as we shall see, *Blade Runner* and *Matrix*, Mastorna also seems to share ground with Samuel R. Delany's 1976 sci-fi novel *Triton* (a utopian/dystopian planet), in which women can become men and men women, as suggested by Mastorna's father. In the novel, the investigation of identity, desire and gender leads to considerations of democracy, liberalism and otherness (in the words of Kathy Acker, in her

introduction to the Wesleyan University reprint, entitled *Trouble on Triton*, Hanover, 1996, xii), topics similarly investigated in *Mastorna* and elsewhere by Fellini. Joanna Russ's *The Female Man* (1975) uses the technique of parallel worlds to question how different societies might produce different versions of the same person. Postmodernism throws up similar issues, of course: Dick Higgins defines the postcognitive questions asked by artists from the 1960s on as: 'Which world is this. What is to be done in it? Which of my selves is to do it?' (in *A Dialectics of Centuries*, 1978). The shifting of roles and gender is foreshadowed in *Mastorna* by the cabaret artist, a man dressed as a woman, whose peculiar language includes the word *mutter* (mother), which the hostess translates as *esposa* (wife). The cabaret artist turns out not to have a single identity: he is also the hotel porter and has two families. Later, when Mastorna phones his wife, he too is duplicated, both dialling and picking up (as Winton sees himself in *What Mad Universe*). There are also near-duplications: the cabaret artist's wife and one of Armandino's lovers have a similar name (Grete/Greta), and all the hostesses may or may not be the same woman.

Mastorna's journey involves shedding many loads and this might be thought, ultimately, to lead to a lack of ontological grounding. In other words, if all the elements of identity are up for grabs, the words 'I', 'you' and so on become meaningless, a state of affairs that Mastorna's Lethe-bathed father envisages with relish. In what appears to be a casual, bumbling fashion, the Deputy Station Master replaces one personal pronoun with another, as if it were a matter of course: 'It is we, that is to say, you …' Mastorna makes progress when he declares that nothing in the film of 'his' life has anything to do with 'him'.

This ontological questioning, characteristic of the postmodern, was registered in a number of novels in the 1960s, such as Thomas Pynchon's *The Crying of Lot 49* (1966) whose narrator Oedipa Maas empathizes with the theatre director and projector of the planetarium, causing her to ponder: 'Shall I project a world?' Pynchon's novel also contains a definition of miracles that is pertinent to *Mastorna*: 'You know what a miracle is … another world's intrusion into this one. Most of the time we coexist peacefully, but when we do touch there's cataclysm.' In *Mastorna*, both the initial reprieve from the plane crash and the return to Florence are described as miraculous, and both may be cataclysmic. Pynchon's vocabulary seems to partake equally of the worlds of religion, spiritualism and science fiction, and pinpoints their intersection (or collision).

Brian McHale discusses postmodern science fiction and colliding worlds extensively in *Postmodernist Fiction* (Oxford: Routledge, 1987) and his treatment throws up numerous possible interpretations for *Mastorna*. For example, his reading of the ending of Robert Coover's *The Origin of the Brunists* (1966) coincides with what Zanelli and Cavazzoni say of Fellini's script: the protagonist escapes the 'esoteric enclave' of the Brunists, derived in part from Berger and Luckmann (in *The Social Construction of Reality*) and moves away from a world lacking in social interaction towards 'the paramount reality of our everyday lives with others, here and now' (20).

McHale cites two postmodern novels whose territory is anticipated by *Mastorna*: Philip Dick's *Ubik* (1969) and Muriel Spark's *The Hothouse by the East River* (1973), both of which, he says, 'construct equivocal afterlifes, variants on the "worlds" to come'. The parallels with Spark are particularly striking: 'Inconsistencies and improbabilities begin to creep in, inexplicable events occur. This, too, it turns out has been a death-world, but one initially coinciding at every point with the real-world Manhattan. Spark's dead, victims of the 1944 V-2 blitz of London, act out a perfect simulacrum of the life they *would have lived* had they survived until the 1970s […] This conditional existence starts breaking down from the moment when the dead begin to realize that they have been dead all along. Spark's world, like Dick's, erases itself' (ibid., 64).

McHale also cites Christine Brooke-Rose's *Such* (1966), which suggests another possibility for *Mastorna*: the protagonist of the novel dies and enters a bizarre death-world only to be returned to his former life, where, however, he no longer belongs: 'He is a one-man embodiment of "another world's intrusion into this one" on *both* sides of the boundary,' says McHale (241).

Fellini may have known of an earlier science fiction work, *La Invenciòn de Morel* (1940) by Adolfo Bioy Casares, thought by some to have inspired Resnais and Robbe-Grillet for *L'année dernière à Marienbad* (1961), as well as at least one episode of the television series *Lost*. The novel has just one character intended to be real, all the others being part of a recording by a machine able to reproduce reality. The machine functions imperfectly, creating the impression of two suns and two moons. In the Resnais film, there are similar glitches, as the action freezes, then resumes, the dubbing is out of sync, the geometry of the chateau is impossible and the characters, but not the trees, throw long shadows across its grounds. The narrator of the novel states his belief that: 'we lose immortality because we have not conquered our opposition to death'.

64. The image is recurrent in Fellini's thoughts. Recalling his first Academy Award, he told Costantini: 'Sunset Boulevard seemed covered in gold dust.' Ibid., 36. A similar image came to his mind when he told Costantini of his meeting with Bergman: 'As the rain started to fall even more heavily, Bergman pointed out to me with his very long finger a corner of the swimming pool. Beneath the rain-rippled surface of the water an infinity of little organisms, like a Sumerian alphabet, were whirling around at bacterial velocity. Bergman squatted down on his heels and began talking to the tadpoles with a happy smile on his face. Pasqualone retired a discreet distance to leave us alone […] Just at that moment the clouds opened and the funeral scene was bathed in yellow light. We turned back in silence, without exchanging a word, not even farewells when we parted.' Ibid., 69–70. The image also gets into Fellini's dream about *Mastorna* with the Oriental passenger standing before him 'covered in dust but shining' (see Introduction).

65. This is Maite Carpio's view.

66. In 2003, the BBC science programme *Horizon* screened an episode entitled 'Timetrip', in which theoretical physicists speculated about an advanced society with supercomputing capability reconstructing its own past as a means

of time travel. Such a society, they suggested, would also be able to produce billions of simulated universes:

Dr. Nick Bostrom: 'If almost everyone like me are simulated people, and just a tiny minority are non-simulated ones, then I'm probably one of the simulated ones, rather than one of the exceptional non-simulated ones. In other words, you're almost certainly living in an ancestor simulation.'

Prof. Paul Davies: 'The better the simulation gets, the harder it would be to tell whether or not you were in a simulation or in the real thing, whether you live in a fake universe or a real universe. And indeed the distinction between what is real and what is fake would simply evaporate away.'

Prof. Frank Tipler: 'Inside the simulation, you can't tell any difference between the simulated environment – the virtual reality – and the real environment. In fact, this environment we now find ourselves in could be just a simulation.'

Artificially created universes feature in Robert Heinlein's sci-fi novel *The Unpleasant Profession of Jonathan Hoag*, where the constructs are works of art. In the first chapter of *Looking Awry* (Cambridge and London: MIT Press, 1992), Slavoj Zizek analyzes how these universes may relate to the Lacanian concept of the real.

Zizek's comment, in the same chapter, on the ending of *The Woman in the Window*, in which the protagonist 'awakes *in order to continue his dream*' would suggest that Mastorna's return to life is a continuation of death.

67. Cavell calls this 'the fullest image of absolute isolation'. Stanley Cavell, *The World Viewed* (Cambridge, Massachusetts: Harvard University Press, Enlarged Edition, 1979), 159. Cavell must have seen the same version of the Dreyer film as Fellini since the original was not recovered until 1981.

68. This final image is ambiguously suspended between a cinematic effect allowing for Mastorna's return to life with renewed enthusiasm and a glitch in the imitative mechanics of the world, indicating that he is merely in a new simulated reality. But the possibilities do not end there, since we could imagine Mastorna, after the initial shock, believing in, or pretending to believe in, or accepting in disbelief, this world, like another, later fictional character: 'Is it all being mounted for her sake, because she is a writer? Is it someone's idea of what hell will be like for a writer, or at least purgatory: a purgatory of clichés? Whatever the case, she ought to be out on the square [...] A commonplace among commonplaces no doubt, but what does that matter any longer? What does it matter if the happiness of the young couples on the square is a feigned happiness, the boredom of the sentry a feigned boredom, the false notes that the cornet player hits in the upper register feigned false notes?' J.M. Coetzee, *Elizabeth Costello* (London: Vintage, 2004), 206. Later, lovers at a table next to Costello appear to be extras on the set of a dimly remembered film and the afterlife is perceived as an unconvincing sham, yet she finds herself thinking: 'How beautiful it is, this world, even if it is only a simulacrum!' (215). An otherworldly atmosphere also hovers over the opening pages of Coetzee's *The Childhood of Jesus* (London: Harvill *Secker*, 2013), with its utopian/dystopian location and 'cleansing' of former attachments.

Selected Bibliography

In English

Adorno, Theodor, *The Jargon of Authenticity*. London: Routledge, 2003.
Baxter, John, *Fellini*. London: Fourth Estate, 1993.
Bondanella, Peter, ed., *Federico Fellini. Essays in Criticism*. New York: Oxford University Press, 1978.
———, *The Cinema of Federico Fellini*. Princeton: Princeton University Press, 1992.
———, *The Films of Roberto Rossellini*. Cambridge: Cambridge University Press, 1993.
——— and Degli-Esposti, Cristina, ed., *Perspectives on Federico Fellini*. New York: G.K. Hall & Co., 1993.
Brown, Fredric, *What Mad Universe*. New York: Bantam Books, 1949.
Burke, Frank, *Federico Fellini: Variety Lights to La Dolce Vita*. Boston: Twayne, 1984. Series title: Twayne's filmmakers series.
———, *Fellini's Films: From Postwar to Postmodern*. New York: Twayne Publishers; London: Prentice Hall International, 1996. Series title: Twayne's filmmakers series.
——— and Waller, Marguerite R., ed., *Federico Fellini: Contemporary Perspectives*. Toronto: Toronto University Press, 2002.
Casares, Adolfo Bioy, transl. Suzanne Jill Levine, *The Invention of Morel*. New York: New York Review Books, 2003.

Cavell, Stanley, *The World Viewed*, enlarged edition. Cambridge, Massachusetts and London: Harvard University Press, 1979.
Chandler, Charlotte, *I, Fellini*. London: Bloomsbury, 1996.
Conard, Mark T., ed., *The Philosophy of Neo-Noir*. Lexington: The University Press of Kentucky, 2009.
Coetzee, J.M., *Elizabeth Costello*. London: Vintage, 2004.
———, *Slow Man*. London: Secker & Warburg, 2005.
Costantini, Costanzo, ed. *Conversations with Fellini*. San Diego, New York, London: Harvest Original, 1995.
Degli-Esposti, Cristina, ed., *Postmodernism in the Cinema*. Oxford, New York: Berghahn Books, 1998.
Fellini, Federico, *The Book of Dreams*. New York: Rizzoli International, 2008.
———, ed., Anna Keel and Christian Strich, transl. Isabel Quigley, *Fellini on Fellini*. London: Methuen, 1976.
Grossman, David, transl. Jessica Cohen, *Writing in the Dark*. London: Bloomsbury, 2008.
Gundle, Stephen, *Death and the Dolce Vita, the Dark Side of Rome in the 1950s*. Edinburgh: Canongate, 2012.
Hay, James, *Popular Film Culture in Fascist Italy: The Passing of the Rex*. Bloomington: Indiana University Press, 1987.
Heinlein, Robert A., *The Unpleasant Profession of Jonathan Hoag*. London: New English Library, 1976.
Hoffman, Michael, introduction to Franz Kafka's *Amerika*. New York: New Directions, 2002.
Jung, C. G., *The Collected Works*, vol. 17. Princeton: Princeton University Press, 1954.
Kezich, Tullio, *Federico Fellini, His Life and Work*. London: I.B. Tauris, 2007.
McHale, Brian, *Postmodernist Fiction*. London: Routledge, 1987.
Miller, D.A., *8½*. London: Palgrave Macmillan on behalf of the British Film Institute, 2008.
Mulhall, Stephen, *The Wounded Animal, J.M. Coetzee and the Difficulty of Reality in Literature & Philosophy*. Princeton and Oxford: Princeton University Press, 2009.

Murray, Edward, *Fellini, the Artist*. New York: F. Ungar Pub. Co., 1976.

Rosenbaum, Jonathan, *Discovering Orson Welles*. Berkeley and Los Angeles: University of California Press, 2007.

Shiel, Mark, *Italian Neorealism. Rebuilding the Cinematic City*. London: Wallflower, 2006.

Silverman, Kaja, *Male Subjectivity at the Margins*. New York and London: Routledge, 1992.

Stubbs, John Caldwell, ed., *Moraldo in the City and A Journey with Anita* (Champaign: University of Illinois Press, 1983).

———, *Federico Fellini as Auteur, Seven Aspects of his Films*. Carbondale: Southern Illinois University Press, 2006.

Tarkovsky, Andrei, *Time Within Time, The Diaries 1970–1986*. London and Boston: Faber and Faber, 1994.

Wallace, David Foster, *Consider the Lobster*. London: Abacus, 2005.

Zizek, Slavoj, *Looking Awry*. Cambridge and London: MIT Press, 1992.

In Italian

Argentieri, Mino, *Il cinema italiano dal dopoguerra a oggi*. Rome: Editori Riuniti, 1998.

Arpa, A., *L'arpa di Fellini*. Rome: Edizioni dell'Oleandro, 2001.

Bernhard, Ernst, *Mitobiografia*, ed. Hélène Erba-Tissot, transl. Gabriella Bemporad. Milan: Adelphi, 1969.

Berretto, Paolo, ed., *Azione! Come i grandi registi dirigono gli attori*. Rome: Edizioni minimim fax/Fondazione cinema per Roma, 2007.

Bispuri, Ennio, *Interpretare Fellini*. Rimini: Guaraldi, 2003.

Borin, Fabrizio, 'Il tempo del cinema e la sua immaginazione. Gli universi del fantastico di Andrej Tarkovskij e Federico Fellini', in *Visionaria*, ed. Dario Marzola. Alessandria: Edizioni Falsopiano, 2008.

Brunetta, Gian Piero, *Guida alla storia del cinema italiano, 1905–2003*. Turin: Einaudi, 2003.

———, *Il cinema neorealista italiano. Da Roma città aperta a I soliti ignoti*. Bari: Editori Laterza, 2009.

Buzzati, Dino, *I sette messaggeri* (The Seven Messengers). Milan: Oscar Mondadori, 1984, re-titled *Il sacrilegio* (The Sacrilege).

Caldiron, Orio, *Giuseppe Rotunno, la verità della luce*. Rome: Skira Editore/Fondazione Centro Sperimentale di Cinematografia, 2007.

Calvino, Italo. 'Autobiografia di uno spettatore', Preface to *Quattro film di Federico Fellini*. Turin: Einaudi, 1974.

Cardinale, Claudia, trans. Paola Lanterna, *Le stelle della mia vita*. Casale Monferrato: Edizioni Piemme, 2006.

Casanova, Alessandro, *Scritti e immaginati – I film mai realizzati di Federico Fellini*. Rimini: Guaraldi Universitaria, 2005.

Cavalli, Ennio, *10 Fellini ½ raccontando ricordi*. Rimini: Guaraldi, 1994.

Cini, Roberta, *Nella città delle donne. Femminile e Sogno nel cinema di Federico Fellini*. Tirrenia: Edizioni del Cerro, 2008.

Ellwood, David W., and Brunetta, Gian Piero, *Hollywood in Europa. Industria, politica, pubblico del cinema 1945–1960*. Florence: La Casa Usher, 1991.

Fellini, Federico, *Fare un film*. Turin: Einaudi, 1980.

———, *Giulietta*. Genova: Il melangolo, 1994.

———, *Intervista sul cinema*, ed. Giovanni Grazzini. Rome/Bari: Editori Laterza, 2004.

———, *Il libro dei sogni*. Milan: Rizzoli, 2007.

———, *Ciò che abbiamo inventato è tutto autentico, lettere a Tullio Pinelli*. Venice: Marsilio, 2008.

———, *Il viaggio di G. Mastorna*, ed. Ermanno Cavazzoni. Macerata: Quodlibet Compagnia Extra, 2008.

———, *L'arte della visione, conversazioni con Goffredo Fofi e Gianni Volpi*. Brindisi: Donzelli Editore, 2009.

Flaiano, Ennio, *Diario notturno*. Milan: Adelphi, 1994.

Fofi, Goffredo, *I grandi registi della storia del cinema*. Rome: Donzelli editore, 1995.

Guidorizzi, Mario, *Cinema italiano d'autore. I parte 1930–1965*. Verona: Cierre edizioni, 2006

———, *Cinema italiano d'autore. II parte, 1966–2011*. Verona: Cierre edizioni, 2008.

Iarussi, Oscar, *C'era una volta il futuro – L'Italia della dolce vita*. Bologna: il Mulino, 2011.

Kezich, Tullio, and Levatesi, Alessandra, *Dino De Laurentiis, la vita e i film*. Milan: Feltrinelli, 2009.

———, *Federico Fellini, la vita e i film*. Milan: Feltrinelli, 2002.

———, *Noi che abbiamo fatto* La dolce vita. Palermo: Sellerio, 2009.

———, *Federico Fellini. Il libro dei film*. Milan: Rizzoli, 2009.

Marzola, Dario, ed., *Visionaria, il cinema fantastico tra ricordi sogni e allucinazioni*. Alessandria: Edizioni Falsopiano, 2008.

Mastroianni, Marcello, *Mi ricordo, sì, io mi ricordo*. Milan: Baldini & Castaldi, 1997.

Medici, Antonio, *Neorealismo*. Rome: Dino Audino, 2008.

Menghi, Céline, 'Lacan con Fellini. La Cosa ci riguarda' in *La Psicoanalisi*. Rome: Casa Editrice Astrolabio, 43–44, Jan–June, July–Dec 2008.

Mollica, Vincenzo, ed., *Il Fumetto e il Cinema di Fellini*. Montepulciano: Editori del Grifo, 1984.

Moscariello, Angelo, *Come si guarda un film*. Rome: Dino Audino, 2007.

Munoz, Andrea, *Viaggio al termine dell'Italia. Fellini politico*. Soveria Mannelli: Rubbettino, 2012.

Pasolini, Pier Paolo, 'Soggettiva libera indiretta e cinema di poesia' in *Estetica e cinema*, ed. Daniela Angelucci. Bologna: Il Mulino, 2009.

Provenzano, Roberto, *Invito al cinema di Federico Fellini*. Milan: Mursia, 1995.

Quaglietti, Lorenzo, *Storia economico-politica del cinema italiano, 1945–1980*. Rome: Editori Riuniti, 1980.

Rossi, Moraldo, *Fellini & Rossi: il sesto vitellone*. Recco (Genova): Le mani; Bologna: Cineteca del Comune di Bologna, 2001.

Scolari, Giovanni, *L'Italia di Fellini*. Rimini: Edizioni Sabinæ, 2008.

Secchiaroli, Tazio, *G. Mastorna opera incompiuta*. Palermo: Sellerio, 2000.

Solmi, Angelo, *Storia di Federico Fellini, i suoi primi quarant'anni e la scalata visionaria a* La dolce vita. Milan: Betelgeuse, 2008.

Tobino, Mario, *Le libere donne di Magliano*. Milan: Oscar Mondadori, 1963.

Verdone, Mario, *Federico Fellini*. Milan: Editrice Il Castoro, 1994.

Vitti, Antonio, ed., *Ripensare il neorealismo: cinema, letteratura, mondo*. Pesaro: Metauro, 2008.

Zanelli, Dario, *L'inferno immaginario di Federico Fellini*. Rimini: Guaraldi, 1995.

Zanzotto, Andrea, *Il cinema brucia e illumina – intorno a Fellini e altri rari*, ed. Luciano De Giusti. Venice: Marsilio, 2011.

Zavattini, Cesare, *Opere, Cinema*, ed. Valentina Fortichiari and Mino Argentieri. Milan: Bompiani, 2002.

DVD

Carpio, Maite, 'Mysterious Journey of Fellini' in *Fellini's Magic*, Umbrella World Cinema, 2003.

Index

A
Adorno, Theodor, 195
  and authenticity, 175
Arpa, A., 193

B
Barad, Judith, 201
Bergman, Ingmar, 146, 201
  planned collaboration with, 186
Bergman, Ingrid, 188
Bernhard, Ernst, 139, 182
  death of, 8
  and entelechy, 9
  influence of, 8–9, 156
  Mitobiografia, 9
Bondanella, Peter, ix–xii, 13
Brooke-Rose, Christine, 200
Brown, Fredric, 1, 199
  and storyline of *What Mad Universe*, 180
Burke, Frank, 13, 193
Burke, Kenneth, 9
Buzzati, Dino, vii, 142, 182, 193
  contribution to *Mastorna*, 140
  disagreements with, 4–5
  and the esoteric, 8–9
  illness of, 155
  and inspiration for *Mastorna*, 10, 171

C
Capra, Frank, 193
  It's a Wonderful Life and *Mastorna*, 167–78
Cardinale, Claudia, 4
Carpio, Maite, 149, 154, 201
Casanova, Alessandro, 12
Casares, Adolfo Bioy, 200
  and *L'année dernière à Marienbad*, 200
Cavazzoni, Ermanno, xi, 194, 200
  and rebirth interpretation of *Mastorna*, 178–79, 182, 200
Cavell, Stanley, 202
censorship (Madame Anastasia), 186–87
Chandler, Charlotte, 176, 192
Coetzee, J.M.,
  visions of the afterlife in novels by, 186, 202
Conard, Mark T., 201
Coover, Robert, 200
Costantini, Costanzo, 140, 185, 201

D
Degli-Esposti, Cristina, 189
Delany, Samuel, R., 199
De Laurentiis, Dino, vii, 1, 3, 4, 12, 141, 143, 144, 145, 146,

148, 152, 161, 174, 175, 178, 185, 191, 193, 195
backing for *Mastorna*, 1
explanation for the failure to make *Mastorna*, 149
reaction to Fellini backing out, 154–57
De Santis, Giuseppe, 187
De Sica, Vittorio, 140, 143, 144, 147, 187
Dick, Philip K., 200
Di Venanzo, Gianni, 9, 140, 141
Dreyer, Carl Theodor, 183, 202

F
Fellini, Federico,
8½, vii, ix, 1, 3, 5, 6, 7, 12, 13, 137, 139, 140, 141, 145, 146, 147, 148, 150, 154, 155, 156
A Director's Notebook, 7, 13, 141, 142, 149, 152, 168, 170, 189–91
Amarcord, ix, 7, 10, 13, 142, 144, 157, 166
Book of Dreams, x, 155
E la nave va, 5, 10
Fellini Roma, ix, 10, 13
Giulietta degli spiriti, 3, 4, 13, 137, 139, 140, 141, 155, 191
I clowns, 13
I vitelloni, 13, 158, 175
Il Casanova, 9, 12, 13, 194
La città delle donne, ix, 10, 13, 137, 140, 186
La dolce vita, ix, 4, 5, 6, 7, 13, 139, 140, 141, 147, 148, 150, 154, 160, 166, 167, 169, 182, 184, 191
La strada, 13, 158
La voce della luna, ix, 149
Le notti di Cabiria, 158, 159
Le tentazioni del dottor Antonio, 6, 140
Prova d'orchestra, 10, 140
Satyricon, ix, 9, 13, 138, 140, 143, 147, 152, 157, 178, 180, 186, 191
Toby Dammit, ix, 7, 8, 10, 138, 142, 148, 194
Un'agenzia matrimoniale, 139, 184
attitude to scripts, 5
and Catholicism, 137, 147, 169, 171, 173, 188
on fascism, 7, 171, 173
illness of, 156–57
letter to De Laurentiis backing out of the film, 156
letter to De Laurentiis explaining the film, 1–3, 194, 195–98
as postmodern auteur, 148–49
other screenplays for unmade films,
Le libere donne di Magliano, 160–61
Moraldo va in città, 158–60
Viaggio con Anita, 161–65
and superstition, x, 155
Flaiano, Ennio, 139–40, 158, 184, 185, 192
Franchi, Franco, 143, 144

G
Geduld, Carolyn, 13
Gherardi, Piero, 141, 155, 191
Grimaldi, Alberto, 152, 157
Grossman, David, 13
Guerra, Tonino, 9

H
Heidegger, Martin, 177, 195
Heinlein, Robert, A., 202

… Index

I
I Ching, 8, 155
Ingrassia, Ciccio, 143, 144

J
Jung, C.G., 8, 13, 137, 183

K
Kafka, Franz, 11, 14, 146, 161, 195
  Amerika, 7, 140, 184–85
Kezich, Tullio, 148, 154, 155, 184, 192, 193
Kieslowski, Krzysztof, 185
Kurosawa, Akira, 186

L
Laurel and Hardy, 135, 143, 199

M
Magritte, René, 151, 191
Manara, Milo, 10
Masina, Giulietta, 139, 158
Mastorna, 15–136
  abandoning of project for, 149–57
  and authenticity, 170–73, 180, 195
  collaboration on screenplay for, 4, 5, 9, 146
  as Dantescan journey, x, 3, 5, 10, 146, 195
  gender assignment in, 174, 199
  and identity, 171, 174, 178–79
  inspiration for, 10, 171
  and *It's a Wonderful Life*, 167–78
  memory in, 5, 160, 175, 179, 194, 197–98, 201
  and ontological grounding, 199
  original ideas for, 141–49
  plundered for other films, 10
  uncompleted trilogy with *8½* and *La dolce vita*, vii, 5–7 and *What Mad Universe*, 180, 199
Mastroianni, Marcello, 4, 5, 10, 12, 143, 144, 154, 161, 186, 191, 192, 198
  as Mastorna, xiv, 16, 54, 95, 136, 142, 153
  re-enacted screen test for *Mastorna*, 149–52
  screen test for *Mastorna*, 10, 142
McHale, Brian, 200
Menghi, Céline, 187
Miller, D.A., 187
Mina, 142–44
Mollica, Vincenzo, 9
Mulhall, Stephen, 177, 193

N
neorealism, 4, 144, 147, 148, 173, 184, 187, 188, 189

O
Ophuls, Max, 186, 193
Osiris, Wanda, 144

P
painters providing visual inspiration for Fellini's films, 191
Pasolini, Pier Paolo, 139, 140, 143, 144, 147, 185
Petri, Elio, 144, 198
Pinelli, Tullio, 4, 13, 140, 158, 160, 161, 175, 184, 192, 193
Pizzi, Luigi, 141, 142
Plato, Er myth, 178, 179
Pynchon, Thomas, 200

R

Rizzoli, Angelo, 3, 139, 144, 191
Rondi, Brunello, vii, 4, 140, 142, 146, 184
Rossellini, Roberto, 138, 148, 185, 186, 187
  Fellini distances himself from, 188
  and influence on Fellini, 4, 188
Rossi, Moraldo, 188
Rotunno, Giuseppe, 13, 141, 142
Russ, Joanna, 199

S

Secchiaroli, Tazio, 142, 191
science fiction,
  Blade Runner, 199, 201
  duplication and replicants, 199
  films produced by De Laurentiis, 12
  implanted memories, 201
  simulated universes, 200, 201–2
  Solaris, 175, 199
Shelley, Mary, 181
Spark, Muriel, 200
Stamp, Terence, 14
Strehler, Giorgio, 10, 14, 154
Stubbs, John C., 192

T

Tarkovsky, Andrei, 13, 193
Tobino, Mario, 158, 160–61
Tognazzi, Ugo, 143, 154, 157
Totò, 142, 143

W

Wallace, David Foster, 179, 195
Waller, Marguerite, 192, 193
Welles, Orson, viii, 3, 185, 188

Z

Zanelli, Dario, 6, 145, 146, 147, 178, 179, 180, 182, 184, 194, 200
Zapponi, Bernardino, vii, 7, 9, 10, 13, 186, 191
Zavattini, Cesare, 139, 184, 187, 189
Zizek, Slavoj, 202